All comics herein are the property of their respective
artist(s) and may not be used or reproduced without
explicit permission except for review purposes. All comics
made for and used with permission by ABO.
ABO is a collective of volunteers supported by community
donations and various daring bank heists.
60% of the profits from the sale of this anthology sent to
the artist or their family members. The remaining 40%
divided evenly between Black & Pink International and
towards funding future ABO projects and schemes.

Front Cover by Michael Eaton & Woof
Back Cover art by Gabriel Wyatt

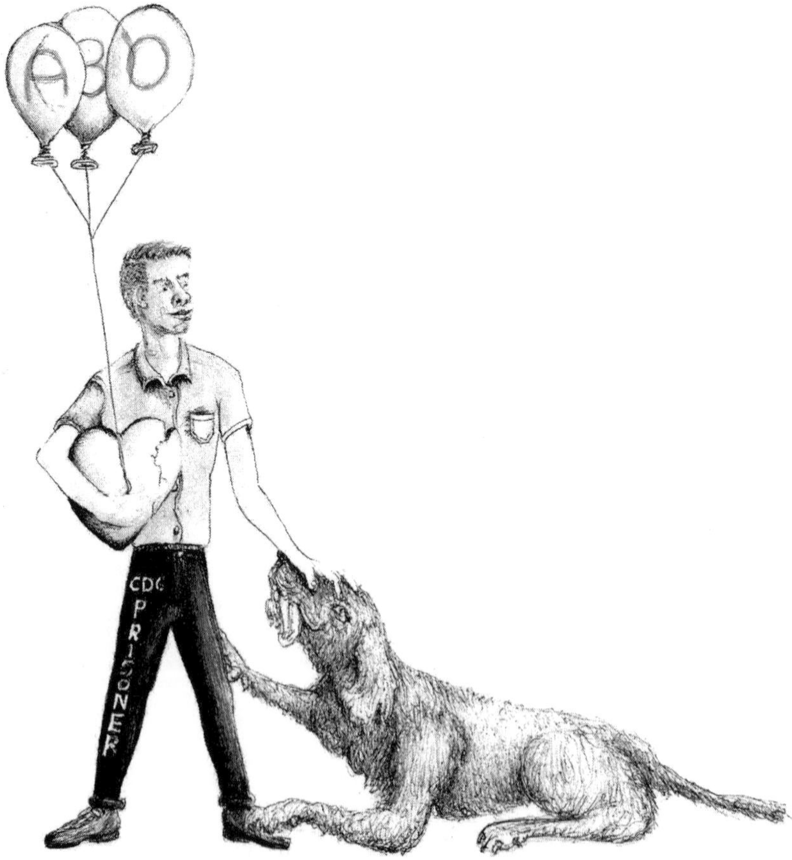
A
B
O
CDC
PRISONER

THANK YOU

We would not have been able to get this done without the help of an amazing cast of very sweet and powerful babies. Thank you.

Sen B & Alex R * Anna A & The A-Team * Ben Passmore * Elia
Michael E * Xy * Nell G * Lucas S * Beja A * Nicky & Doug S
Taurean T * Marcus Z * James W * Justin D * Camden B * Dani B
Rae W * Paul K & Emily M * David S * Kane L * Christian T
Hana Z * Edward O * Ryan H * Jeff P & Christie G * Holly & Hex
Quiver * Jesiah W * Marc R * Kim S * Adria C * Krusty W * Owen A
Jellicore * GROW Incubator * 1-2-3-4 GO! * Smalltown Society
Heartillery * Copyslut * Lil Debbie and the Crusaders
Flying Over Walls * Black & Pink * No Walls Collective
Austin Anarchist Black Cross * Trans Pride Initiative * Beast Bay

And of course all of our incarcerated friends, family,
lovers and contributors.

Forever yours in solidarity,
Casper, Io & WOOF

contents

DEC. 2017 ✳ NUMBER 1

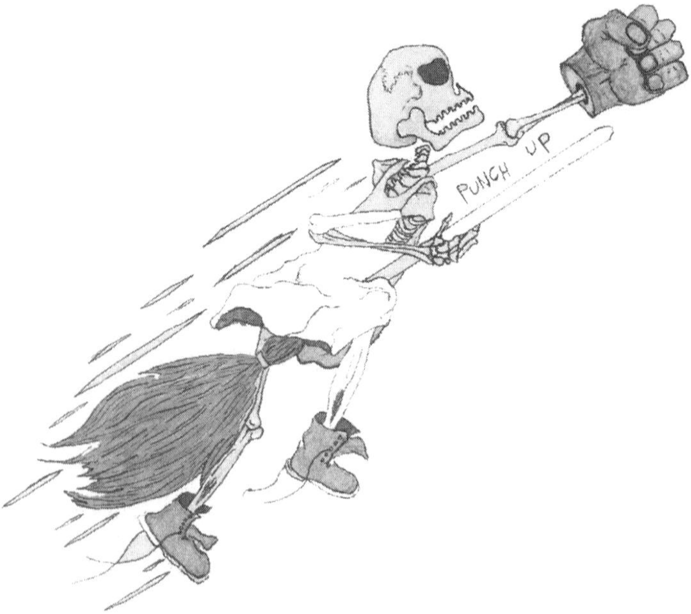

PUNCH UP

Making Comix Under Prison Conditions

What is it like to be locked-up... to have a world inside of you that no one knows about... so much to say: Dreams within dreams?

I can not speak for every prison artist because each prison is different. Even on the same prison unit — there will be differences depending on what cell block or dorm you live on and what officers are working at the time.

Likewise each artist is unique. With that in mind I will attempt to answer this question from my own experiances and those of other artists I know.

Being a prison artist often requires some McGuiver like creativity as we come up with ways to invent ways to make common tools and materials found at your local craft store.

In the future I hope to create a comix series illustrating prison art techniques in

1

general.

On the subject of comix art ... I had to borrow a protractor, because I don't normally use straight edges in my drawings. So measurements and lay-out creation was definately new.

We make shade sticks from pages of cross-word puzzles rolled up tightly. I use tootsie-pop sticks for fine detail shading.

We recieved some very helpful guidelines and instructions from ABO COMIX on how to create a home-made zine. Those instructions provided us with a frame to fill with our art.

However for me, logistacally, there was a lot of pre-production. I first created a script of dialogue. After the script was written, I then numbered and divided those scenes into cells (ironic?) within the comix. Deciding on which scene would be the center piece was pivotal to the process. Lastly I created a basic story board

sketch and then began the final draft. The whole process from start to finish for the comix "Time and Chance" took me 3 days. Not to mention, lots of cups of coffee because simular to the volunteers at ABO COMIX - I have a "day-job" as well.
For every artist you see represented in this anthology, there are many more who started, yet never finished. The ones I know either had too many other art projects they were doing for commissary items or they were free-style artists who draw intuitively. Let's face it people don't come to prison because they are good at setting priorities, time management, and following instructions. All of those skills are needed for every artist who wants to make a comix.
In this school of hard knocks I've learned that success doesn't happen overnight. It takes hardwork: preperation. planning. as well as execution.

Likewise no one succeeds on their own with out help.

I'd like to thank everyone at ABO COMIX as well as all the readers who support their vision.

None of us can change our past - yet together - we all can create a better future.

In Solidarity,

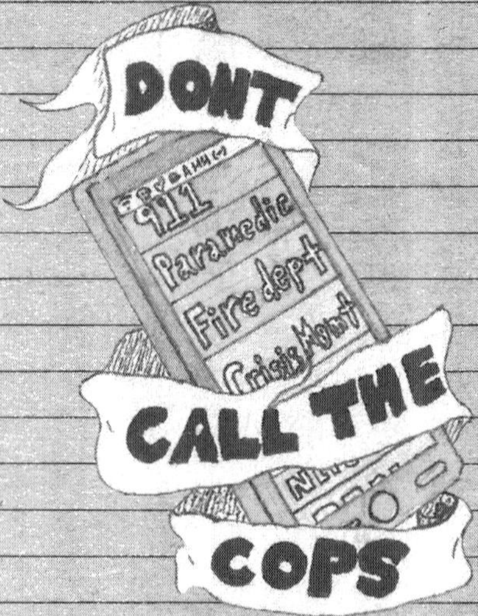
DONT
911
Paramedic
Fire dept
CALL THE
COPS

About This Anthology

Hi, we're the dorks who put this together. We're a squad of queer anarchist goblins; we live amongst you in this kookoo bananas world defined by the oh-so-scary crisis propelling it. And is there anything that symbolizes that crisis better than the god-damn Prison Industrial Complex? We've got big feelings about the PIC, like:

fuck-that-thing-holy-shit-how-did-we-let-this-become-normal?

We've also got big, more posi feelings about comics. It made sense to smash the two together into this book ya got as a way to give our comrades on the inside a vehicle for their stories, and a way to raise money for their commissaries and families.

The PIC is personal for a lot of us. It's torn our families apart. It's stolen some of our best people. It's been literal insult to injury for those practicing resistance. Prison is violence. So is poverty. And for people in poverty, prison is an ever present threat. Sometimes the things we must do to survive, and to try and escape our demoralizing reality for even a moment, carry the risk of incarceration. For our friends of color, and for the queers whose existence is a visible threat to hetero/homo-normativity, that threat hangs all the heavier. Poverty is the food that nourishes the carceral state into a hideous ouroboros of scapegoats and free labor.

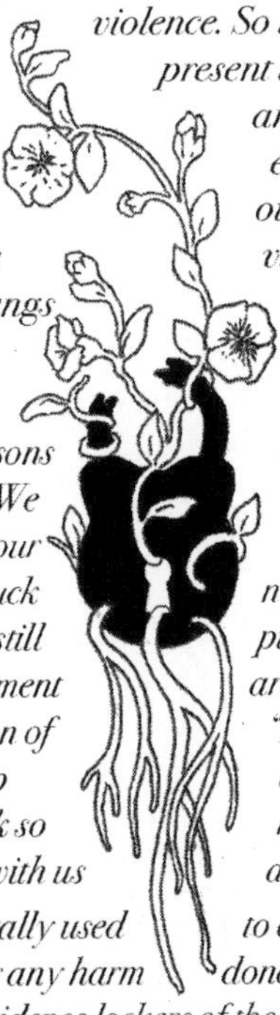

Because of this and more reasons than we could list, we do not believe in reforming prisons. We believe in abolishing them. Maybe you don't agree with our hot take on a world without prisons, cops, borders and truck nuts... but maybe we can agree that it's objectively horrifying we still put humans in cages – that corporations who profit off punishment are on some dystopian super-villain shit – and that the very notion of "Law and Order" in a rigged system is a gargantuan psyop designed to convince us our neighbors are disposable... ok so maybe we aren't all on the same page yet. Dear reader, stick with us a while longer, and you'll see!

Crime is a wacky word generally used to define offenses to the state, unrelated to its root causes or any harm done. Jails exist to satisfy the abstract notion of law, big concrete evidence lockers of the systematic oppression that props up this gross, gross country. But to pretend that without systemic oppression wrongdoing would disappear is utopian goobledy-gook. Without prisons, how would we address actual harm against individuals and communities? With no state to "take away the bad guys," how would we hold ourselves and each other accountable? How can we redefine "justice," not as a punitive process, but as a transformative one? And why wait for the bars to rust to explore these questions?

If you take anything away from these comics, we hope it's the desire to write a penpal in prison. Receiving a letter just might mean the absolute world to someone – it lets them know they are not forgotten. While there are a diversity of tactics to sabotage American values, writing somebody on the inside is the one most likely to get you a new friend!

- ABOcomix

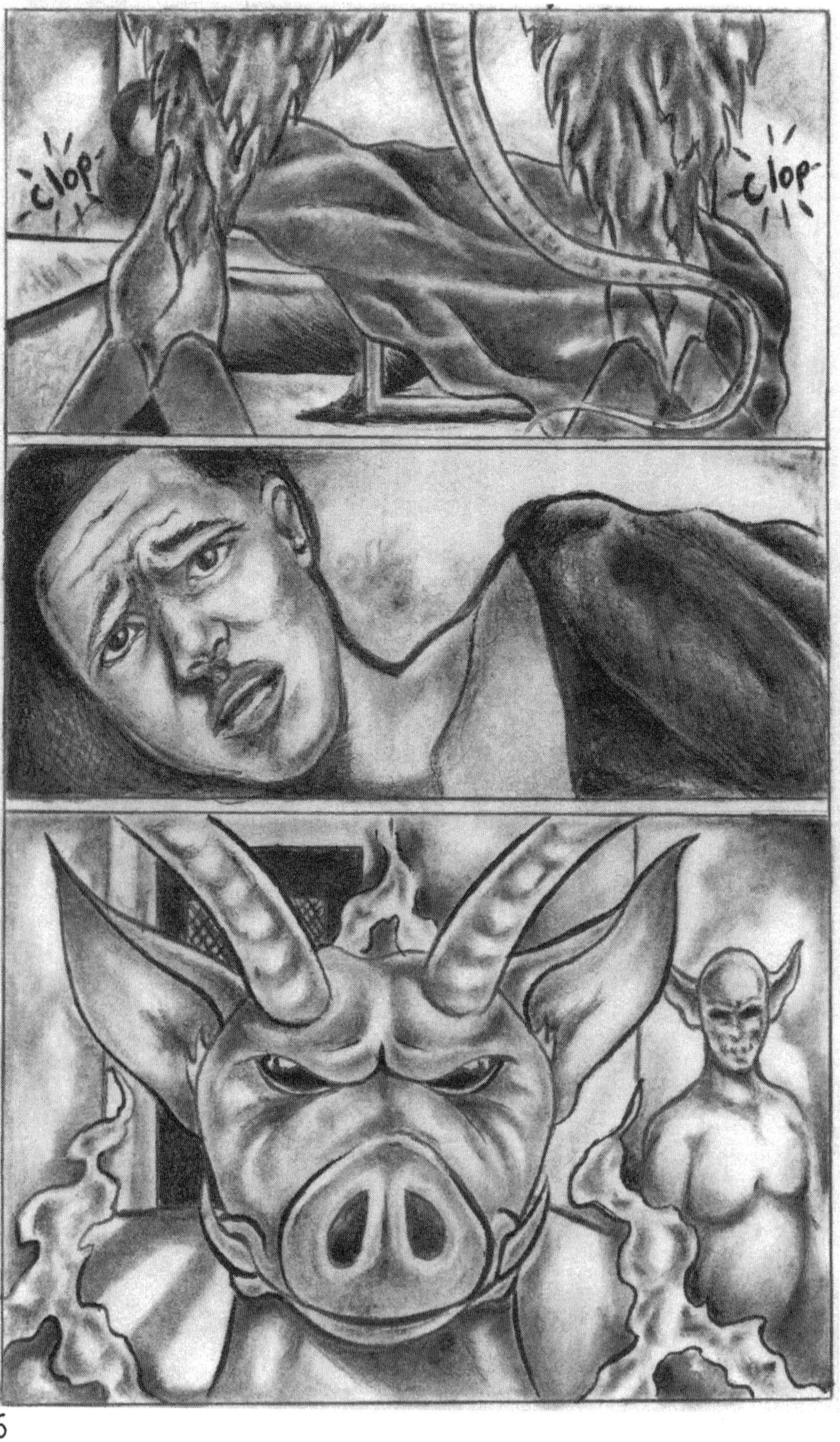
clop
clop

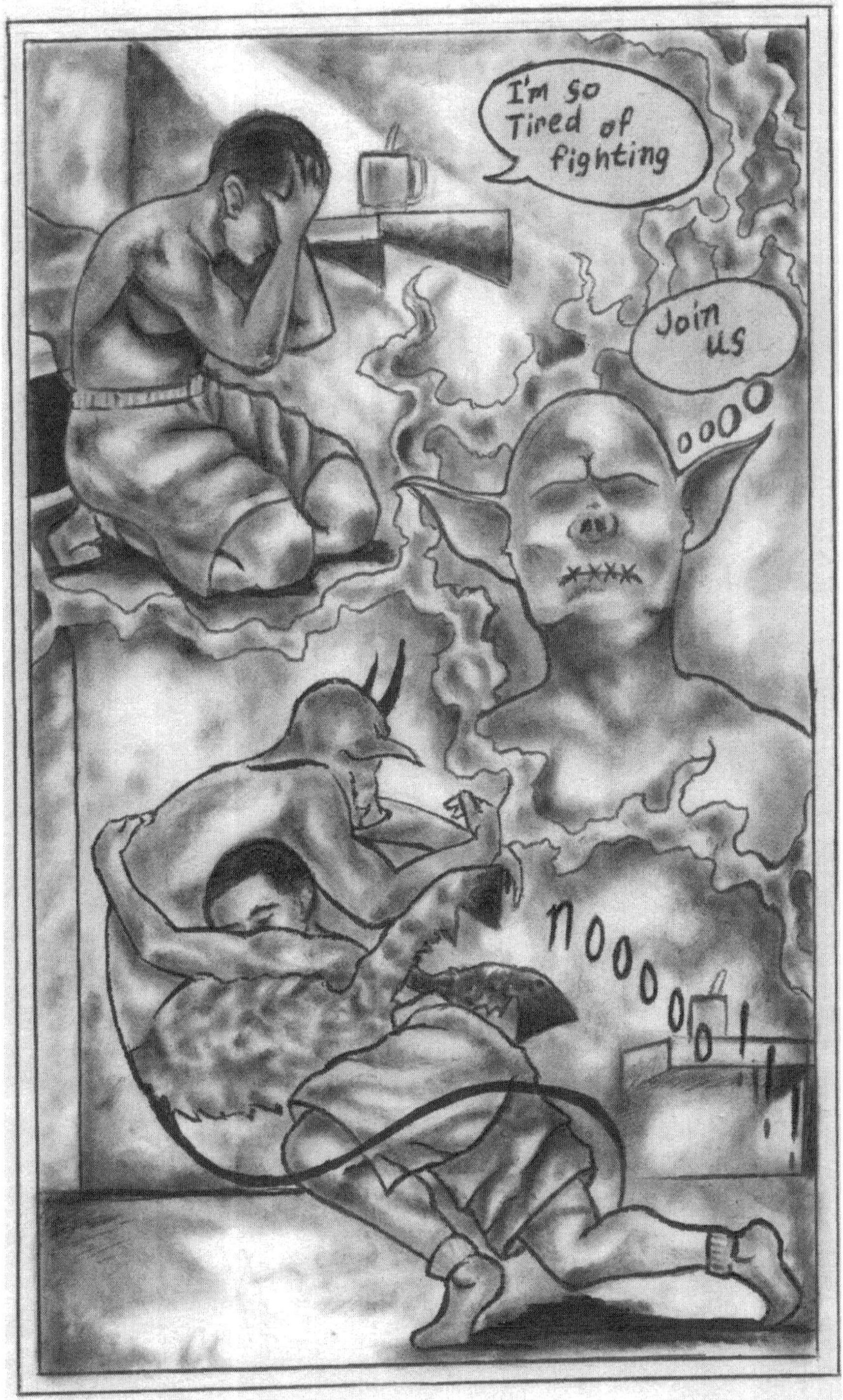
I'm so Tired of fighting
Join us
nooooo!!!

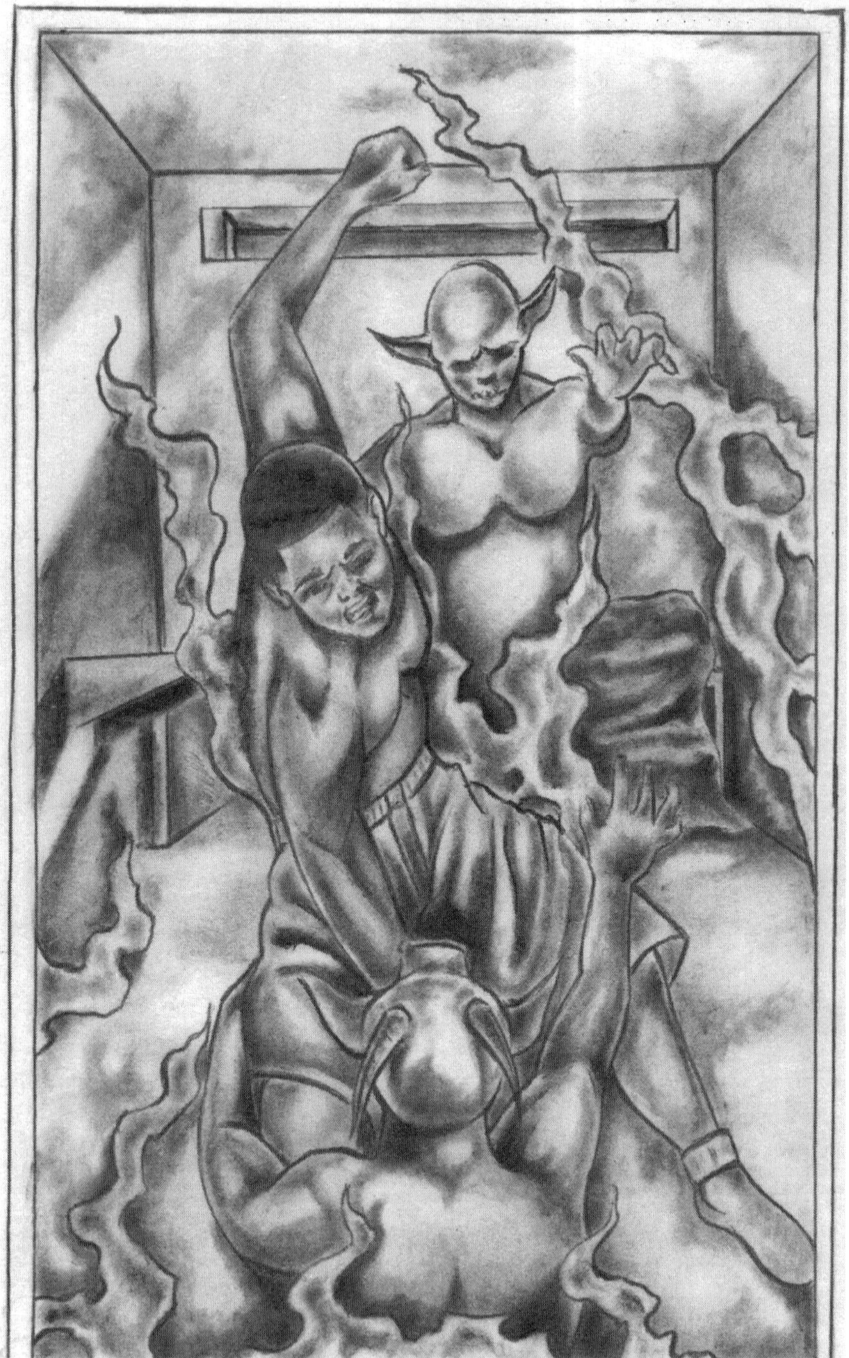

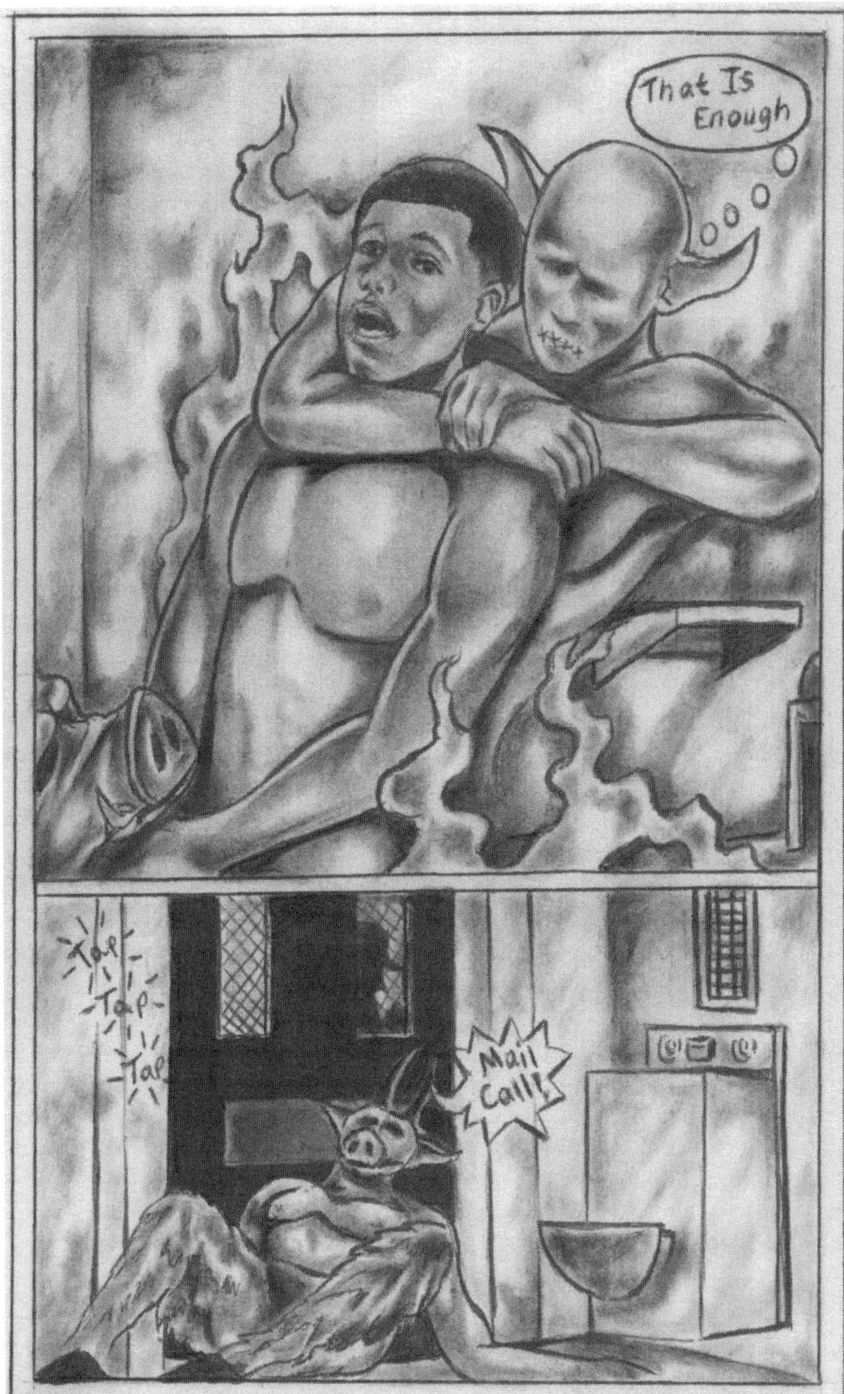
That Is Enough
Tap
Tap
Tap
Mail Call!

POOF
BLACK & Pink
Hello,
I found your name
on the Black & pink web
site. I hope to bring
some light into that
dark place you are.
With love and
Solidarity!
Emma
Write Back Soon!

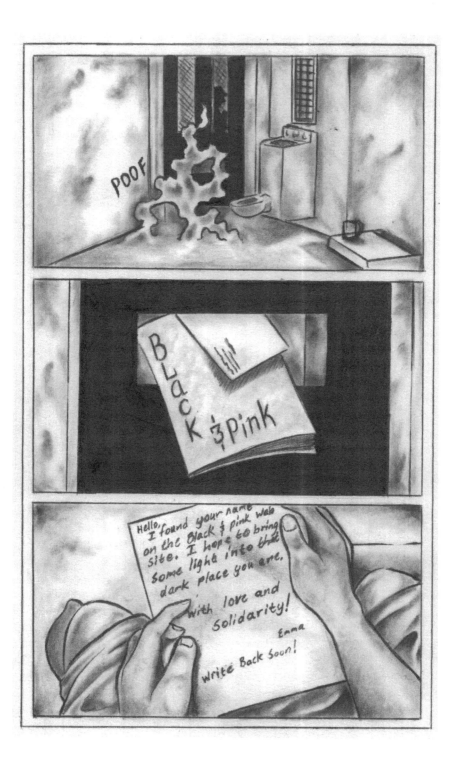

Emma
I want to thank you.
there is noway I can express
in words the importance
of people like you reaching
out to help us in the
fight to maintain.
Your support is the
very thing I needed to
keep the demons at
bay. We need more
beautiful people like
you to support people
in the prison industrial
complex. thank you, thank
you, thank you.
The
Beginning

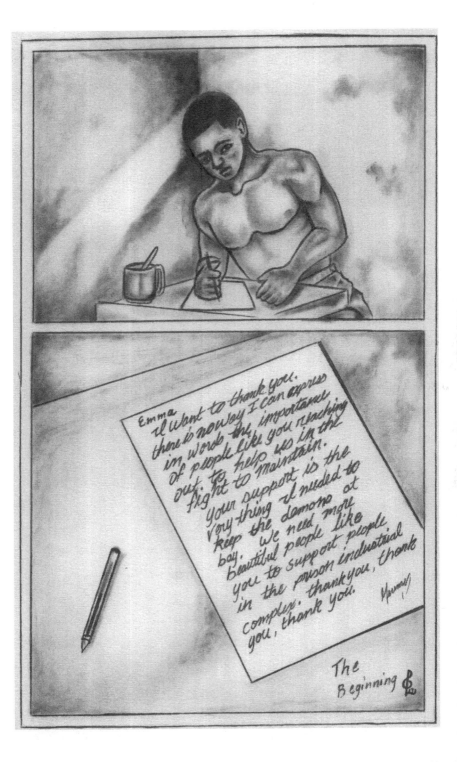

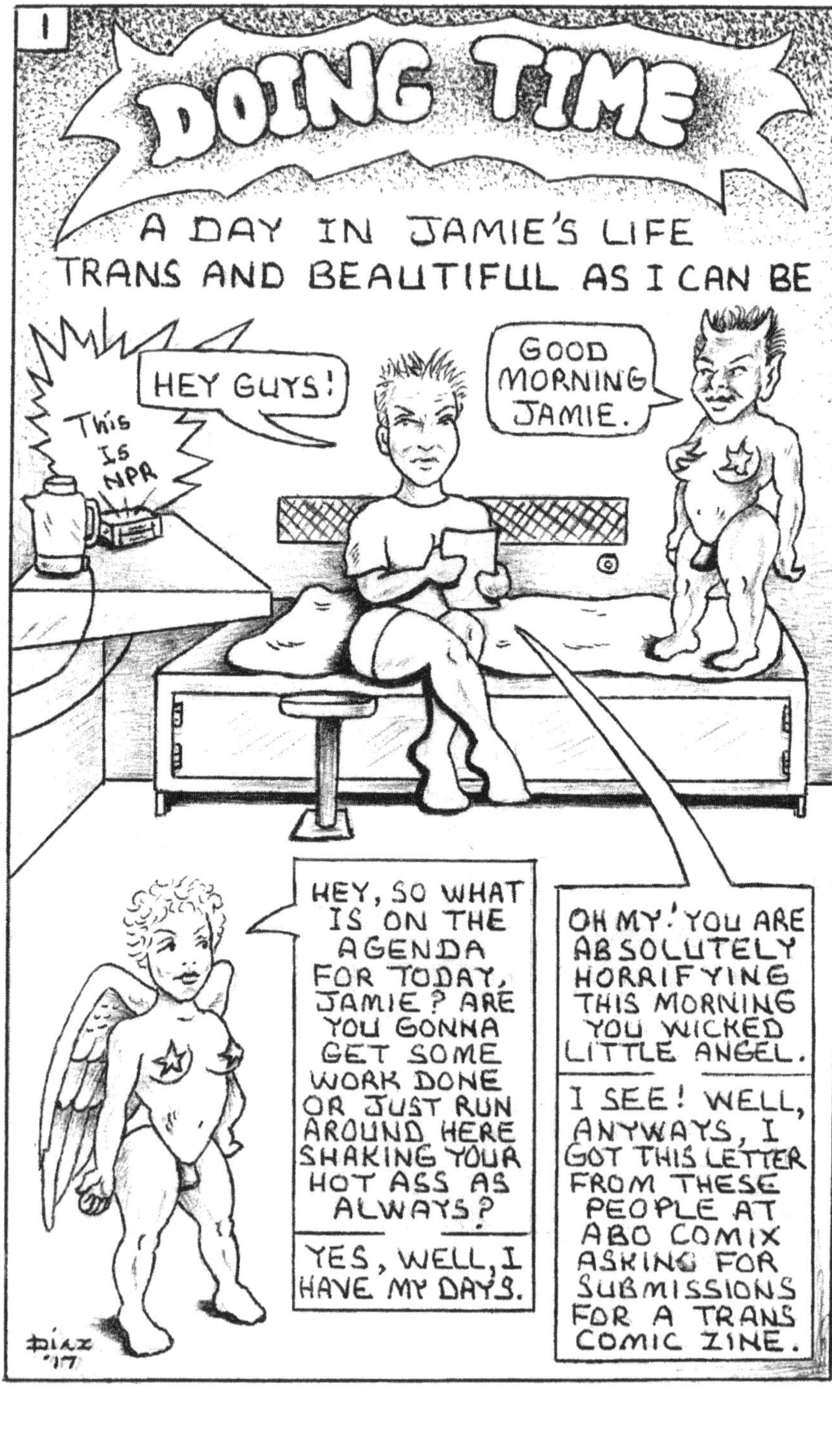
1
DOING TIME
A DAY IN JAMIE'S LIFE
TRANS AND BEAUTIFUL AS I CAN BE
This Is NPR
HEY GUYS!
GOOD MORNING JAMIE.
HEY, SO WHAT IS ON THE AGENDA FOR TODAY, JAMIE? ARE YOU GONNA GET SOME WORK DONE OR JUST RUN AROUND HERE SHAKING YOUR HOT ASS AS ALWAYS?
YES, WELL, I HAVE MY DAYS.
OH MY! YOU ARE ABSOLUTELY HORRIFYING THIS MORNING YOU WICKED LITTLE ANGEL.
I SEE! WELL, ANYWAYS, I GOT THIS LETTER FROM THESE PEOPLE AT ABO COMIX ASKING FOR SUBMISSIONS FOR A TRANS COMIC ZINE.
DIAZ '17

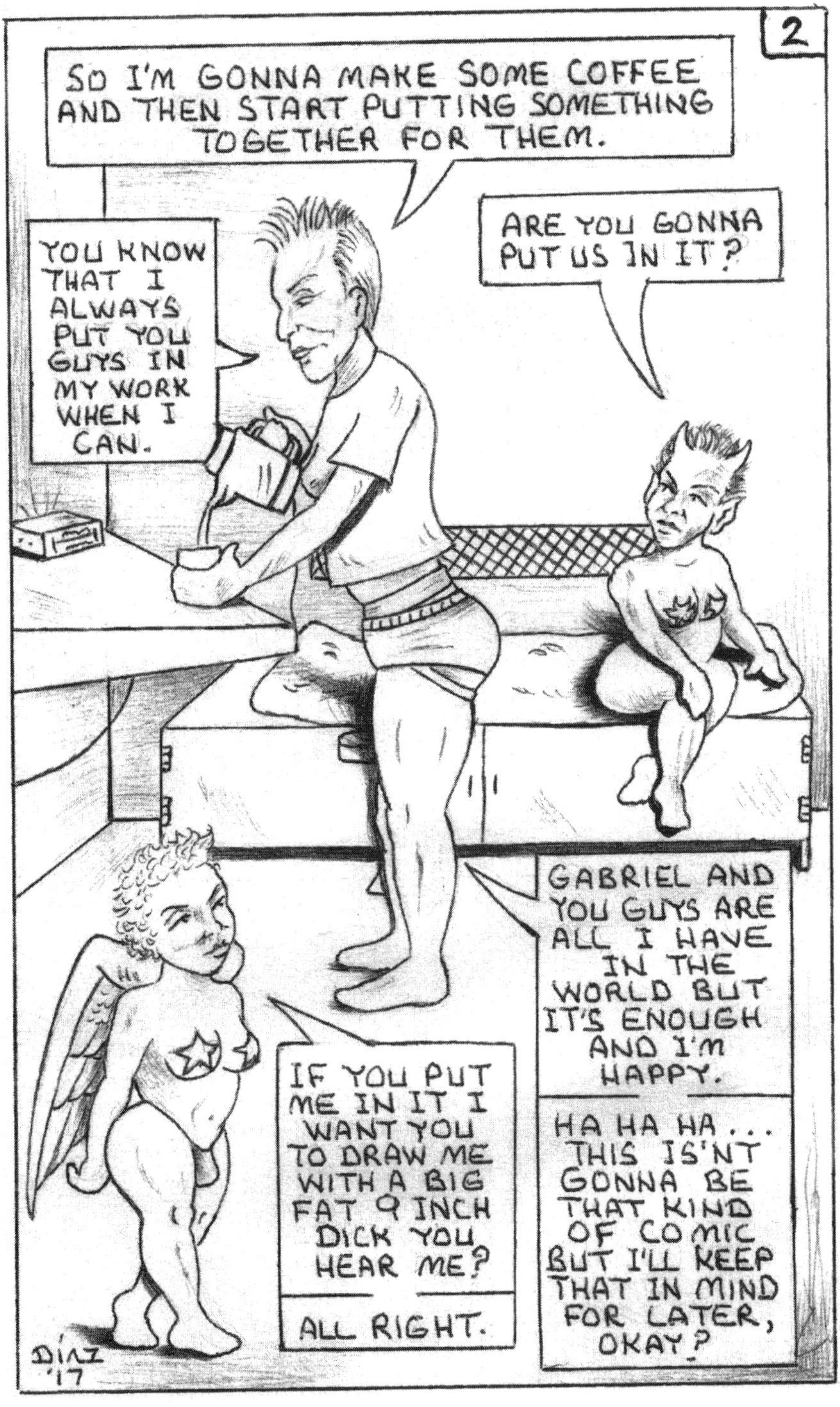
2
SO I'M GONNA MAKE SOME COFFEE AND THEN START PUTTING SOMETHING TOGETHER FOR THEM.
YOU KNOW THAT I ALWAYS PUT YOU GUYS IN MY WORK WHEN I CAN.
ARE YOU GONNA PUT US IN IT?
GABRIEL AND YOU GUYS ARE ALL I HAVE IN THE WORLD BUT IT'S ENOUGH AND I'M HAPPY.
IF YOU PUT ME IN IT I WANT YOU TO DRAW ME WITH A BIG FAT 9 INCH DICK YOU HEAR ME?
ALL RIGHT.
HA HA HA... THIS IS'NT GONNA BE THAT KIND OF COMIC BUT I'LL KEEP THAT IN MIND FOR LATER, OKAY?
DIAZ '17

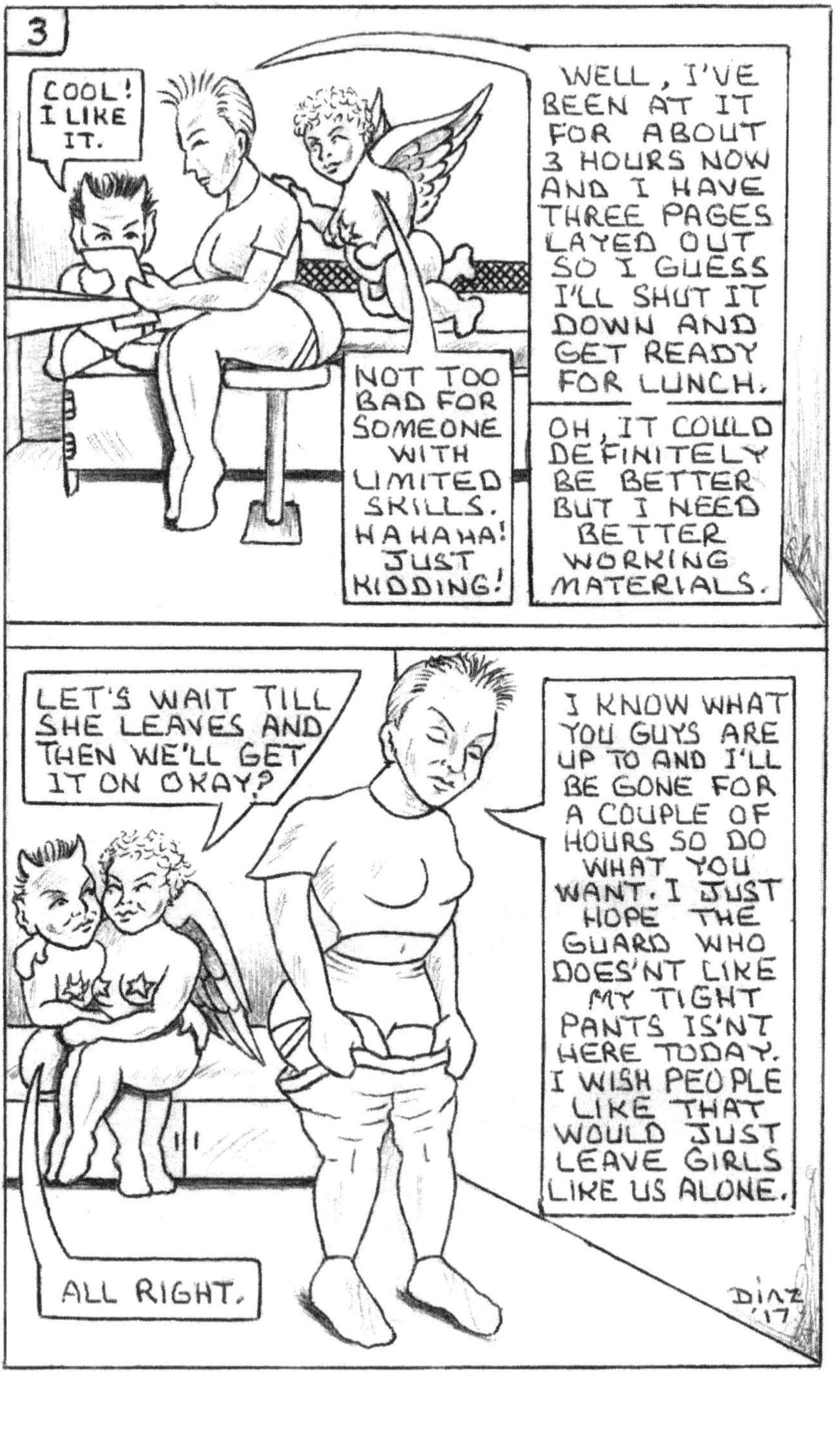
3
COOL! I LIKE IT.
WELL, I'VE BEEN AT IT FOR ABOUT 3 HOURS NOW AND I HAVE THREE PAGES LAYED OUT SO I GUESS I'LL SHUT IT DOWN AND GET READY FOR LUNCH.
NOT TOO BAD FOR SOMEONE WITH LIMITED SKILLS. HAHAHA! JUST KIDDING!
OH, IT COULD DEFINITELY BE BETTER BUT I NEED BETTER WORKING MATERIALS.
LET'S WAIT TILL SHE LEAVES AND THEN WE'LL GET IT ON OKAY?
I KNOW WHAT YOU GUYS ARE UP TO AND I'LL BE GONE FOR A COUPLE OF HOURS SO DO WHAT YOU WANT. I JUST HOPE THE GUARD WHO DOES'NT LIKE MY TIGHT PANTS IS'NT HERE TODAY. I WISH PEOPLE LIKE THAT WOULD JUST LEAVE GIRLS LIKE US ALONE.
ALL RIGHT.
DIAZ '17

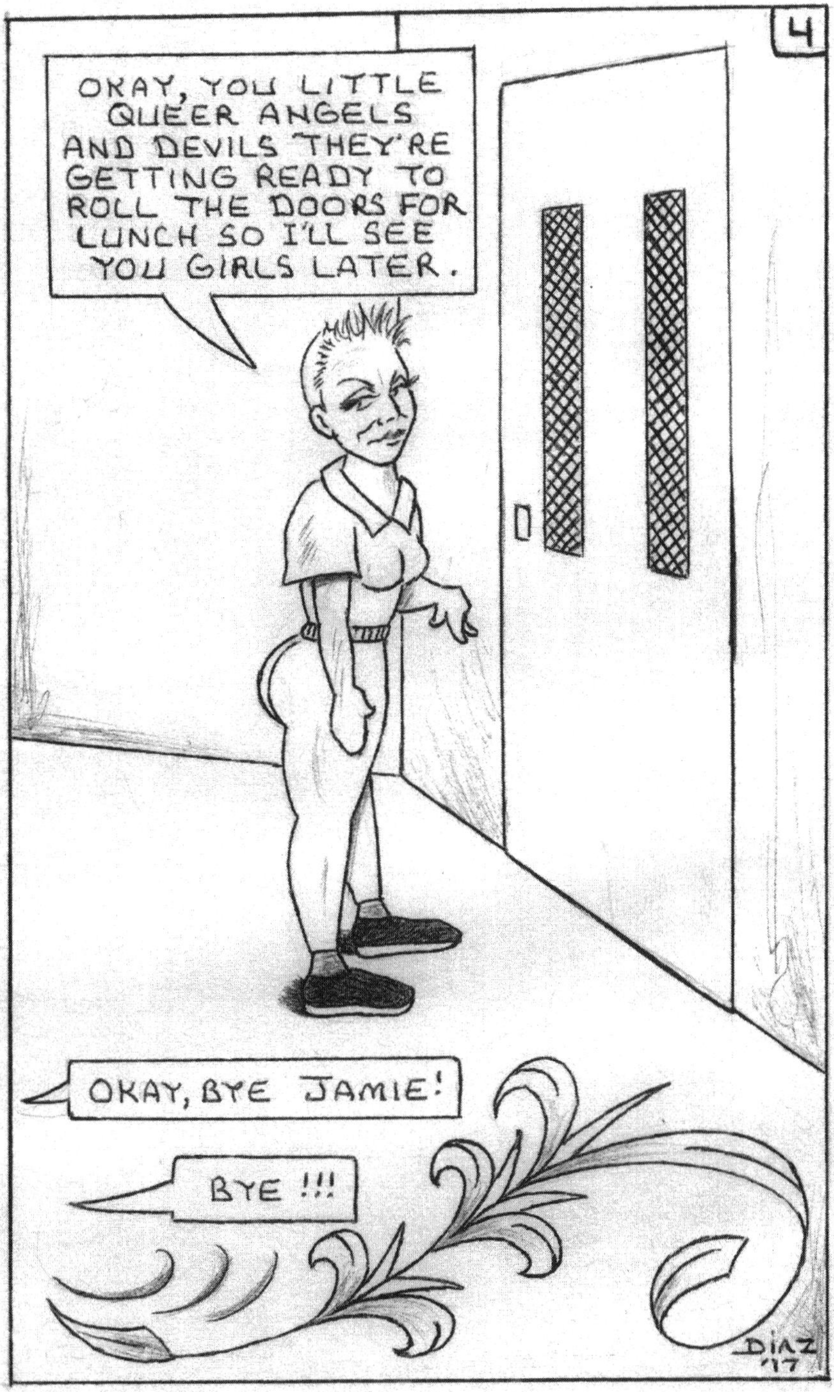
4
OKAY, YOU LITTLE QUEER ANGELS AND DEVILS THEY'RE GETTING READY TO ROLL THE DOORS FOR LUNCH SO I'LL SEE YOU GIRLS LATER.
OKAY, BYE JAMIE!
BYE !!!
DIAZ '17

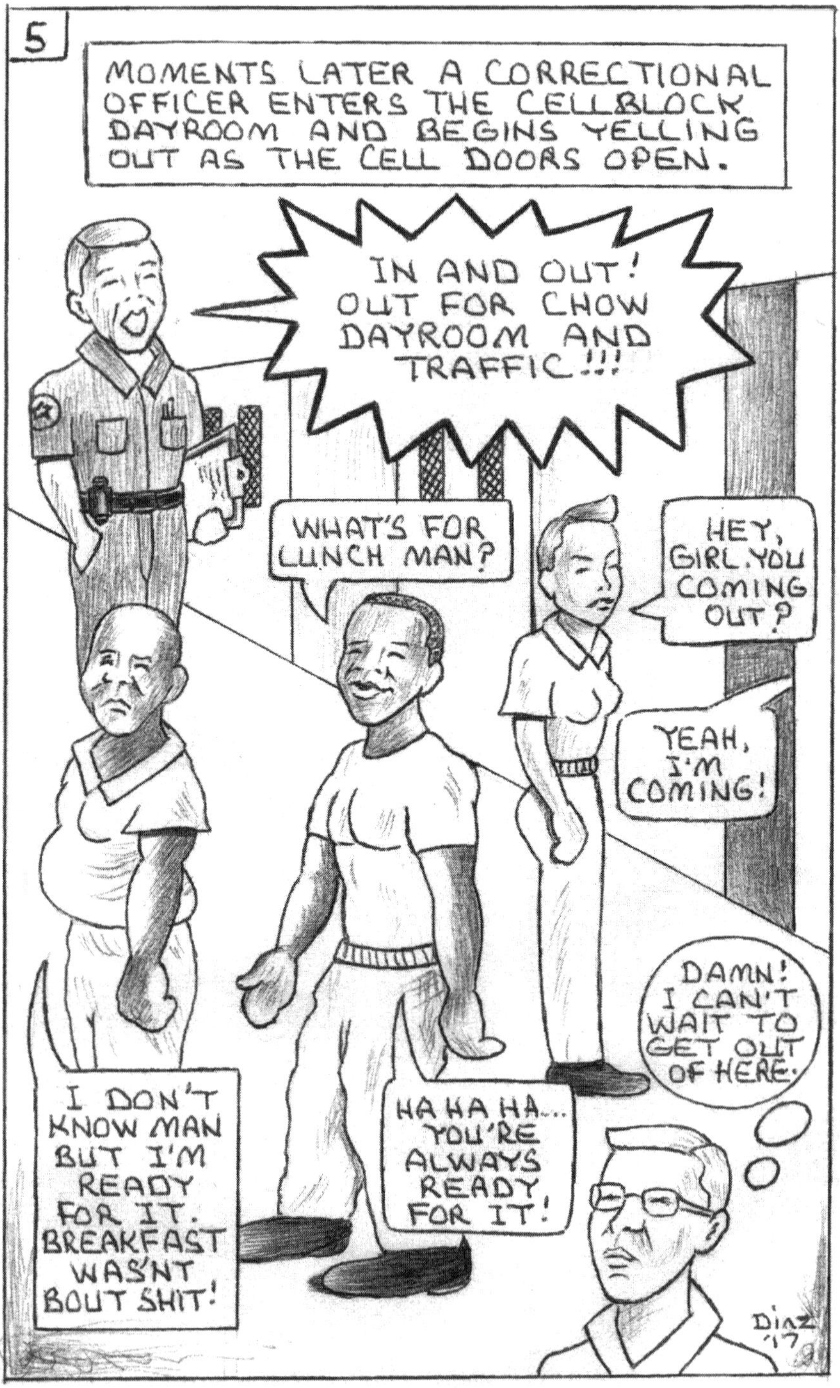
5
MOMENTS LATER A CORRECTIONAL OFFICER ENTERS THE CELLBLOCK DAYROOM AND BEGINS YELLING OUT AS THE CELL DOORS OPEN.
IN AND OUT! OUT FOR CHOW DAYROOM AND TRAFFIC!!!
WHAT'S FOR LUNCH MAN?
HEY, GIRL. YOU COMING OUT?
YEAH, I'M COMING!
DAMN! I CAN'T WAIT TO GET OUT OF HERE.
I DON'T KNOW MAN BUT I'M READY FOR IT. BREAKFAST WAS'NT BOUT SHIT!
HA HA HA... YOU'RE ALWAYS READY FOR IT!
DIAZ '17

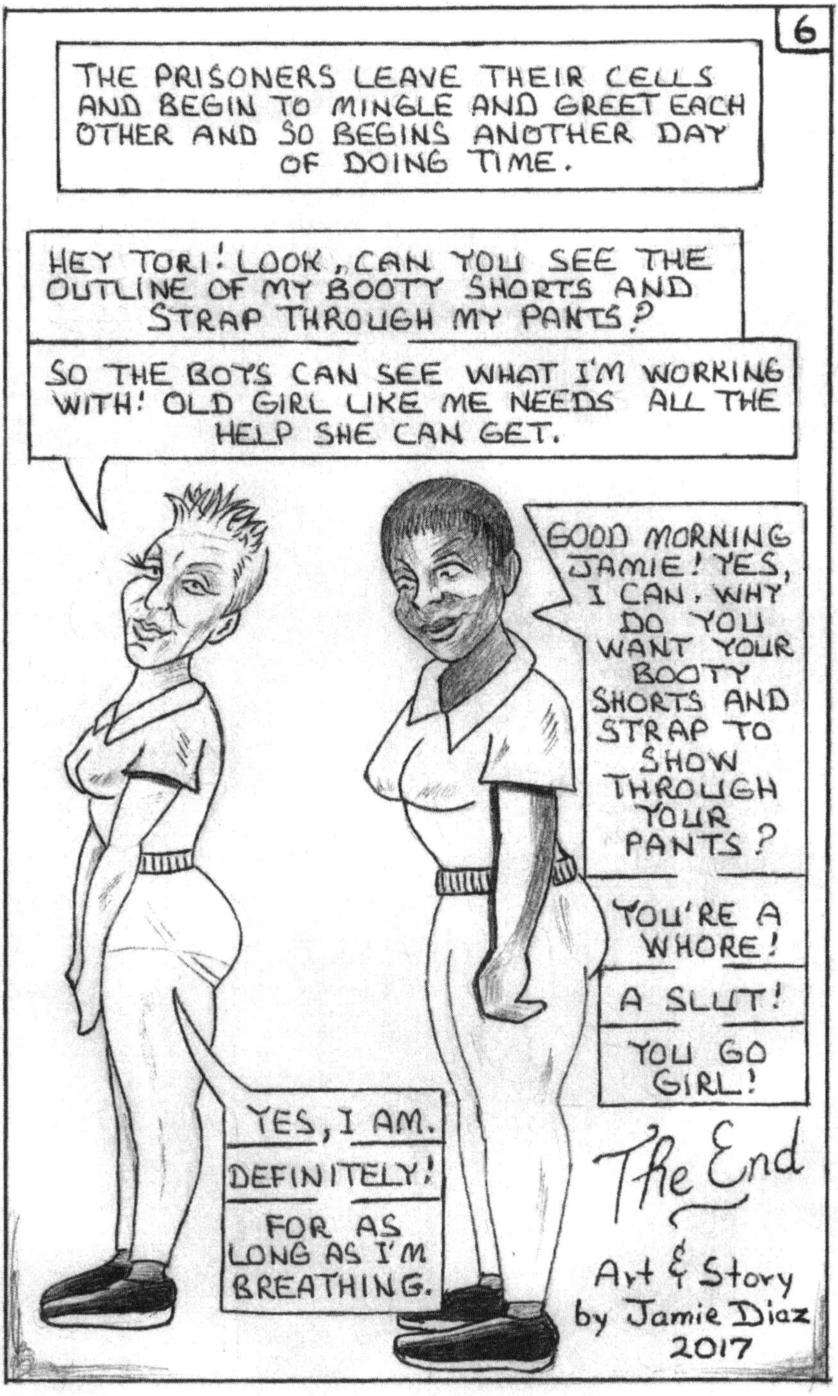
6
THE PRISONERS LEAVE THEIR CELLS AND BEGIN TO MINGLE AND GREET EACH OTHER AND SO BEGINS ANOTHER DAY OF DOING TIME.
HEY TORI! LOOK, CAN YOU SEE THE OUTLINE OF MY BOOTY SHORTS AND STRAP THROUGH MY PANTS?
GOOD MORNING JAMIE! YES, I CAN, WHY DO YOU WANT YOUR BOOTY SHORTS AND STRAP TO SHOW THROUGH YOUR PANTS?
SO THE BOYS CAN SEE WHAT I'M WORKING WITH! OLD GIRL LIKE ME NEEDS ALL THE HELP SHE CAN GET.
YOU'RE A WHORE!
A SLUT!
YOU GO GIRL!
YES, I AM.
DEFINITELY!
FOR AS LONG AS I'M BREATHING.
The End
Art & Story by Jamie Diaz 2017

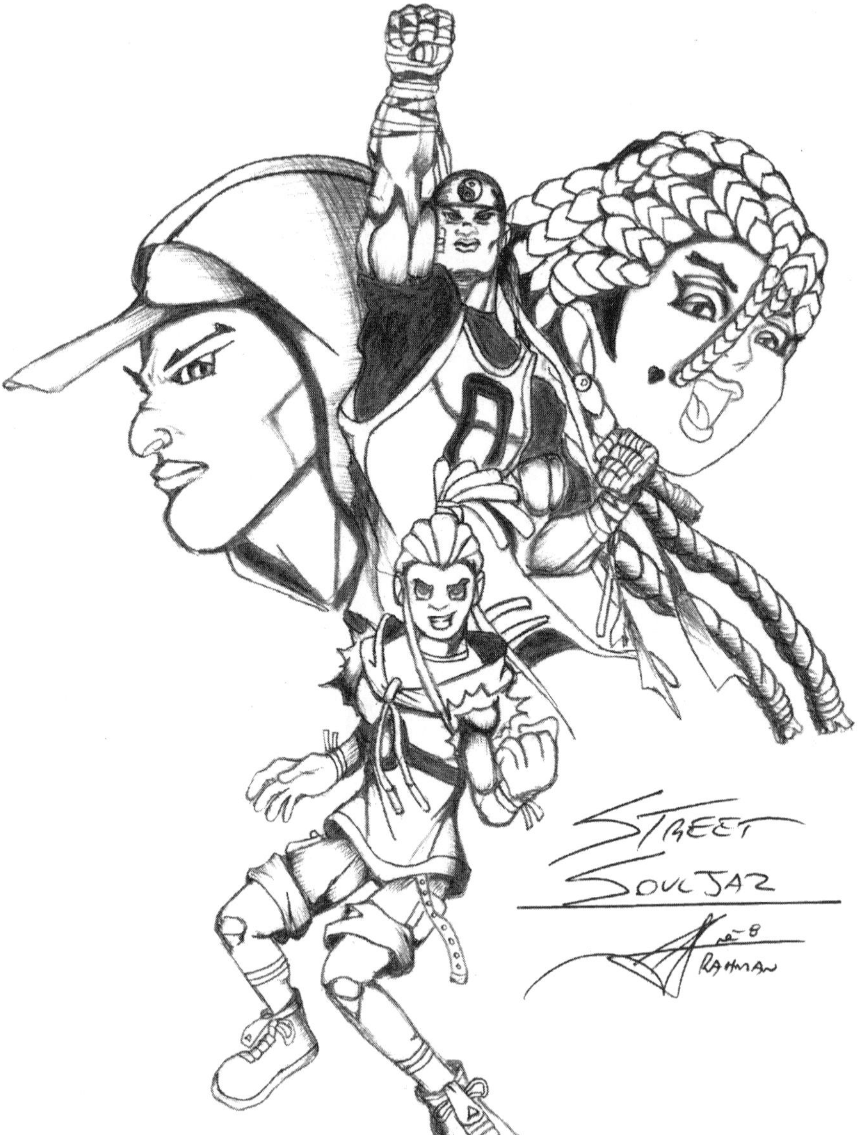
STREET
SOULJAZ
RAHMAN

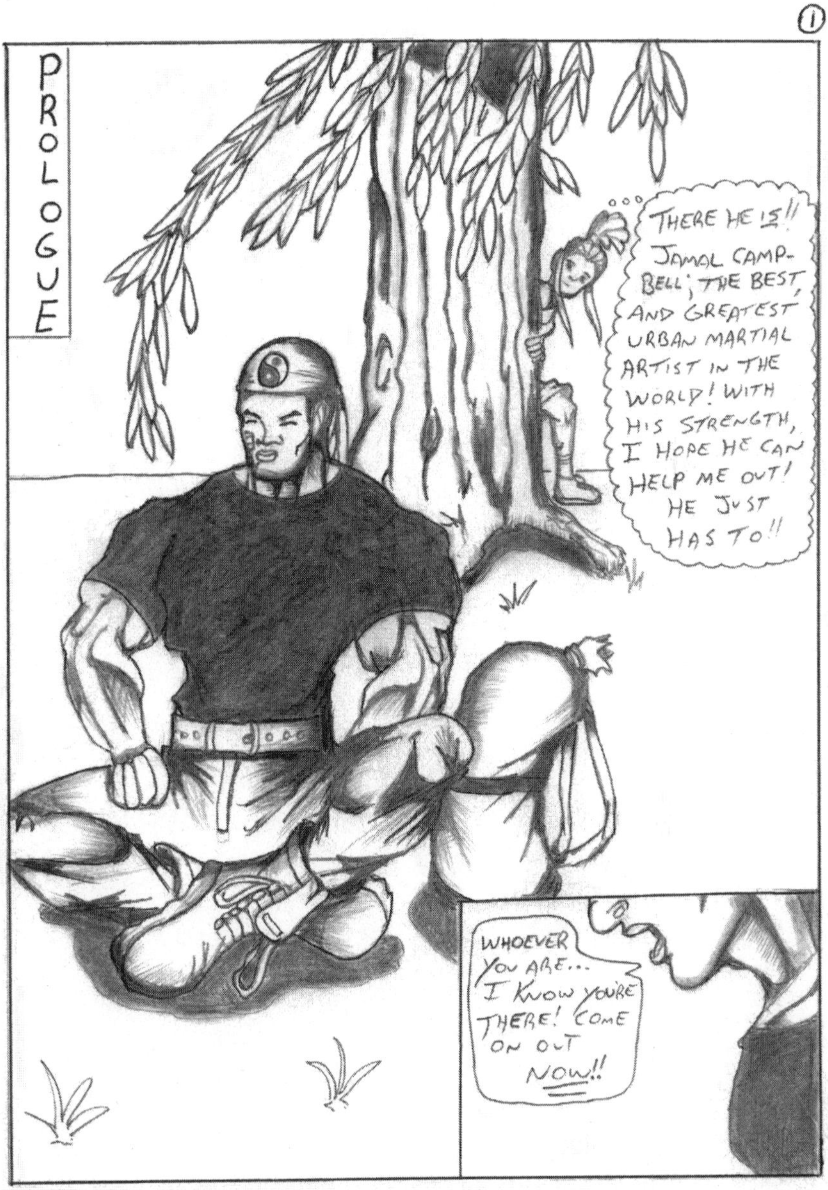

1
PROLOGUE
THERE HE IS!! JAMAL CAMPBELL; THE BEST, AND GREATEST URBAN MARTIAL ARTIST IN THE WORLD! WITH HIS STRENGTH, I HOPE HE CAN HELP ME OUT! HE JUST HAS TO!!
WHOEVER YOU ARE... I KNOW YOU'RE THERE! COME ON OUT NOW!!

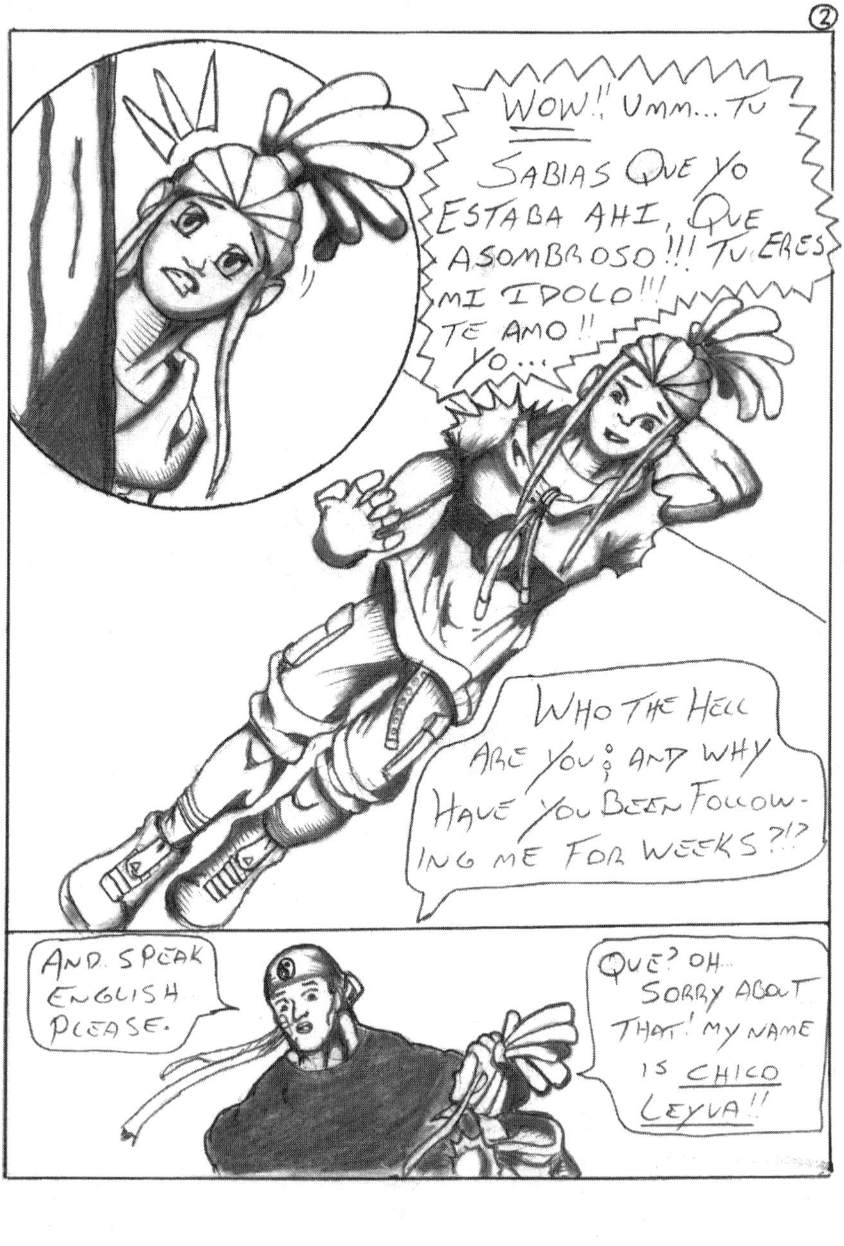
2
WOW!! UMM... TU SABIAS QUE YO ESTABA AHI, QUE ASOMBROSO!!! TU ERES MI IDOLO!!! TE AMO!! YO...
WHO THE HELL ARE YOU¿ AND WHY HAVE YOU BEEN FOLLOW-ING ME FOR WEEKS?!?
AND SPEAK ENGLISH PLEASE.
QUE? OH... SORRY ABOUT THAT! MY NAME IS CHICO LEYVA!!

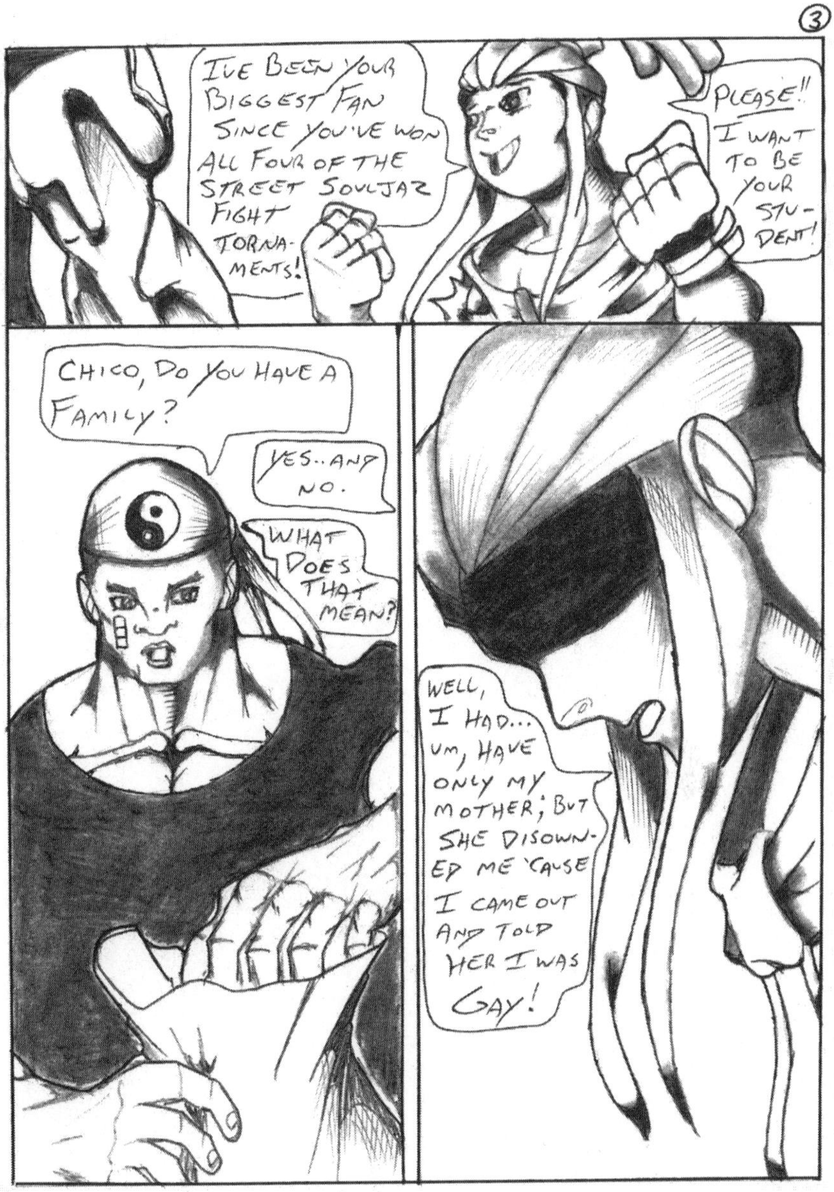
③
IVE BEEN YOUR BIGGEST FAN SINCE YOU'VE WON ALL FOUR OF THE STREET SOULJAZ FIGHT TORNA-MENTS!
PLEASE!! I WANT TO BE YOUR STU-DENT!
CHICO, DO YOU HAVE A FAMILY?
YES..AND NO.
WHAT DOES THAT MEAN?
WELL, I HAD... UM, HAVE ONLY MY MOTHER; BUT SHE DISOWN-ED ME 'CAUSE I CAME OUT AND TOLD HER I WAS GAY!

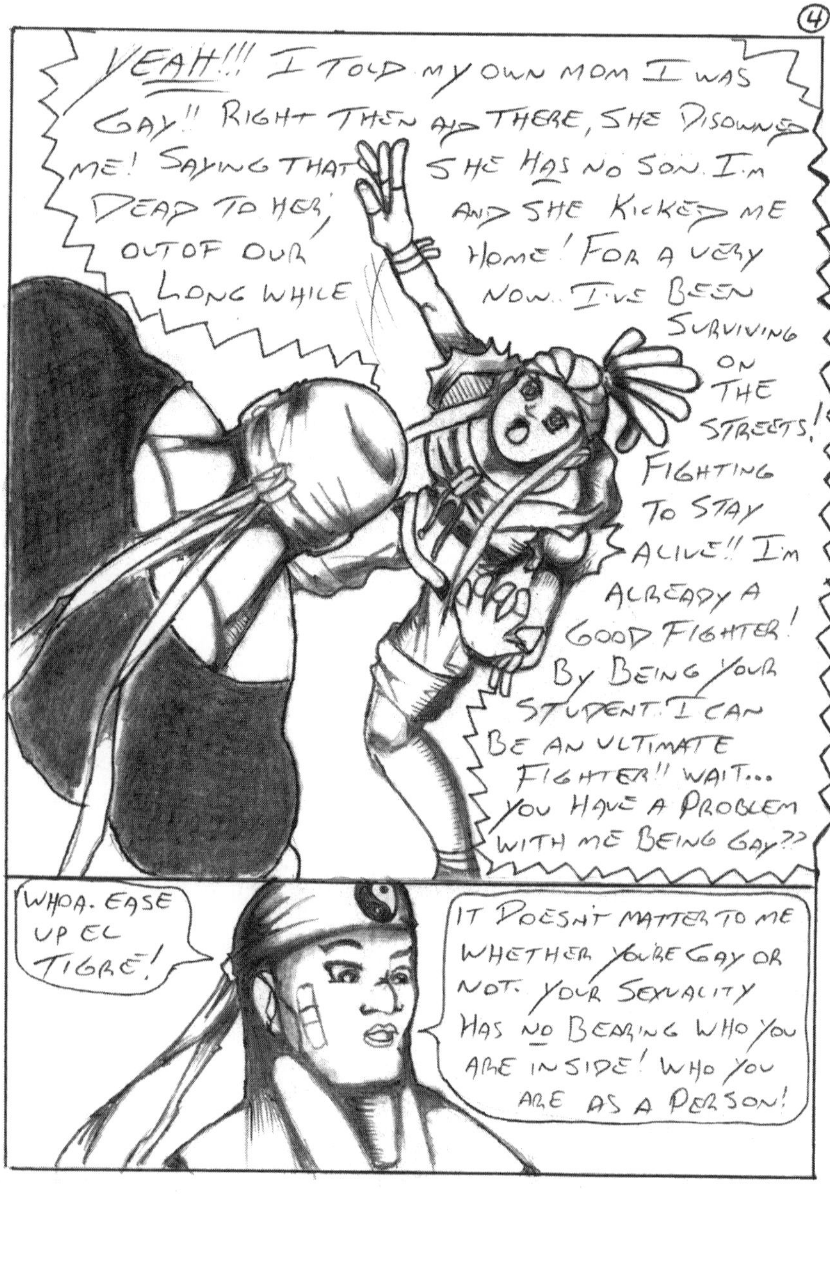
4
YEAH!!! I TOLD MY OWN MOM I WAS GAY!! RIGHT THEN AND THERE, SHE DISOWNED ME! SAYING THAT SHE HAS NO SON. I'M DEAD TO HER, AND SHE KICKED ME OUT OF OUR HOME! FOR A VERY LONG WHILE NOW. I'VE BEEN SURVIVING ON THE STREETS! FIGHTING TO STAY ALIVE!! I'M ALREADY A GOOD FIGHTER! BY BEING YOUR STUDENT. I CAN BE AN ULTIMATE FIGHTER!! WAIT... YOU HAVE A PROBLEM WITH ME BEING GAY??
WHOA. EASE UP EL TIGRE!
IT DOESN'T MATTER TO ME WHETHER YOU'RE GAY OR NOT. YOUR SEXUALITY HAS NO BEARING WHO YOU ARE INSIDE! WHO YOU ARE AS A PERSON!

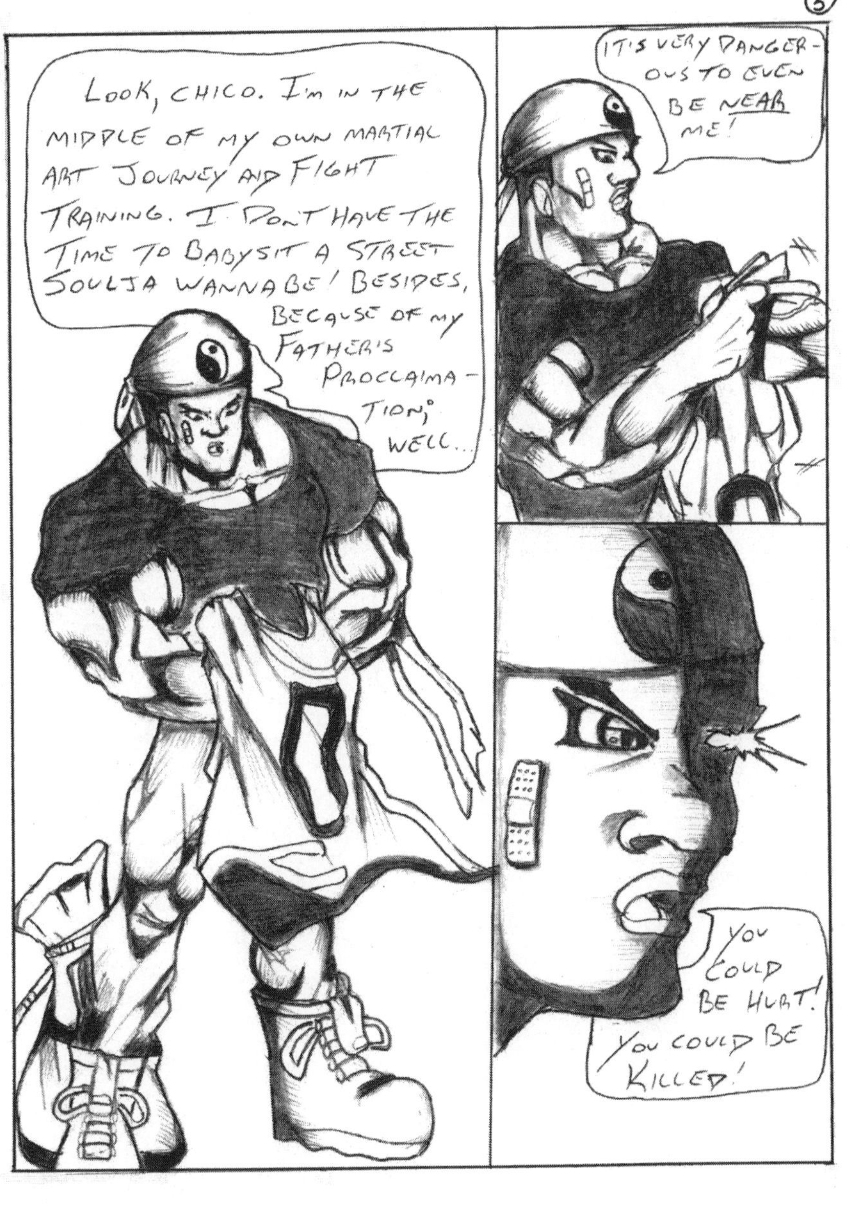
5
LOOK, CHICO. I'M IN THE MIDDLE OF MY OWN MARTIAL ART JOURNEY AND FIGHT TRAINING. I DON'T HAVE THE TIME TO BABYSIT A STREET SOULJA WANNABE! BESIDES, BECAUSE OF MY FATHER'S PROCCLAIMA-TION; WELL...
IT'S VERY DANGER-OUS TO EVEN BE NEAR ME!
YOU COULD BE HURT! YOU COULD BE KILLED!

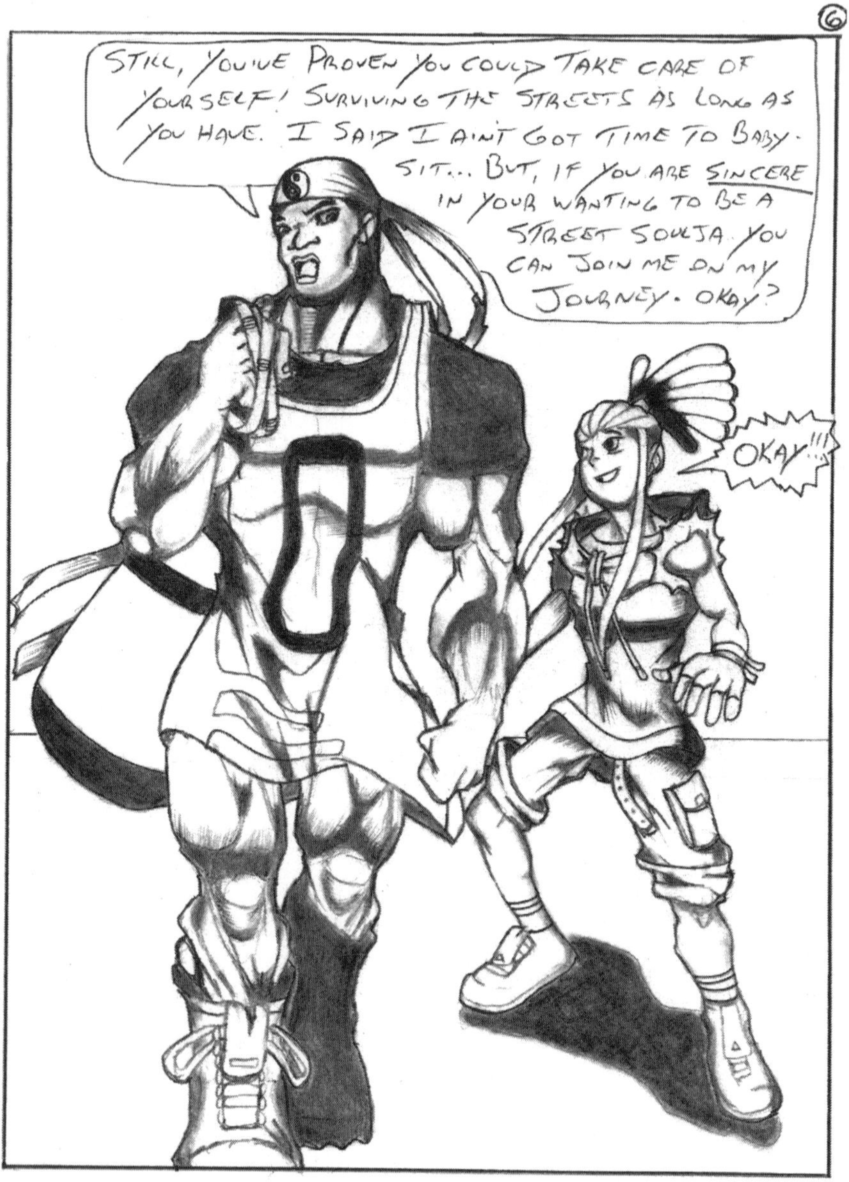
6
STILL, YOU'VE PROVEN YOU COULD TAKE CARE OF YOURSELF! SURVIVING THE STREETS AS LONG AS YOU HAVE. I SAID I AIN'T GOT TIME TO BABY-SIT... BUT, IF YOU ARE SINCERE IN YOUR WANTING TO BE A STREET SOULJA YOU CAN JOIN ME ON MY JOURNEY. OKAY?
OKAY!!!

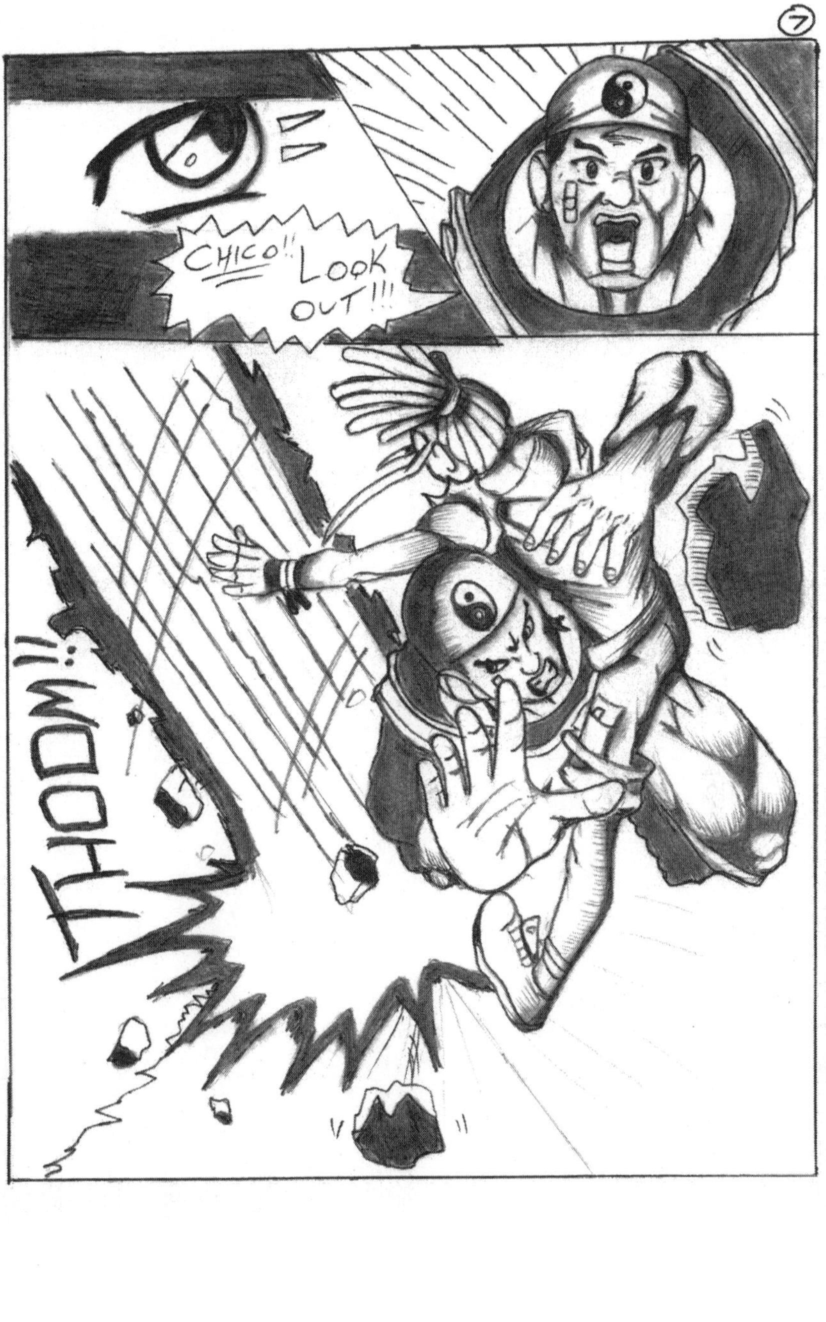
7
CHICO!! LOOK OUT!!!
THOOM!!

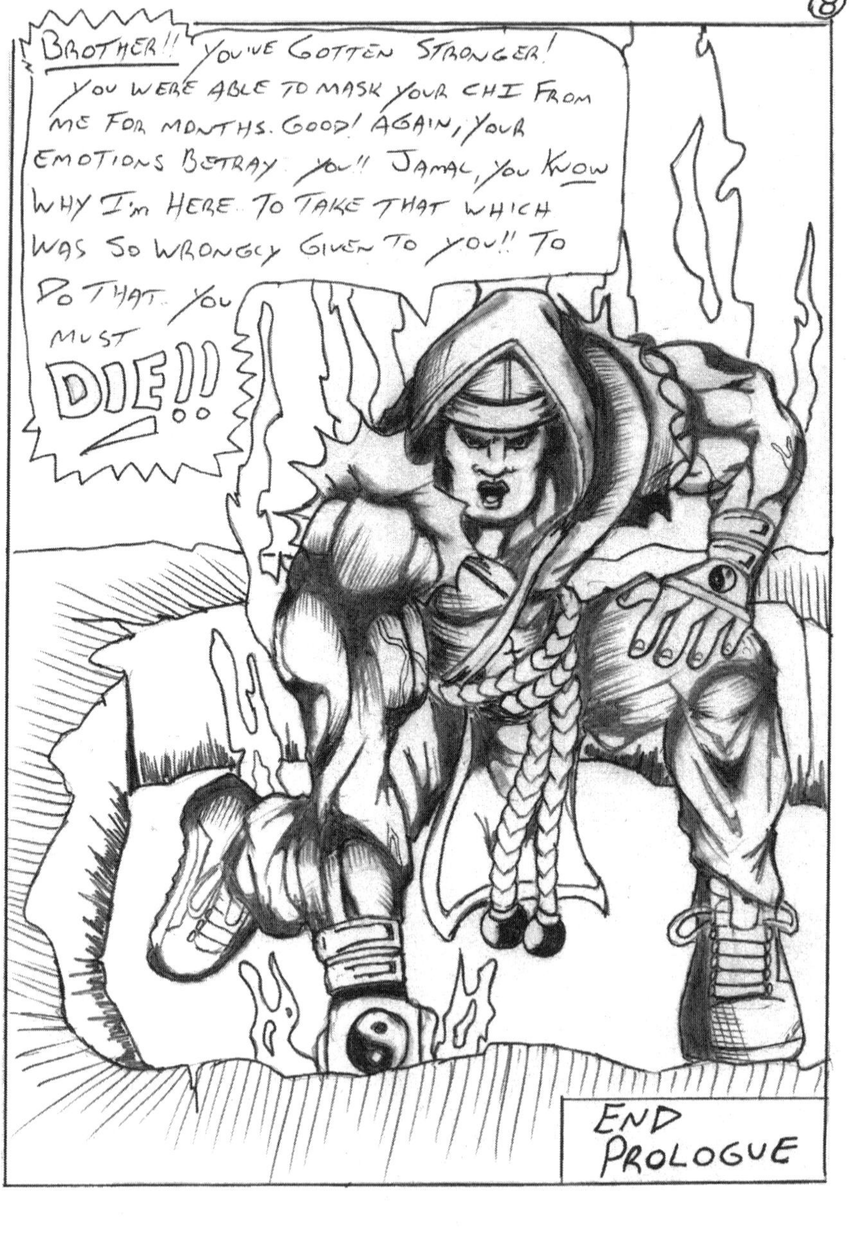
8
BROTHER!! YOU'VE GOTTEN STRONGER! YOU WERE ABLE TO MASK YOUR CHI FROM ME FOR MONTHS. GOOD! AGAIN, YOUR EMOTIONS BETRAY YOU!! JAMAL, YOU KNOW WHY I'M HERE. TO TAKE THAT WHICH WAS SO WRONGLY GIVEN TO YOU!! TO DO THAT, YOU MUST DIE!!
END PROLOGUE

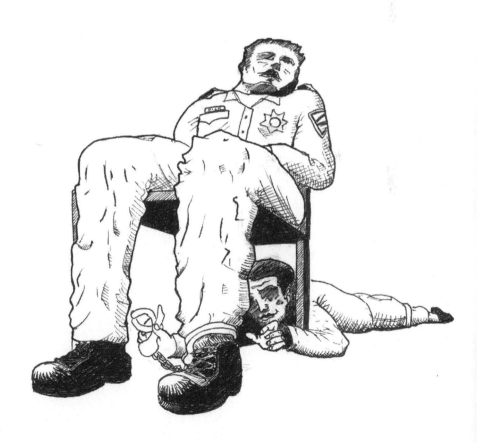

Kevin Bowling
"Kevin and Hell"

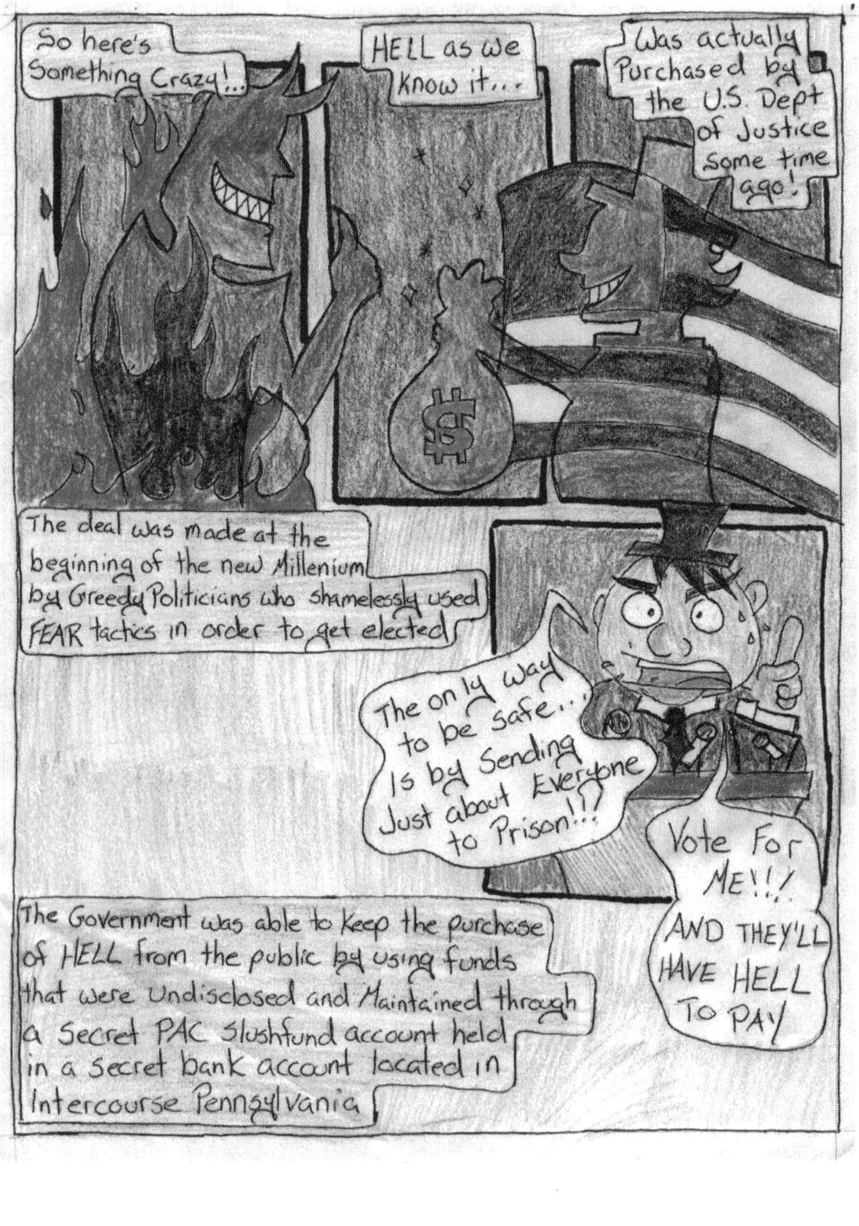
So here's Something Crazy!..
HELL as we know it...
Was actually Purchased by the U.S. Dept of Justice Some time ago!
The deal was made at the beginning of the new Millenium by Greedy Politicians who shamelessly used FEAR tactics in order to get elected
The only way to be safe... Is by Sending Just about Everyone to Prison!!!
Vote For ME!!! AND THEY'LL HAVE HELL TO PAY
The Government was able to keep the purchase of HELL from the public by using funds that were Undisclosed and Maintained through a Secret PAC Slushfund account held in a Secret bank account located in Intercourse Pennsylvania

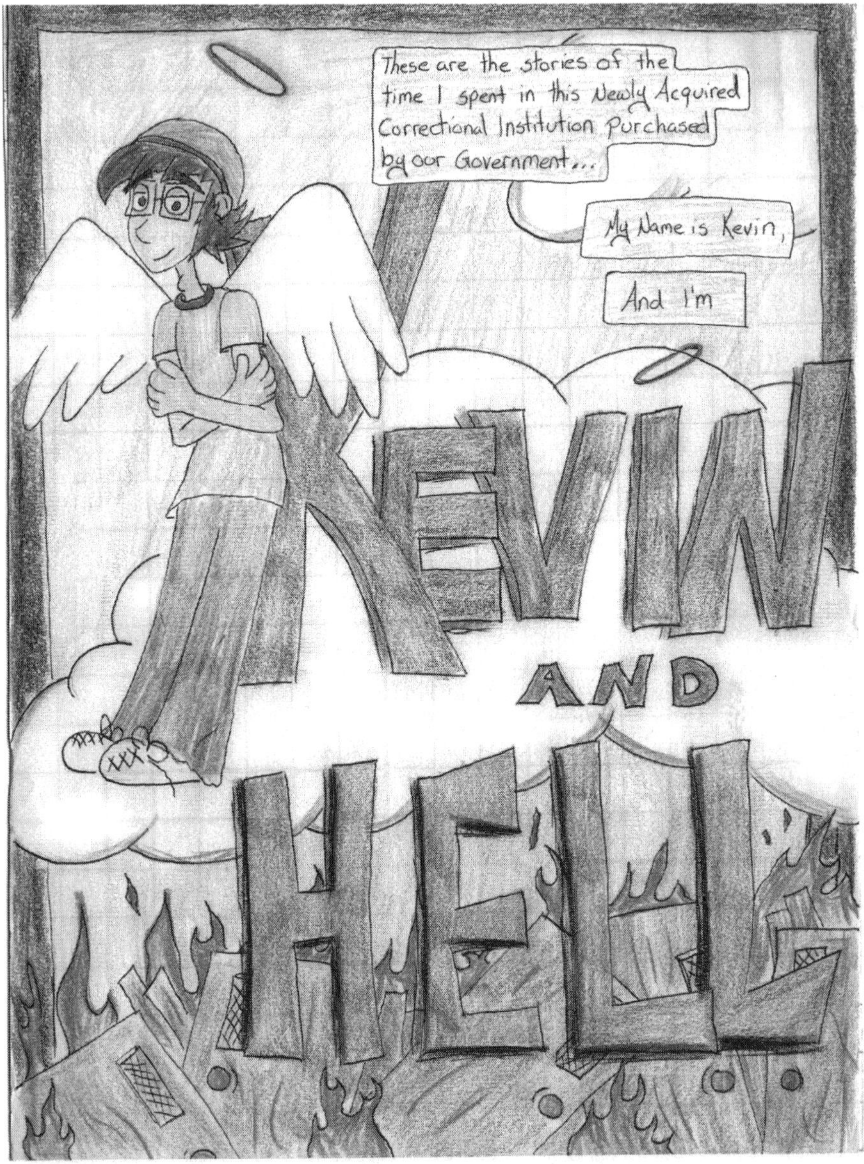
These are the stories of the time I spent in this Newly Acquired Correctional Institution Purchased by our Government...
My Name is Kevin,
And I'm
KEVIN
AND
HELL

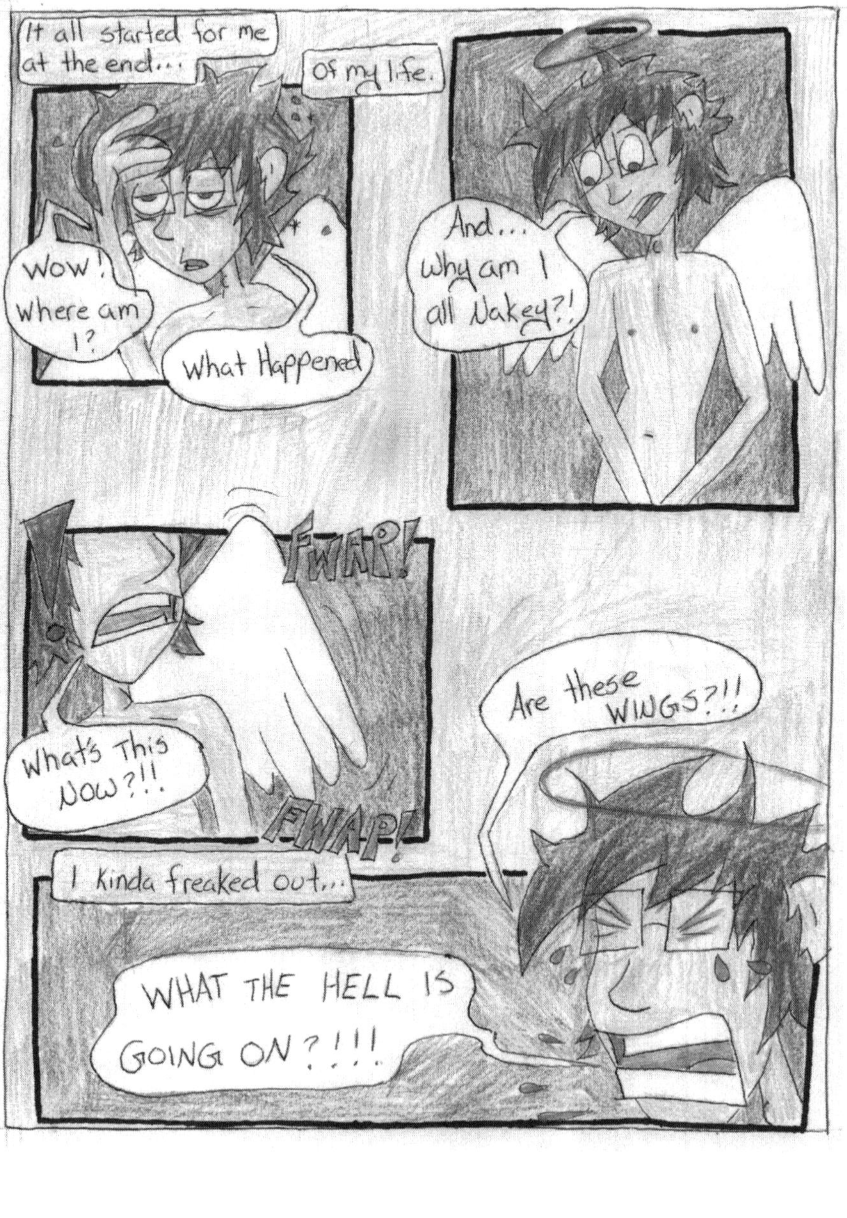

It all started for me at the end...
Of my life.
Wow! Where am I?
What Happened
And... why am I all Nakey?!
FWAP!
What's This NOW?!!
FWAP!
Are these WINGS?!!
I kinda freaked out...
WHAT THE HELL IS GOING ON?!!!

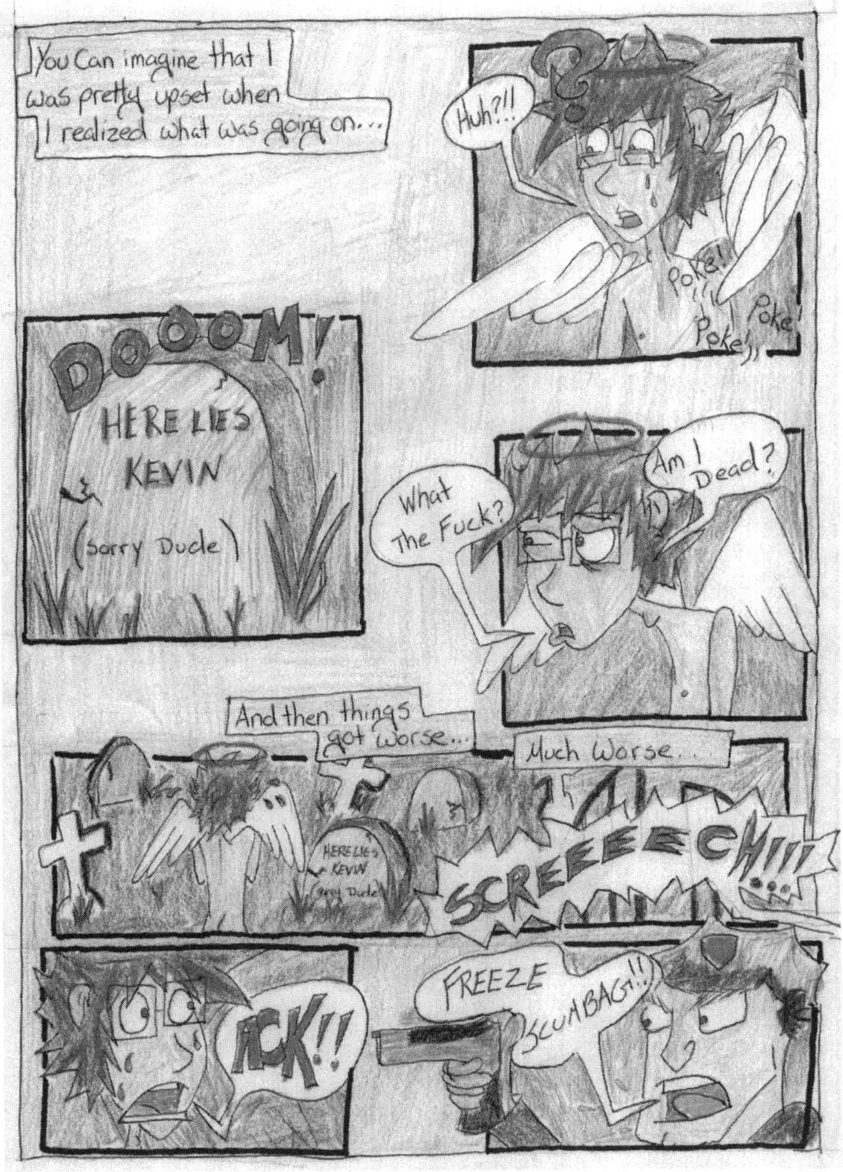
You Can imagine that I was pretty upset when I realized what was going on...
Huh?!!
Poke!
Poke!
Poke!
DOOOM!
HERE LIES KEVIN (Sorry Dude)
What The Fuck?
Am I Dead?
And then things got worse...
Much Worse.
SCREEEEECH!!!
ICK!!
FREEZE SCUMBAG!!

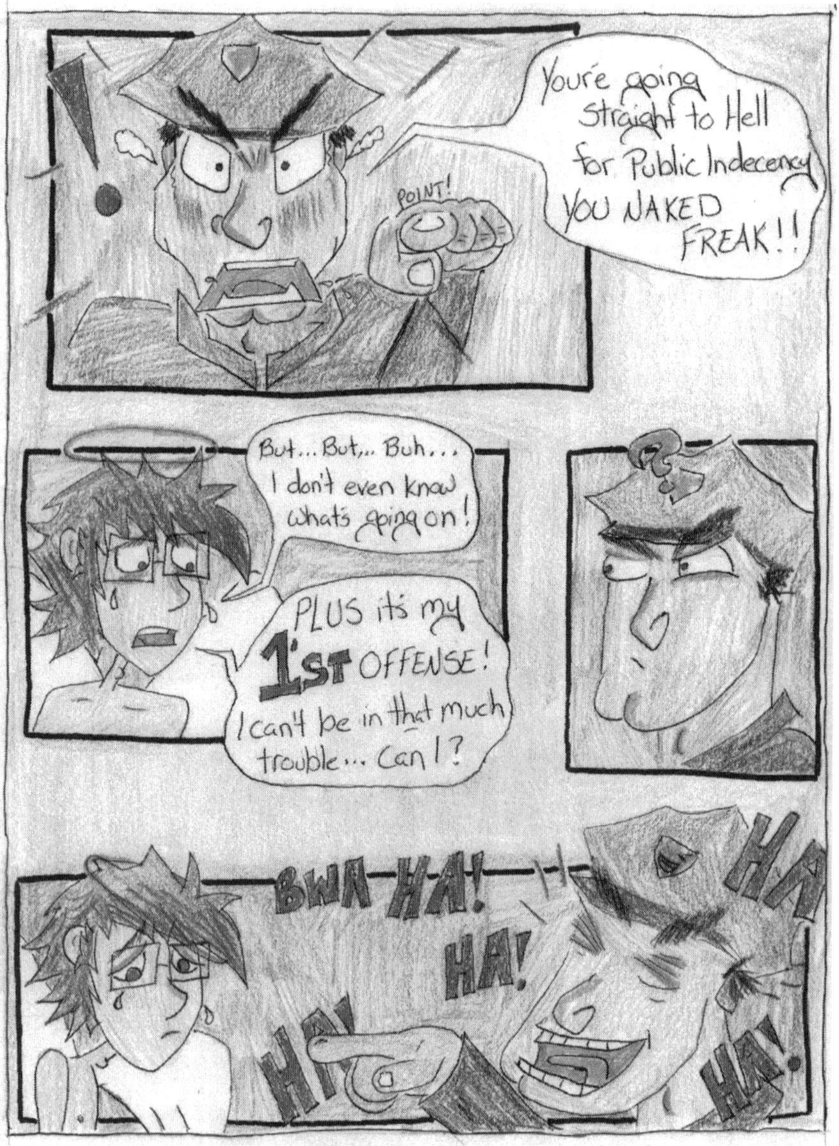
POINT!
You're going Straight to Hell for Public Indecency YOU NAKED FREAK!!
But... But,.. Buh... I don't even know whats going on!
PLUS its my 1ST OFFENSE! I can't be in that much trouble... Can I?
BWA HA!
HA!
HA!
HA!
HA!

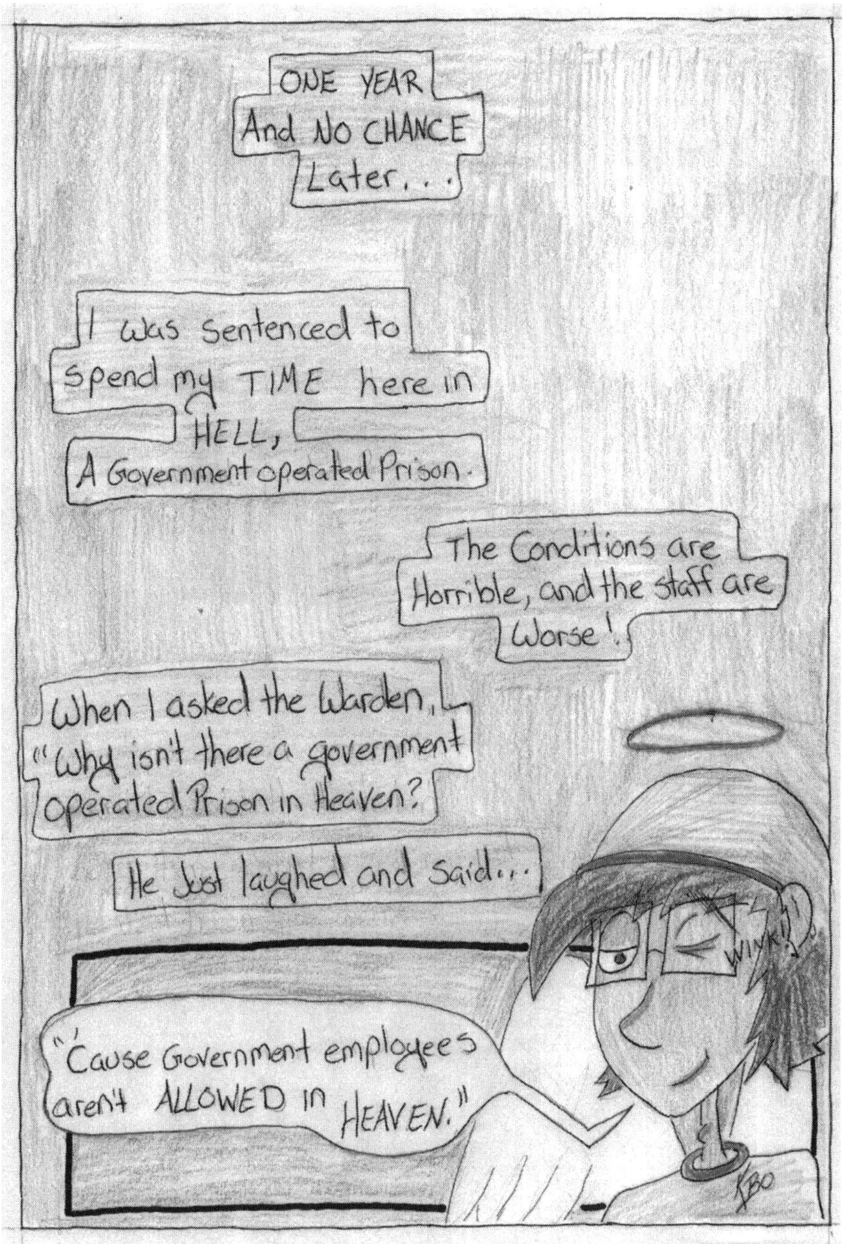
ONE YEAR And NO CHANCE Later...
I was sentenced to spend my TIME here in HELL, A Government operated Prison.
The Conditions are Horrible, and the staff are Worse!
When I asked the Warden, "Why isn't there a government operated Prison in Heaven?
He Just laughed and said...
"'Cause Government employees aren't ALLOWED in HEAVEN."
WINK!
KBO

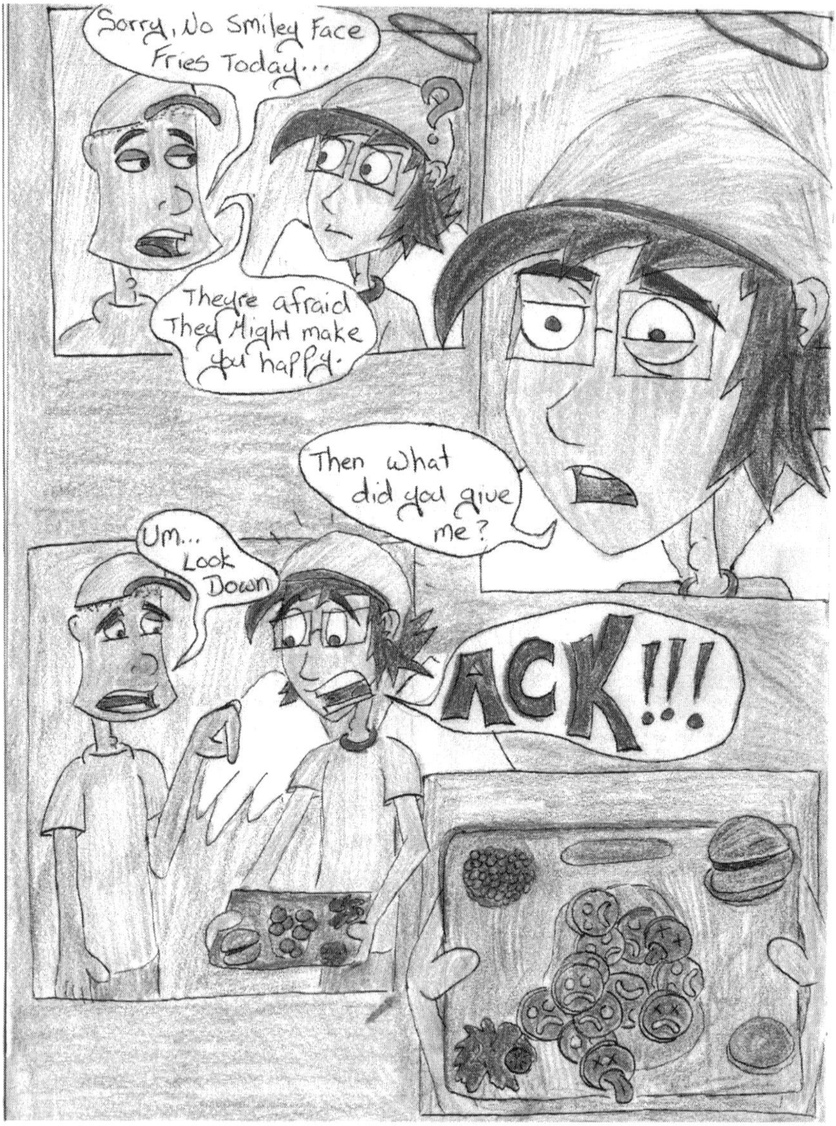
Sorry, No Smiley Face Fries Today...
?
Theyre afraid They Might make you happy.
Then what did you give me?
Um... Look Down
ACK!!!

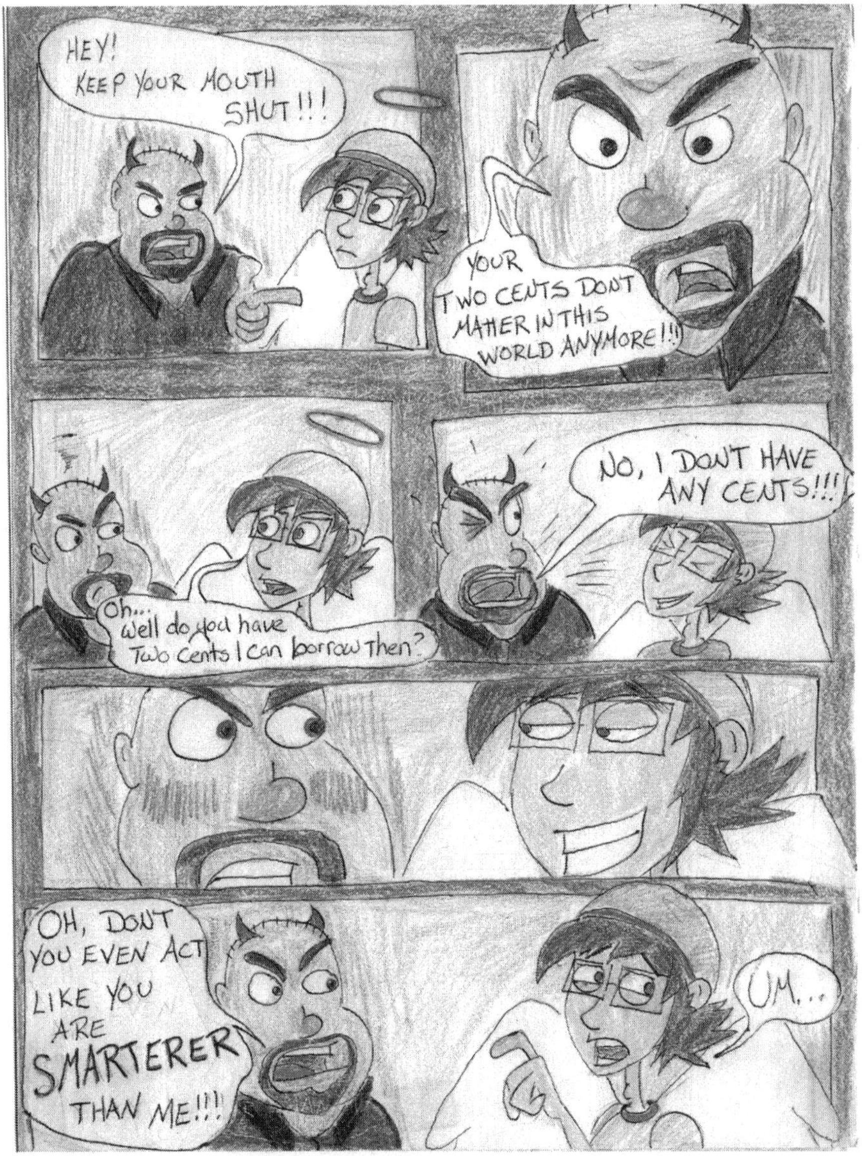
HEY! KEEP YOUR MOUTH SHUT!!!
YOUR TWO CENTS DON'T MATTER IN THIS WORLD ANYMORE!!!
Oh... well do you have Two cents I can borrow Then?
No, I DON'T HAVE ANY CENTS!!!
OH, DON'T YOU EVEN ACT LIKE YOU ARE SMARTERER THAN ME!!!
UM...

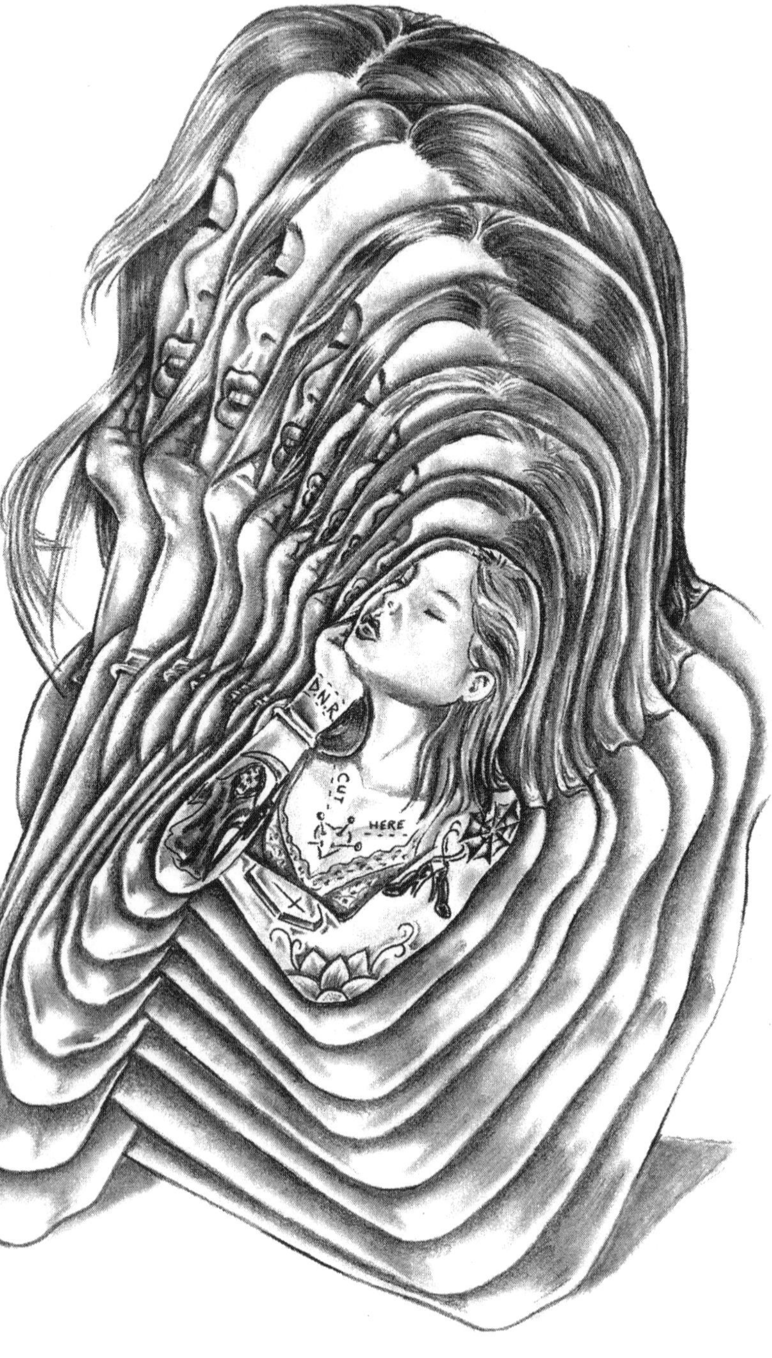
D.N.R
CUT
HERE

E.L. TEDANA

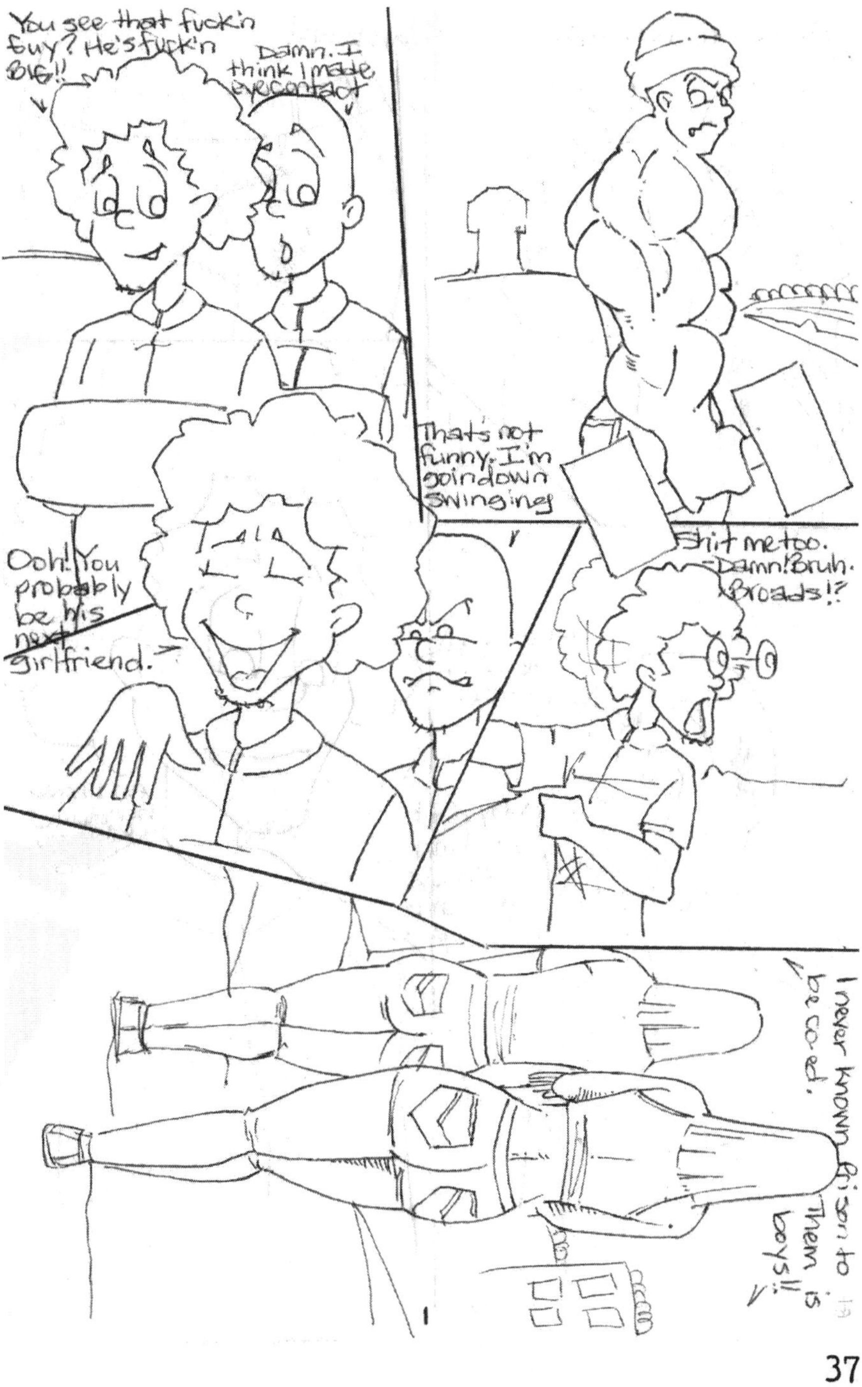
You see that fuck'n guy? He's fuck'n BIG!!
Damn. I think I made eyecontact
That's not funny. I'm goin down swinging
Ooh! You probably be his next girlfriend.
Shit me too. -Damn! Bruh. Broads!?
I never known Fison to be co-ed. Them is boys!!

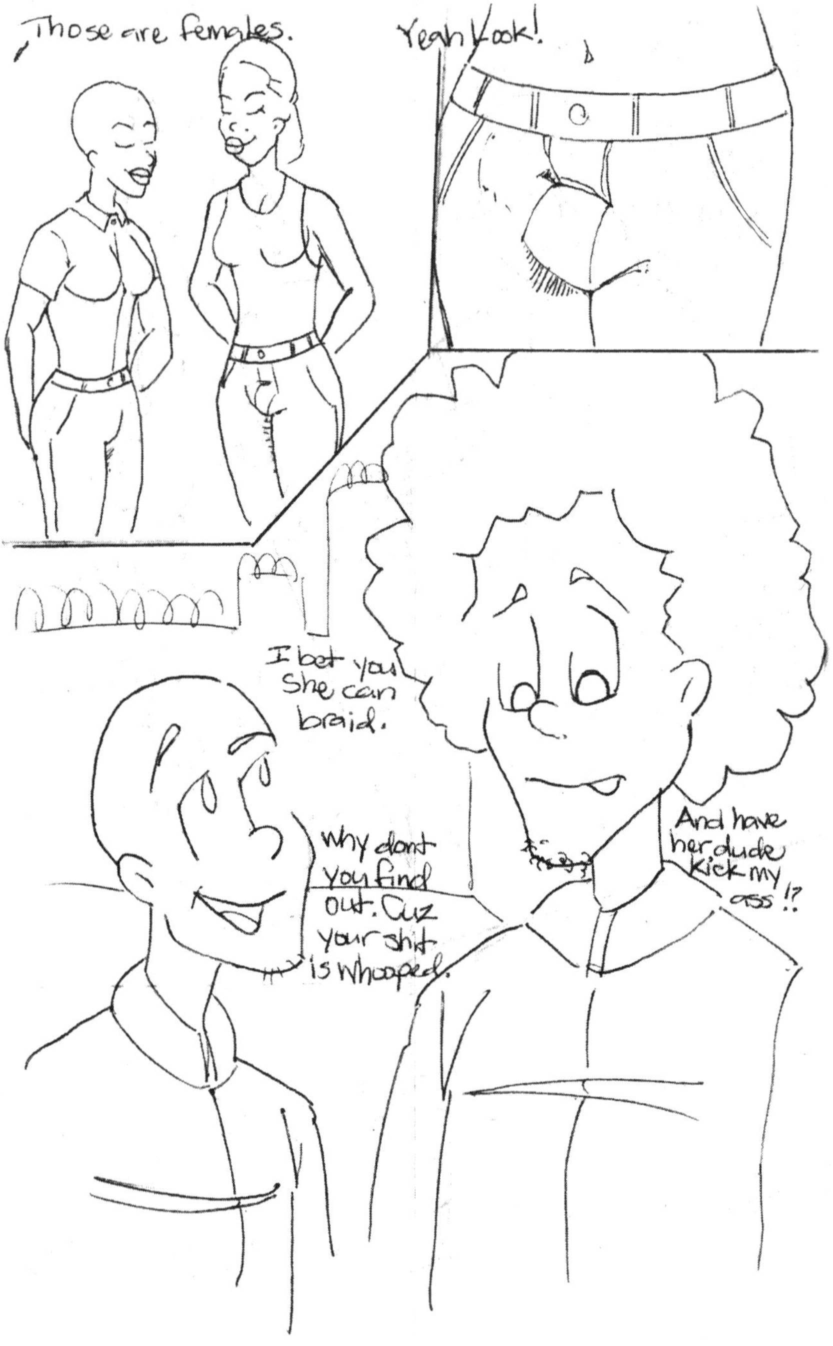

Those are females.
Yeah look!
I bet you She can braid.
Why dont you find out. Cuz your shit is whooped.
And have her dude kick my ass!?

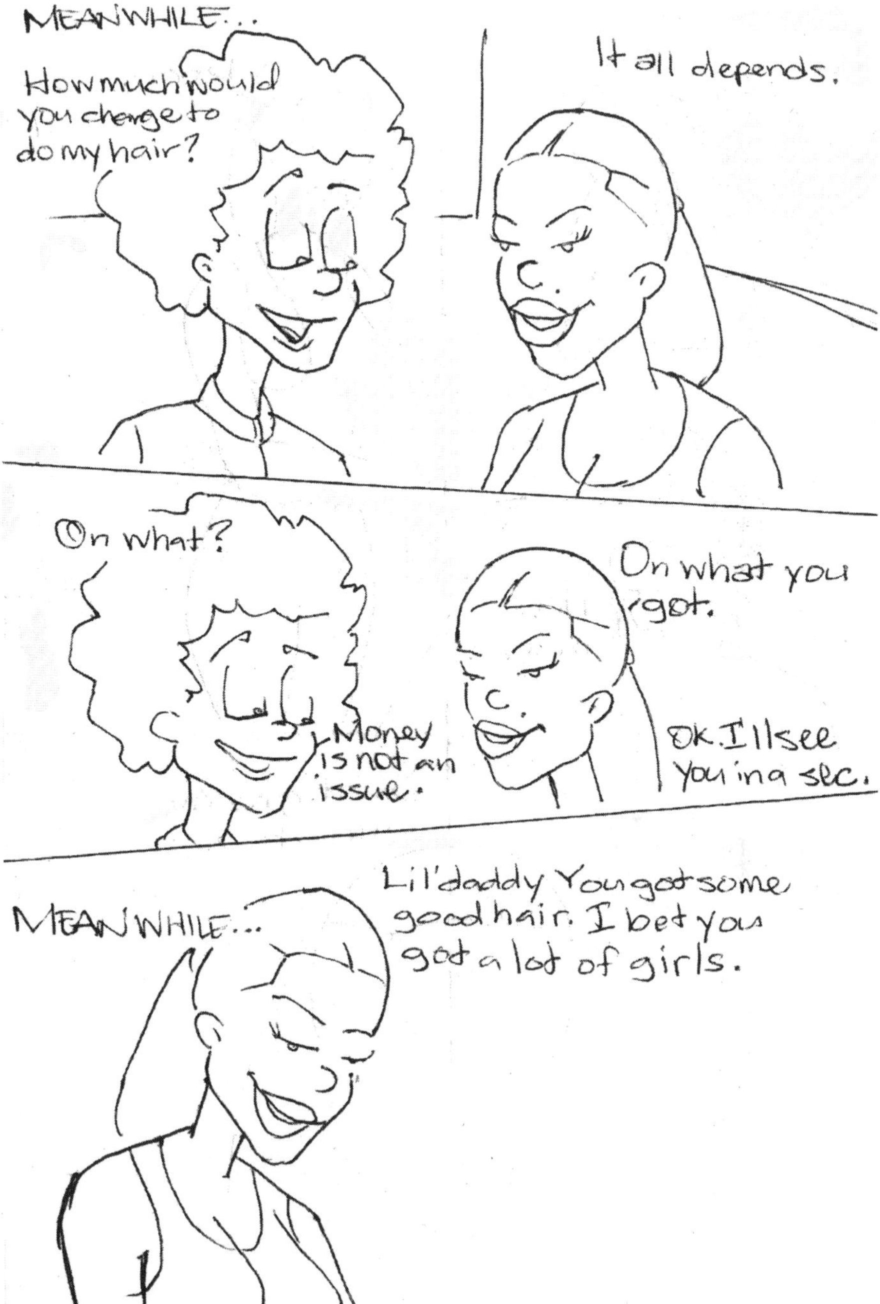
MEANWHILE...
How much would you charge to do my hair?
It all depends.
On what?
On what you got.
Money is not an issue.
OK. I'll see you in a sec.
MEANWHILE...
Lil'daddy You got some good hair. I bet you got a lot of girls.

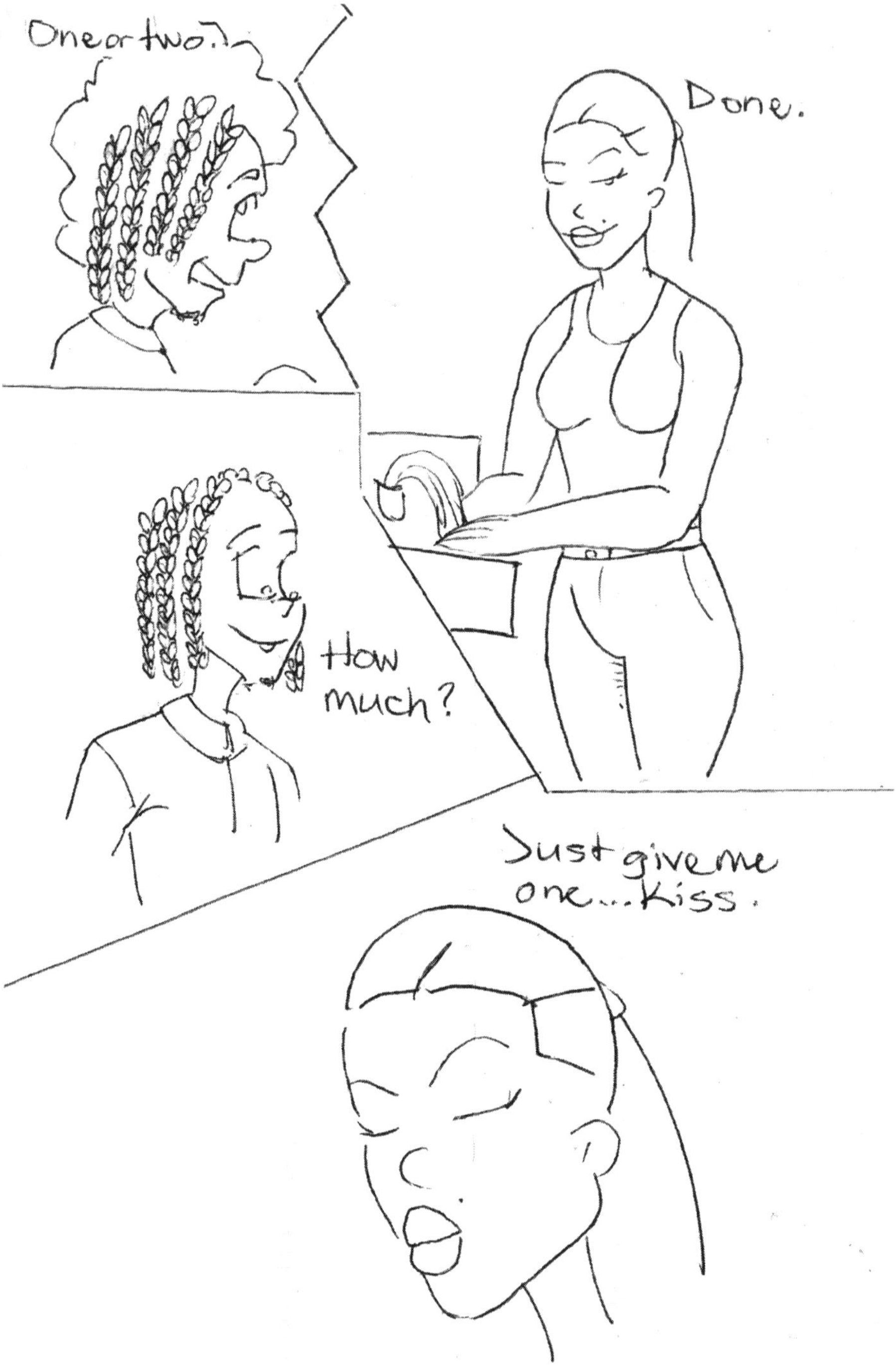
One or two?
Done.
How much?
Just give me one...kiss.

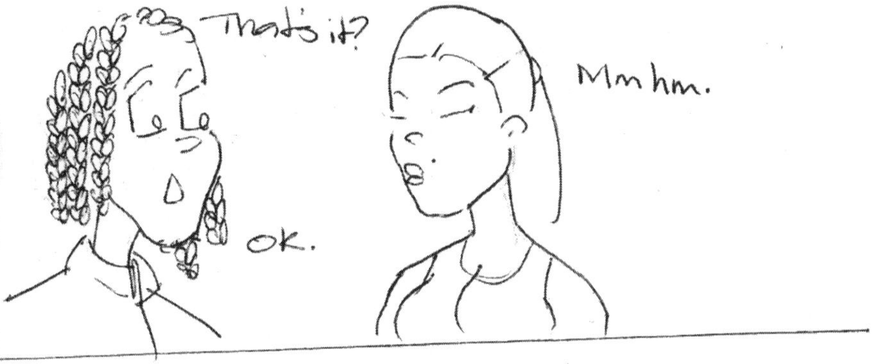
That's it?
Mmhm.
OK.

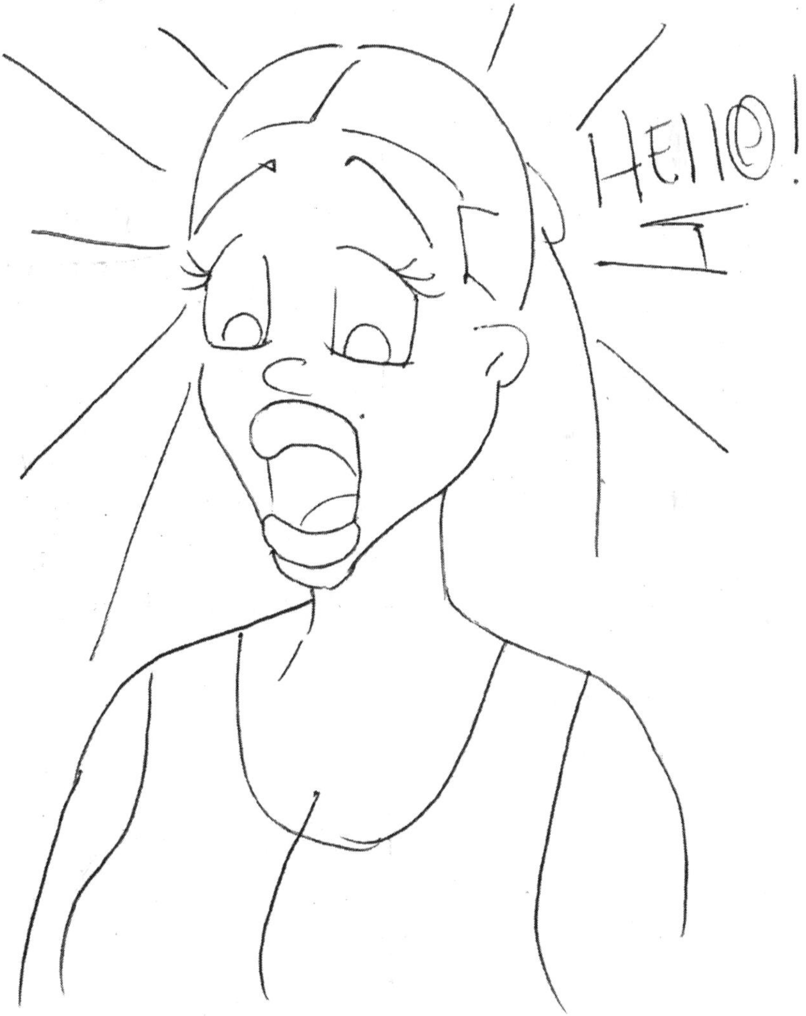
HELLO!

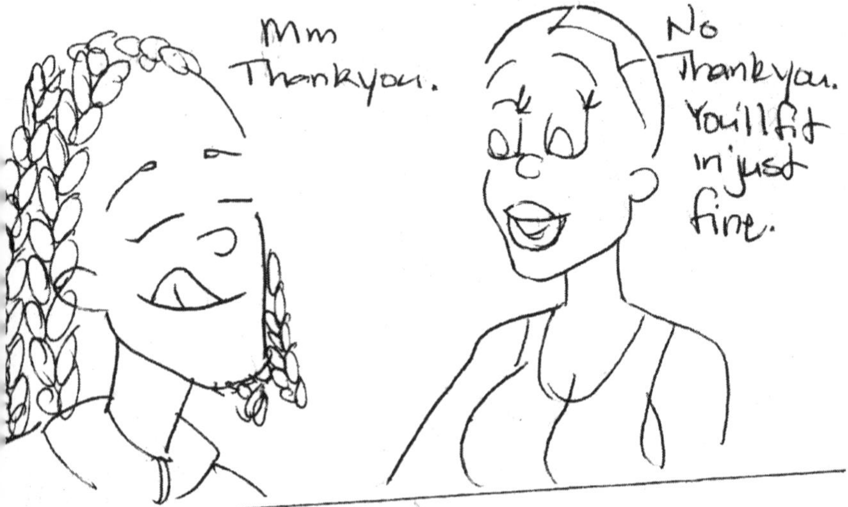
Mm Thankyou.
No Thankyou. You'll fit in just fine.

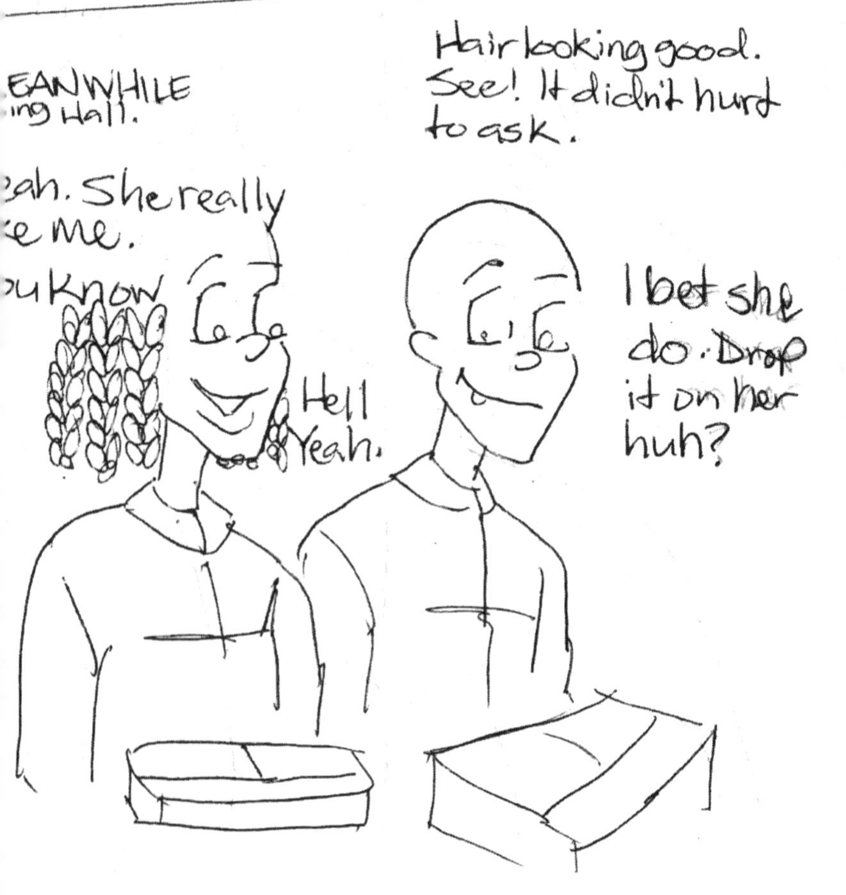
EANWHILE
ing Hall.
Hair looking good. See! It didn't hurt to ask.
ah. She really
e me.
u know
Hell Yeah.
I bet she do. Drop it on her huh?

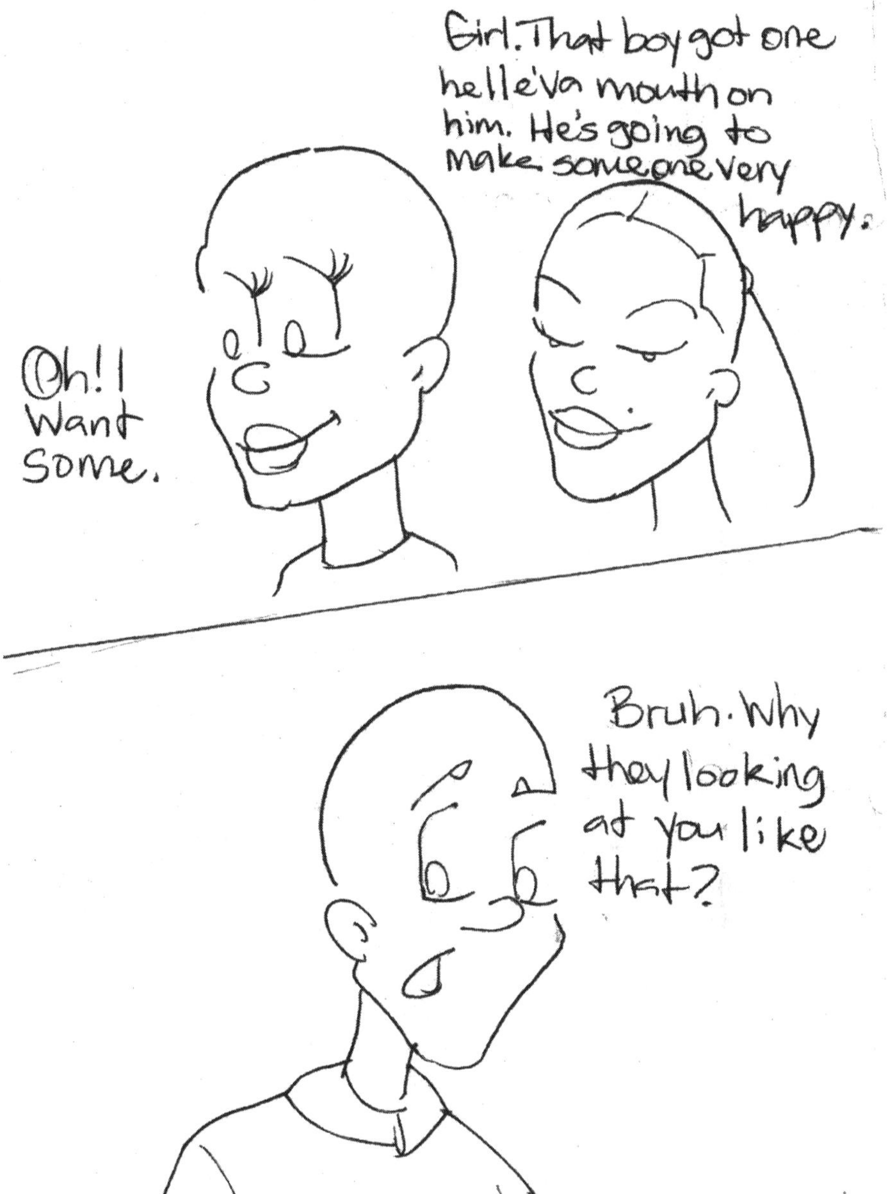
Girl. That boy got one helle'va mouth on him. He's going to make someone very happy.
Oh! I want some.
Bruh. Why they looking at you like that?
END

This page is dedicated to our new friend, Mecca,

and the comic that could have been. He was in the process of creating a submission that was sure to win an Oscar, an Emmy, and a Pabst's Blue Ribbon, but was thrown in solitary for defending a friend from some homophobic chuds who attacked and robbed her. Mecca is recovering from some broken ribs. His belongings, including week's worth of progress on the comic were "misplaced" by the prison. We send all our love his way and look forward to seeing Mecca get out soon, when we will gladly take him up on the help he volunteered to make ABO 2.

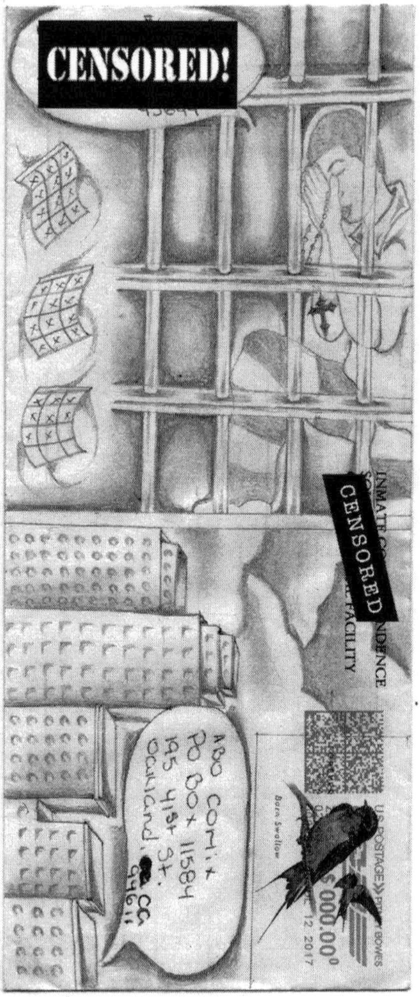
CENSORED!
CENSORED
ABO Comix
PO Box 11584
Oakland,
Barn Swallow
US POSTAGE
$000.00
12 2017

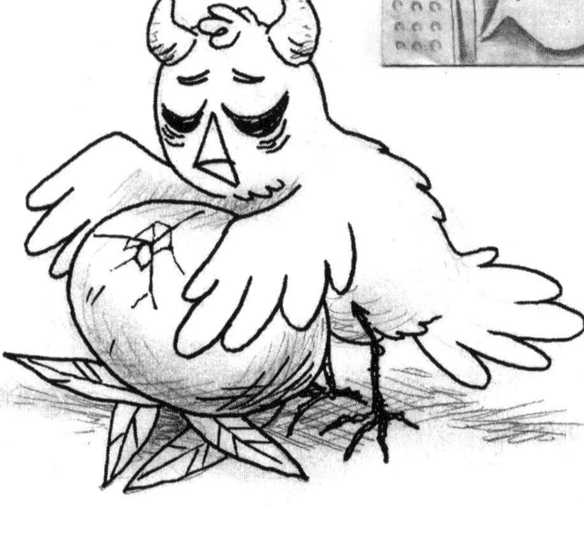

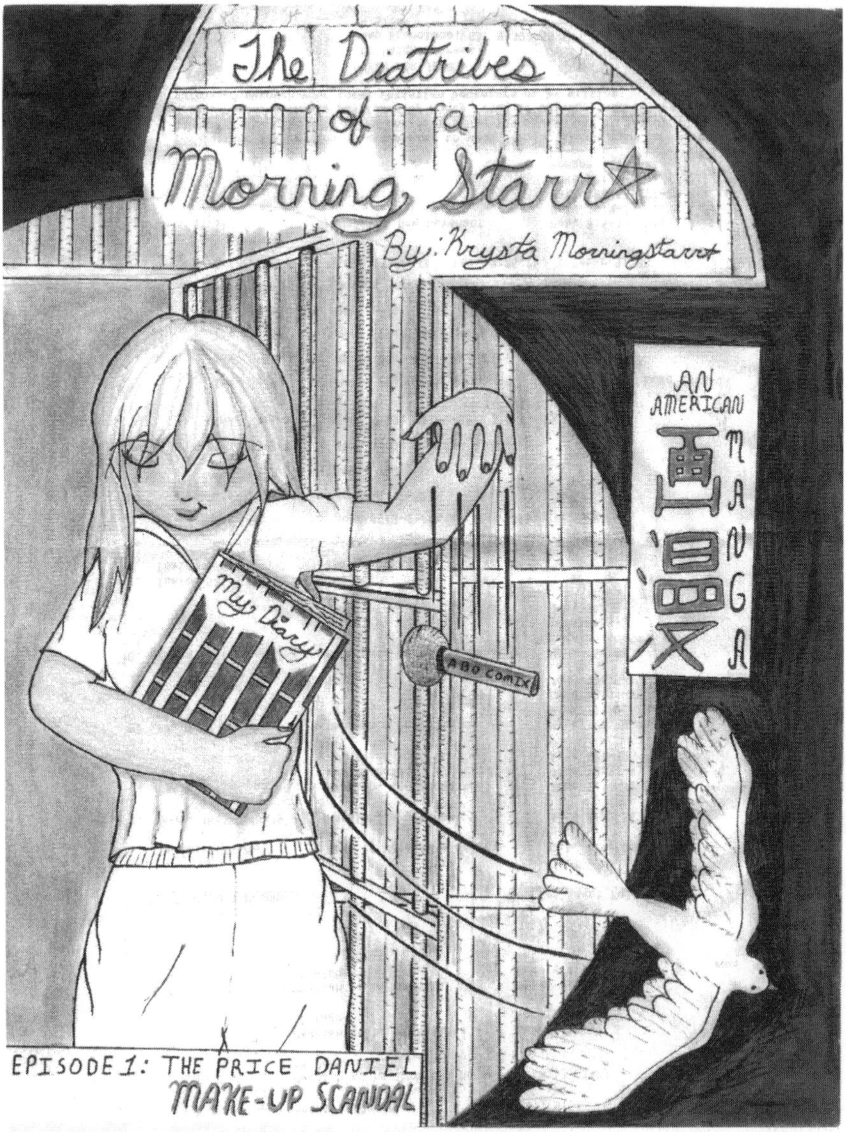
The Diatribes of a Morning Starr
By: Krysta Morningstarr
AN AMERICAN MANGA
漫画
My Diary
ABO COMIX
EPISODE 1: THE PRICE DANIEL MAKE-UP SCANDAL

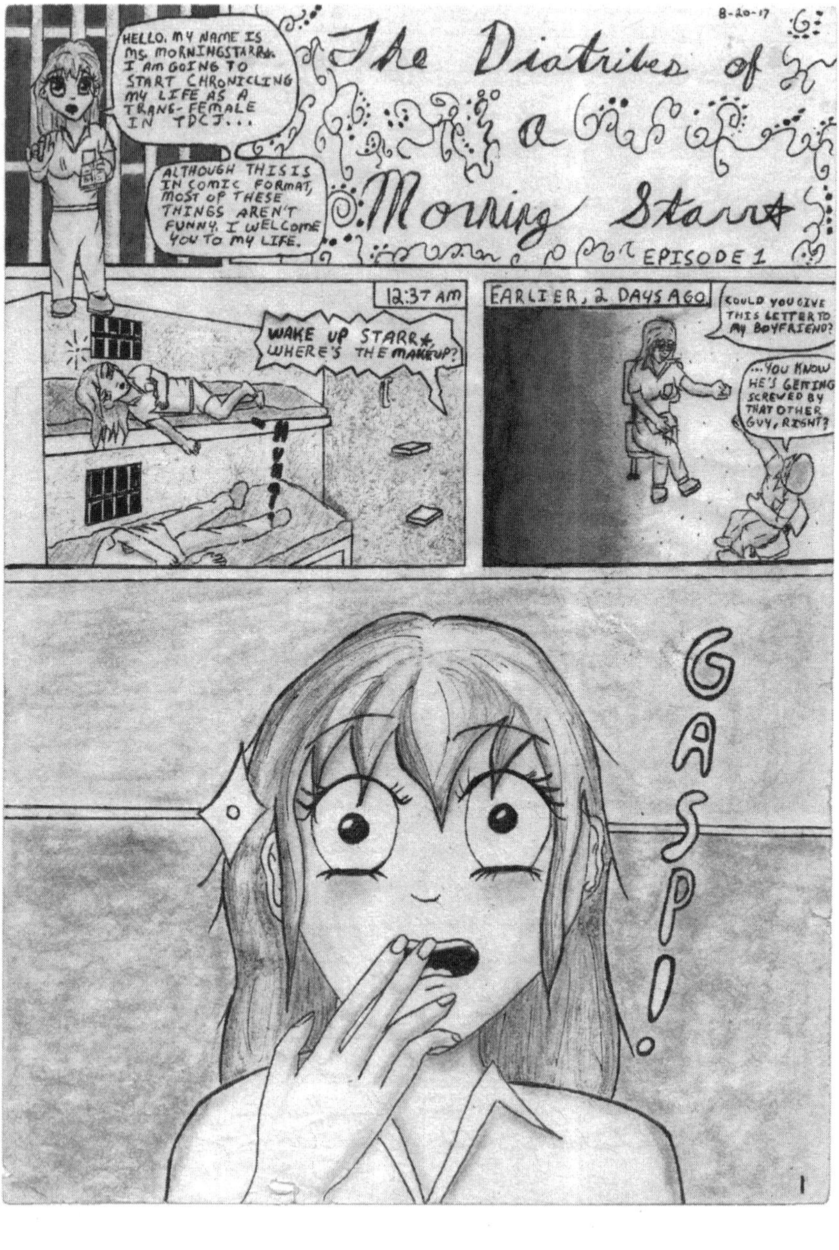
8-20-17
The Diatribes of a Morning Starr
EPISODE 1
HELLO. MY NAME IS MS. MORNINGSTARR. I AM GOING TO START CHRONICLING MY LIFE AS A TRANS-FEMALE IN TDCJ...
ALTHOUGH THIS IS IN COMIC FORMAT, MOST OF THESE THINGS AREN'T FUNNY. I WELCOME YOU TO MY LIFE.
12:37 AM
WAKE UP STARR, WHERE'S THE MAKEUP?
HUH?!
EARLIER, 2 DAYS AGO
COULD YOU GIVE THIS LETTER TO MY BOYFRIEND?
...YOU KNOW HE'S GETTING SCREWED BY THAT OTHER GUY, RIGHT?
GASP!
1

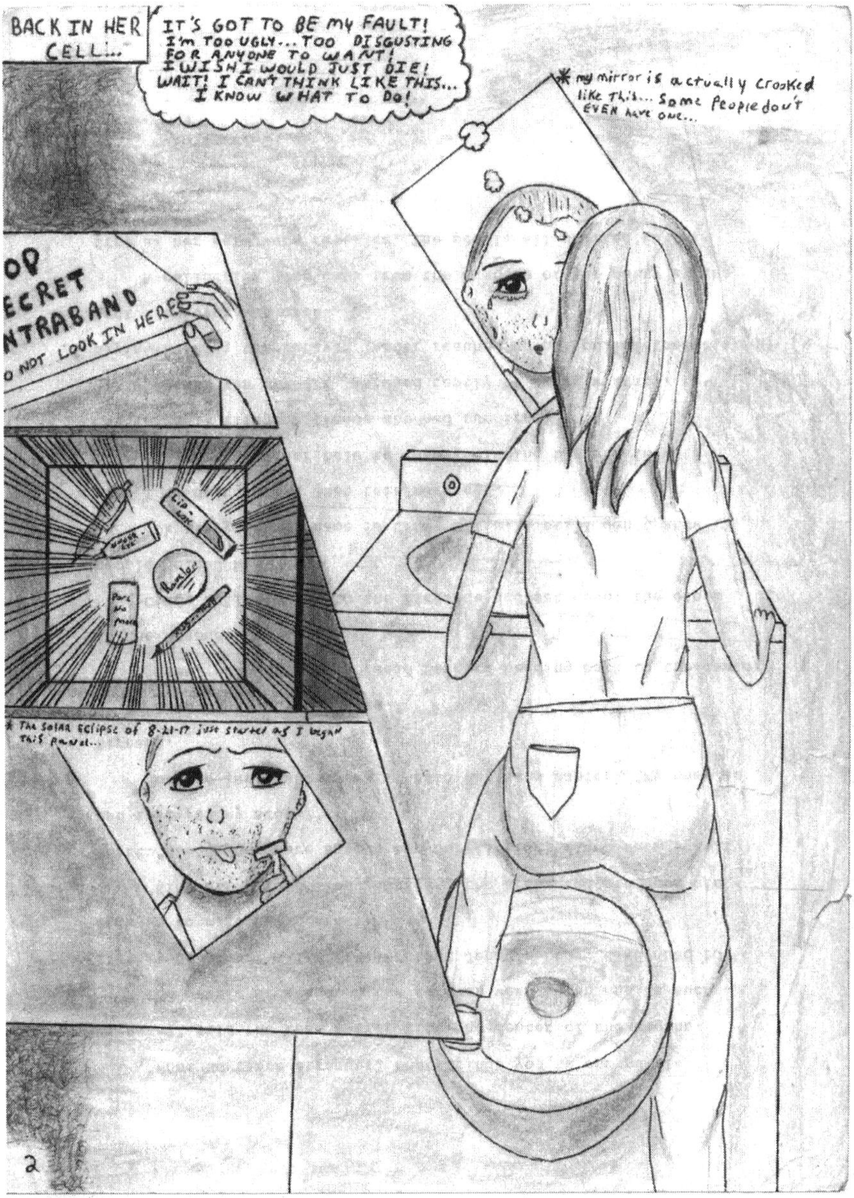
BACK IN HER CELL...
IT'S GOT TO BE my FAULT! I'm TOO UGLY... TOO DISGUSTING FOR ANYONE TO WANT! I WISH I WOULD JUST DIE! WAIT! I CAN'T THINK LIKE THIS... I KNOW WHAT TO DO!
* my mirror is actually crooked like this... Some people don't EVEN have one...
OP
ECRET
NTRABAND
O NOT LOOK IN HERE
* The solar eclipse of 8-21-17 just started as I began this panel...
2

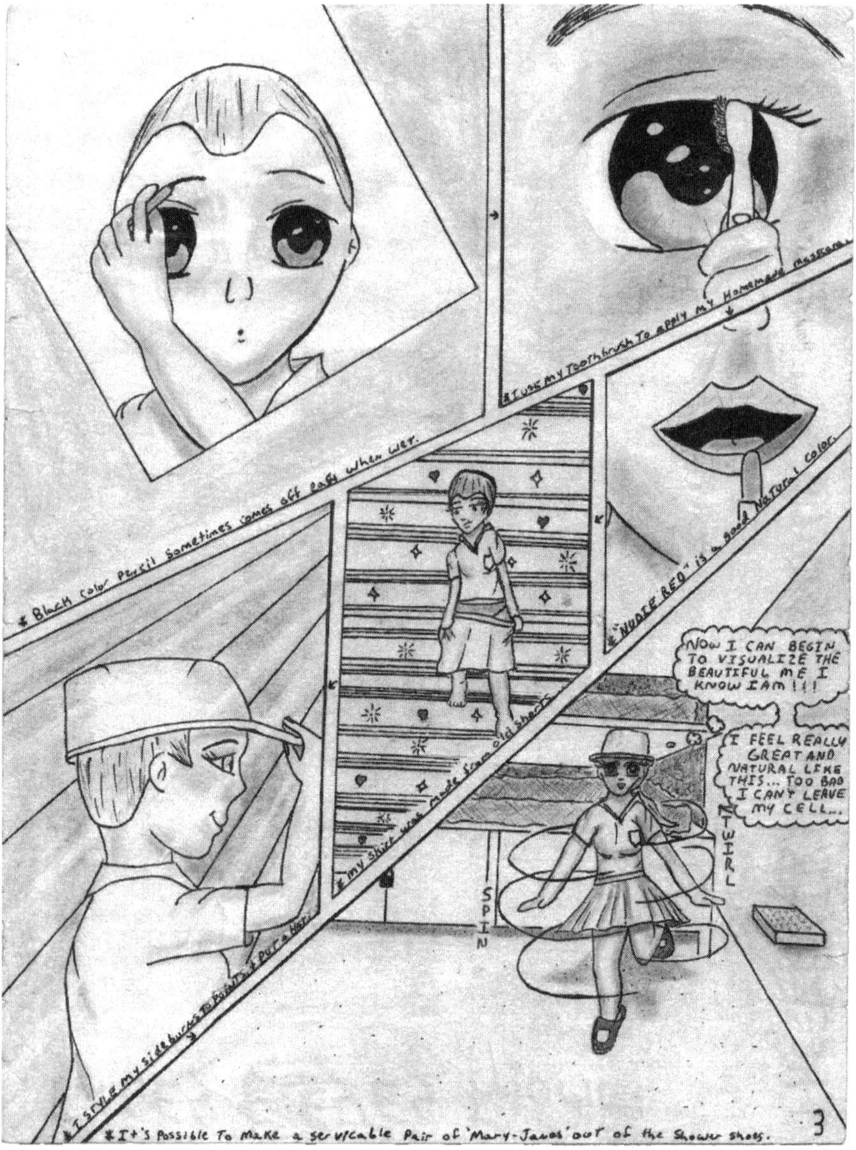

* Black color pencil sometimes comes off easy when wet.
* I use my toothbrush to apply my homemade mascara.
* "NUDIE RED" is a good natural color.
* My shirt was made from old shorts.
* I STYLE my sideburns to points & put a hat.
NOW I CAN BEGIN TO VISUALIZE THE BEAUTIFUL ME I KNOW I AM!!!
I FEEL REALLY GREAT AND NATURAL LIKE THIS... TOO BAD I CAN'T LEAVE MY CELL...
SPIN
TWIRL
* It's possible to make a servicable pair of 'Mary-Janes' out of the shower shoes.
3

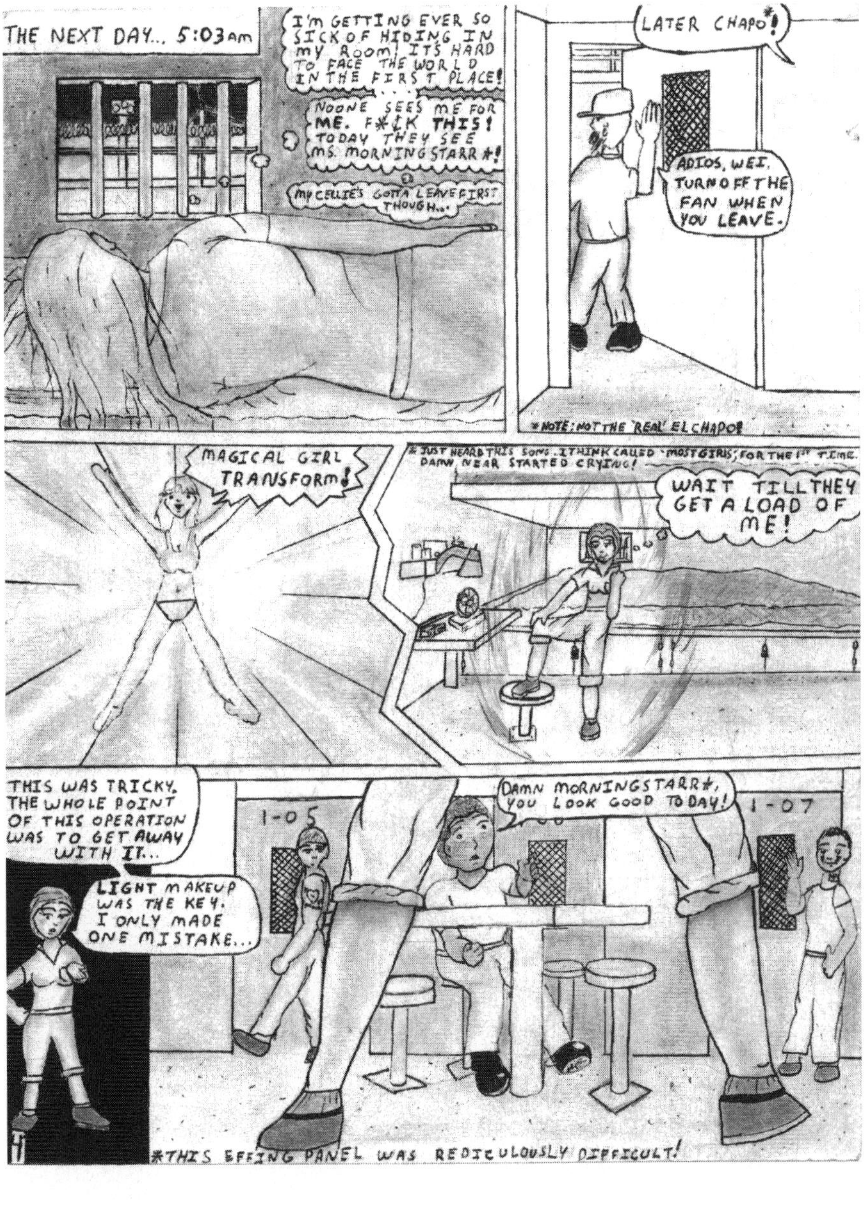
THE NEXT DAY... 5:03am
I'm GETTING EVER SO SICK OF HIDING IN MY ROOM! ITS HARD TO FACE THE WORLD IN THE FIRST PLACE!
NOONE SEES ME FOR ME. F*CK THIS! TODAY THEY SEE MS. MORNING STARR*!
MY CELLIE'S GOTTA LEAVE FIRST THOUGH...
LATER CHAPO*!
ADIOS, WEI. TURN OFF THE FAN WHEN YOU LEAVE.
*NOTE: NOT THE 'REAL' EL CHAPO!
MAGICAL GIRL TRANSFORM!
*JUST HEARD THIS SONG. I THINK CALLED 'MOST GIRLS,' FOR THE 1st TIME. DAMN NEAR STARTED CRYING!
WAIT TILL THEY GET A LOAD OF ME!
THIS WAS TRICKY. THE WHOLE POINT OF THIS OPERATION WAS TO GET AWAY WITH IT...
LIGHT MAKEUP WAS THE KEY. I ONLY MADE ONE MISTAKE...
1-05
DAMN MORNINGSTARR*, YOU LOOK GOOD TODAY!
1-07
*THIS EFFING PANEL WAS REDICULOUSLY DIFFICULT!

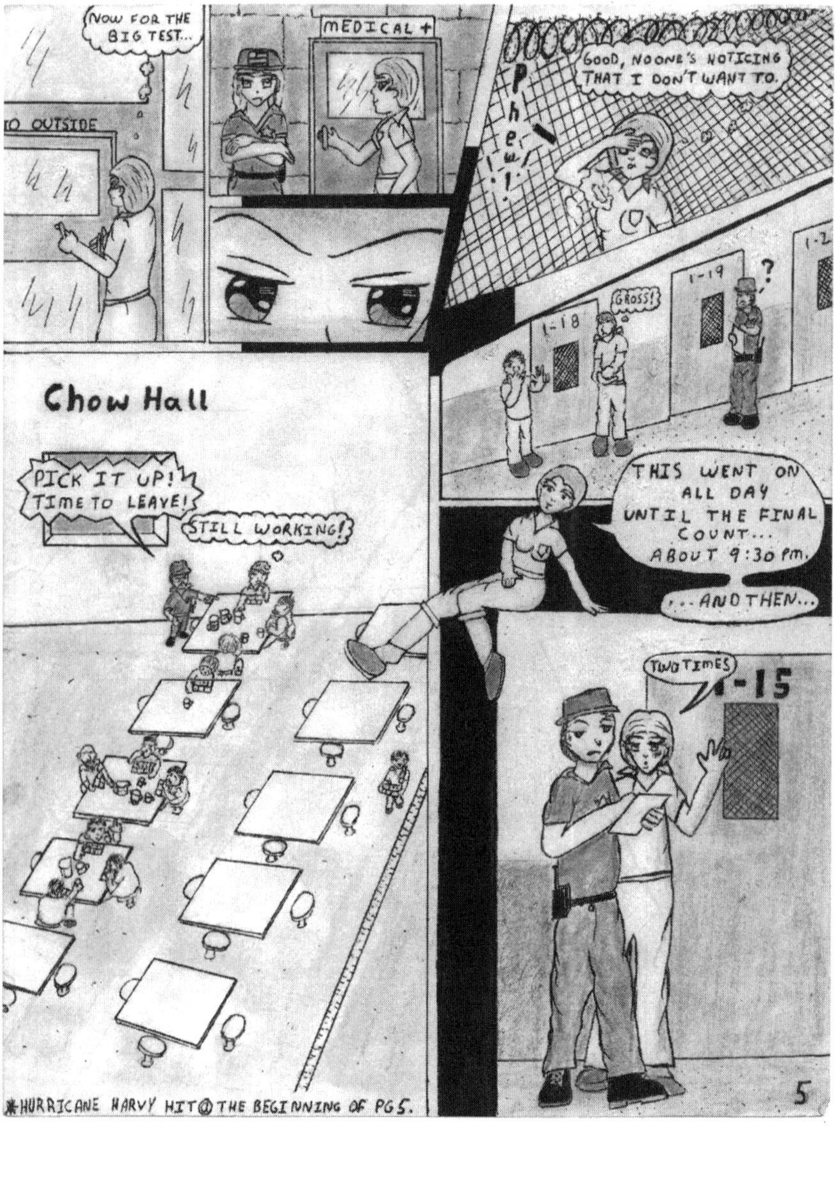
NOW FOR THE BIG TEST...
TO OUTSIDE
MEDICAL +
GOOD, NOONE'S NOTICING THAT I DON'T WANT TO.
Phew!!
1-18
GROSS!
1-19
?
Chow Hall
PICK IT UP! TIME TO LEAVE!
STILL WORKING!
THIS WENT ON ALL DAY UNTIL THE FINAL COUNT... ABOUT 9:30 pm.
...AND THEN...
TWO TIMES
1-15
5
*HURRICANE HARVY HIT @ THE BEGINNING OF PG 5.

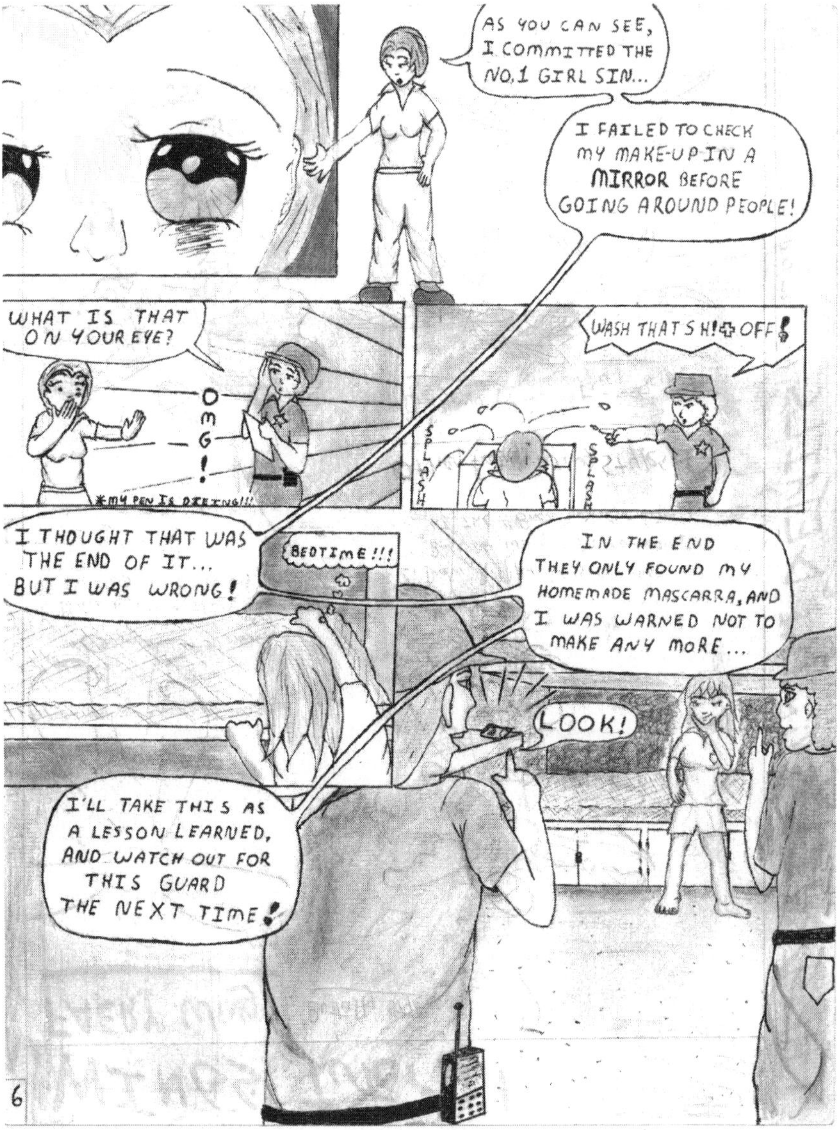
AS YOU CAN SEE, I COMMITTED THE NO.1 GIRL SIN...
I FAILED TO CHECK MY MAKE-UP IN A MIRROR BEFORE GOING AROUND PEOPLE!
WHAT IS THAT ON YOUR EYE?
OMG!
*MY PEN IS DIEING!!!
WASH THAT SH!✚ OFF!
SPLASH
SPLASH
I THOUGHT THAT WAS THE END OF IT... BUT I WAS WRONG!
BEDTIME!!!
IN THE END THEY ONLY FOUND MY HOMEMADE MASCARRA, AND I WAS WARNED NOT TO MAKE ANY MORE...
LOOK!
I'LL TAKE THIS AS A LESSON LEARNED, AND WATCH OUT FOR THIS GUARD THE NEXT TIME!
6

My Diatribe

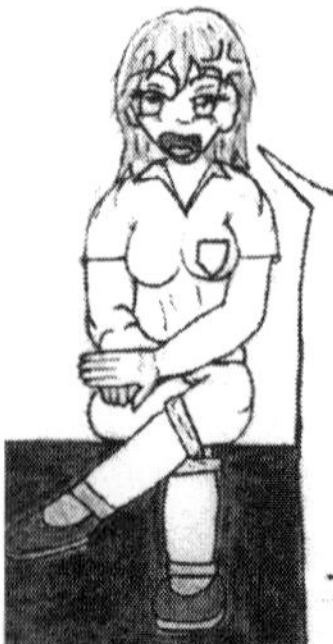

AS I SIT HERE PENNING THE FINAL PAGE IN THIS ENTRY, ONE THING KEEPS COMING TO MIND. I READ SOMEWHERE ONCE THAT TO LIVE THE LIFE OF A **TRANS** IN MODERN AMERICA WAS TO LIVE THE LIFE OF A

GUERILLA OPERATION

NEVER HAS THIS STATEMENT BEEN MORE TRUE THAN FOR ONE STRUGGLING TO FIND ACCEPTANCE, EQUALITY, AND SELF-EXPRESSION IN THE PRISON INDUSTRIAL COMPLEX.

I LEARNED SOMETHING VALUABLE WHEN I WAS TWO YEARS OLD, BUT UNLIKE THE MAJORITY OF PEOPLE, SOCIETY HAS YET TO FORCE ME TO FORGET IT. I LEARNED TO QUESTION **WHY**.

I COULD FILL A BOOK WITH THE SOCIAL AND IDEOLOGICAL 'EXCUCES' PEOPLE HAVE FOR VILLIFYING ONE SUCH AS MYSELF, BUT TO SUM IT UP, ONE NEED STUDY NO FURTHER THAN THEIR LOCAL XTIAN BOOKSTORE. (NEVER MIND THAT THE XTIAN BIBLE IS CAPABLE OF DEMONIZING OR DIEIFYING ANY BEHAVIOR, MATTHEW 5:29-30 GIVES ME A GOOD REASON TO CHOP OFF MY **PENIS**, FOR EXAMPLE...)

DON'T TAKE THIS THE WRONG WAY, THE CONCEPTS OF UNIVERSAL **LOVE** AND NON-JUDGEMENTALISM ARE THE CORNERSTONES OF OF MY BELIEF SYSTEM. ITS JUST THAT THE MESSENGER, MAINSTREAM **RELIGION**, HAS BEEN SUBVERTING THIS GREAT IDEA TO FURTHER ITS OWN **AGENDA** FOR TIME IMMEMORABLE.

SIGH SINCE THINGS ARE THE WAY THEY ARE, THE ONLY ANSWER I HAVE FOUND IS TO ADOPT A POLICY OF GRADUAL AND PERSISTANT NON-CONFORMITY, ACCLIMATING THOSE AROUND YOU TO THE INEVITABLE CHANGE BEING BROUGHT INTO EXISTANCE. KEEP FIGHTING THE GOOD FIGHT!

Thanks for reading! ♥ *Much Love, –*

– Krysta Morningstarr

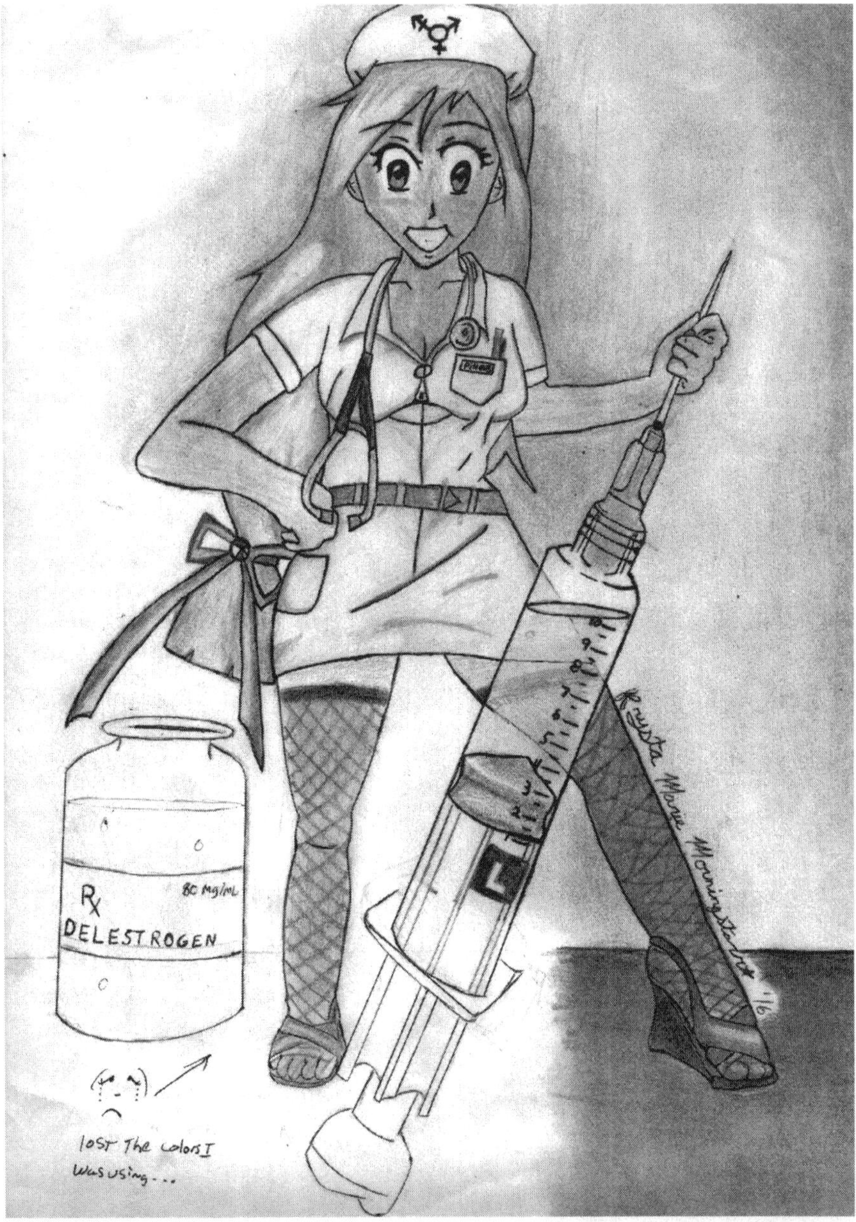
Rx
80 mg/mL
DELESTROGEN
lost The colors I was using...
Krysta Marie Morningstar '16

Daniella Nichole Hope

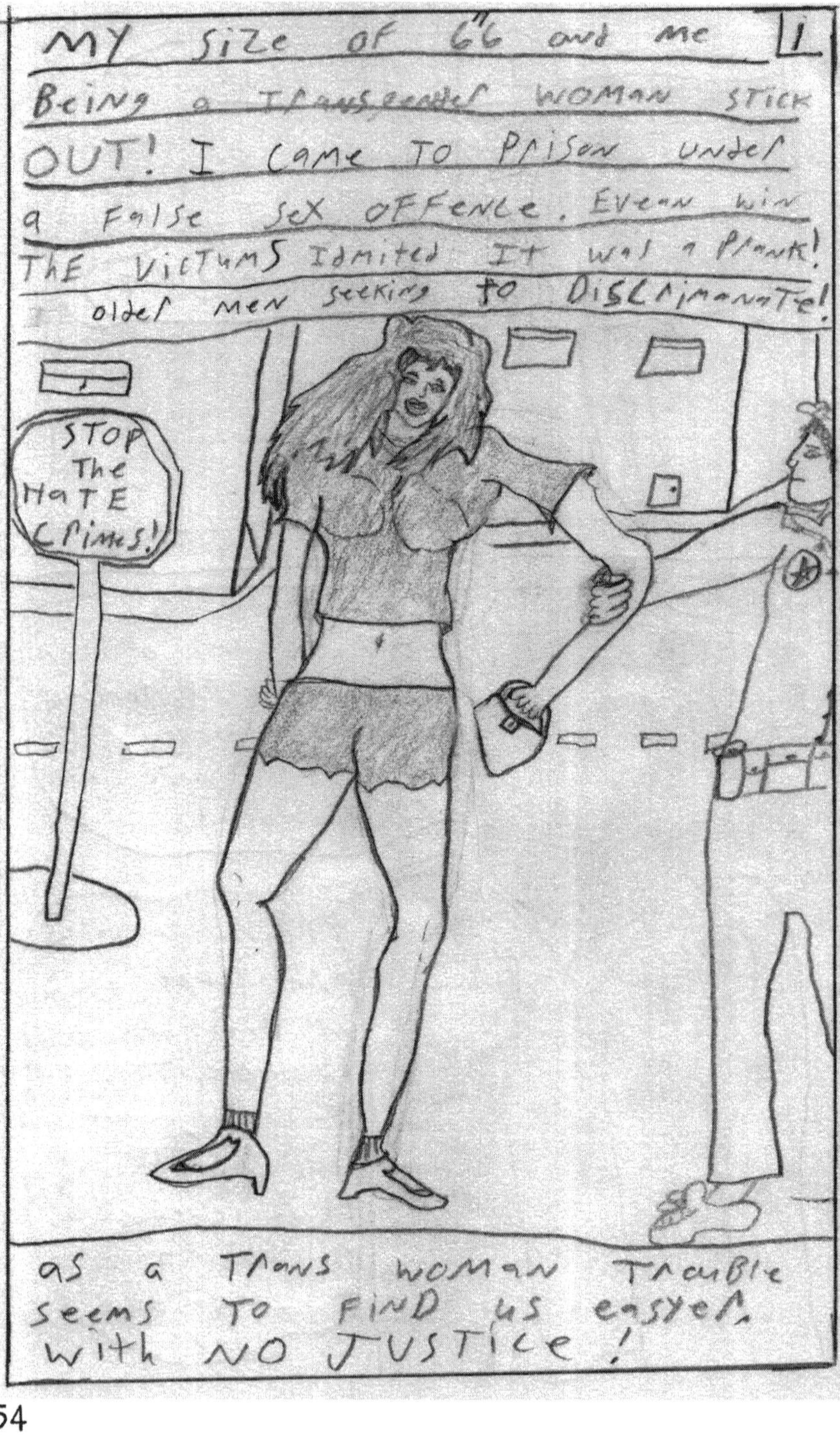
MY SIZE OF 6'6" and me
1
Being a Transgender WOMAN STICK OUT! I Came TO Prison under a False sex offence. Evean win THE Victums Idmited IT was a Prank! older men seeking to Discrimanate!
STOP The HATE Crimes!
as a Trans woman Trouble seems TO FIND us easyer. with NO JUSTICE!

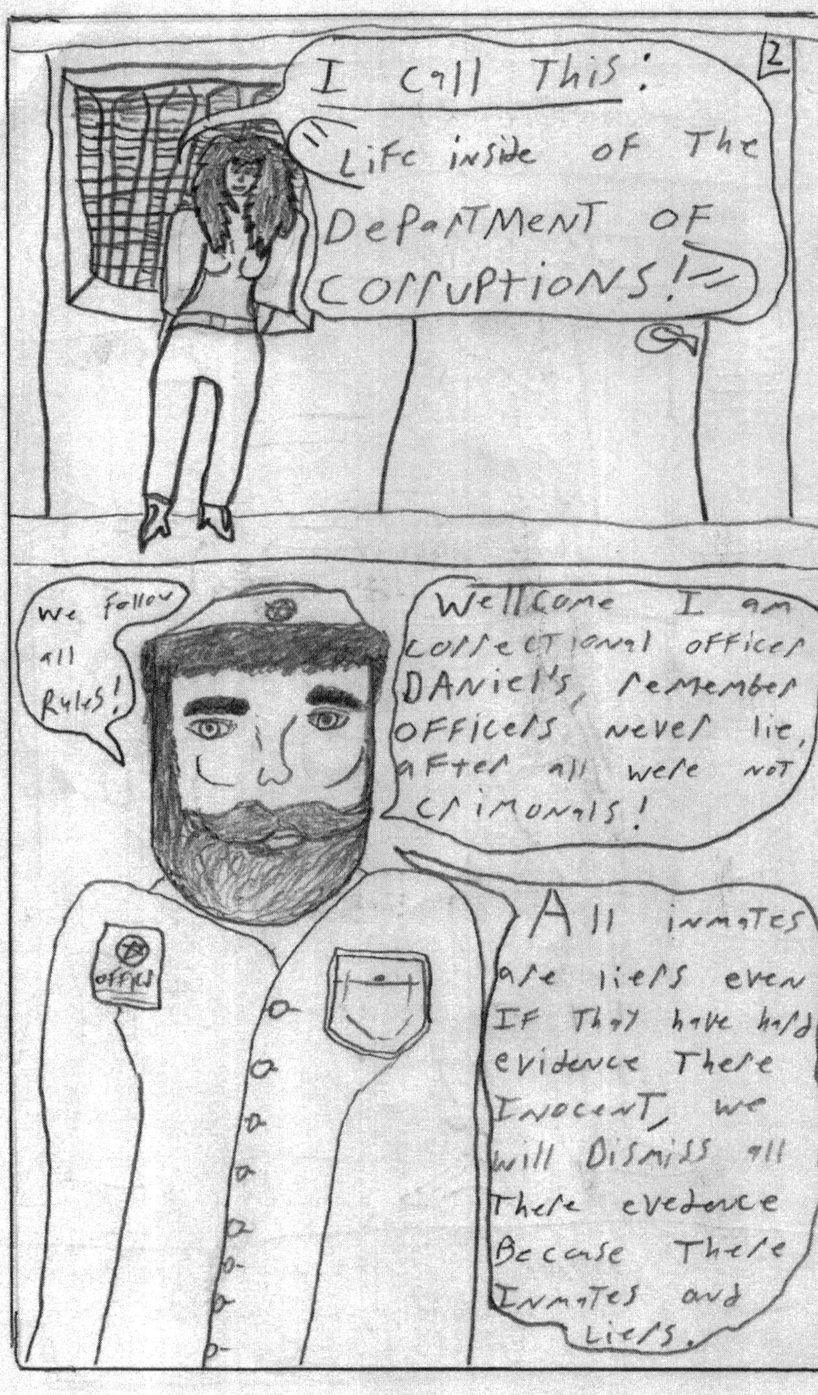
2
I call This:
"Life inside of The Department of Corruptions!"
We follow all Rules!
Wellcome I am correctional officer Daniel's, remember officers never lie, after all were not crimonals!
All inmates are liers even IF They have hard evidence There Inocent, we will Dismiss all There evedence Because There Inmates and Liers.
Officer

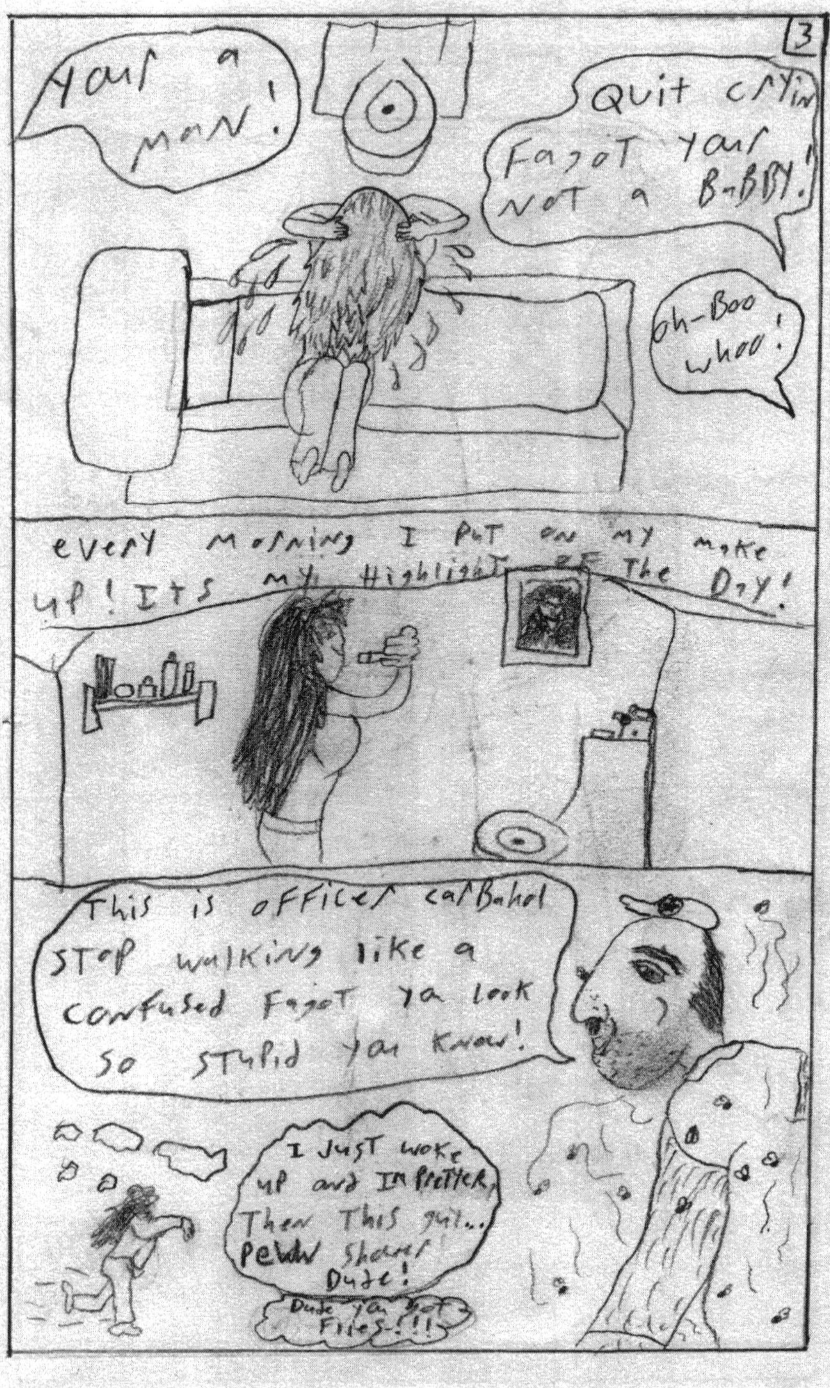
3
Your a MAN!
Quit cryin Fagot your not a BaBBY!
Oh-Boo whoo!
every morning I put on my make up! Its my highlight of The Day!
This is officer carBahal STOP walking like a confused Fagot ya look so STUPID you know!
I JUST woke up and IM pretter, Then This guy... PeWW Shower Dude!
Dude you got Flies-!!!

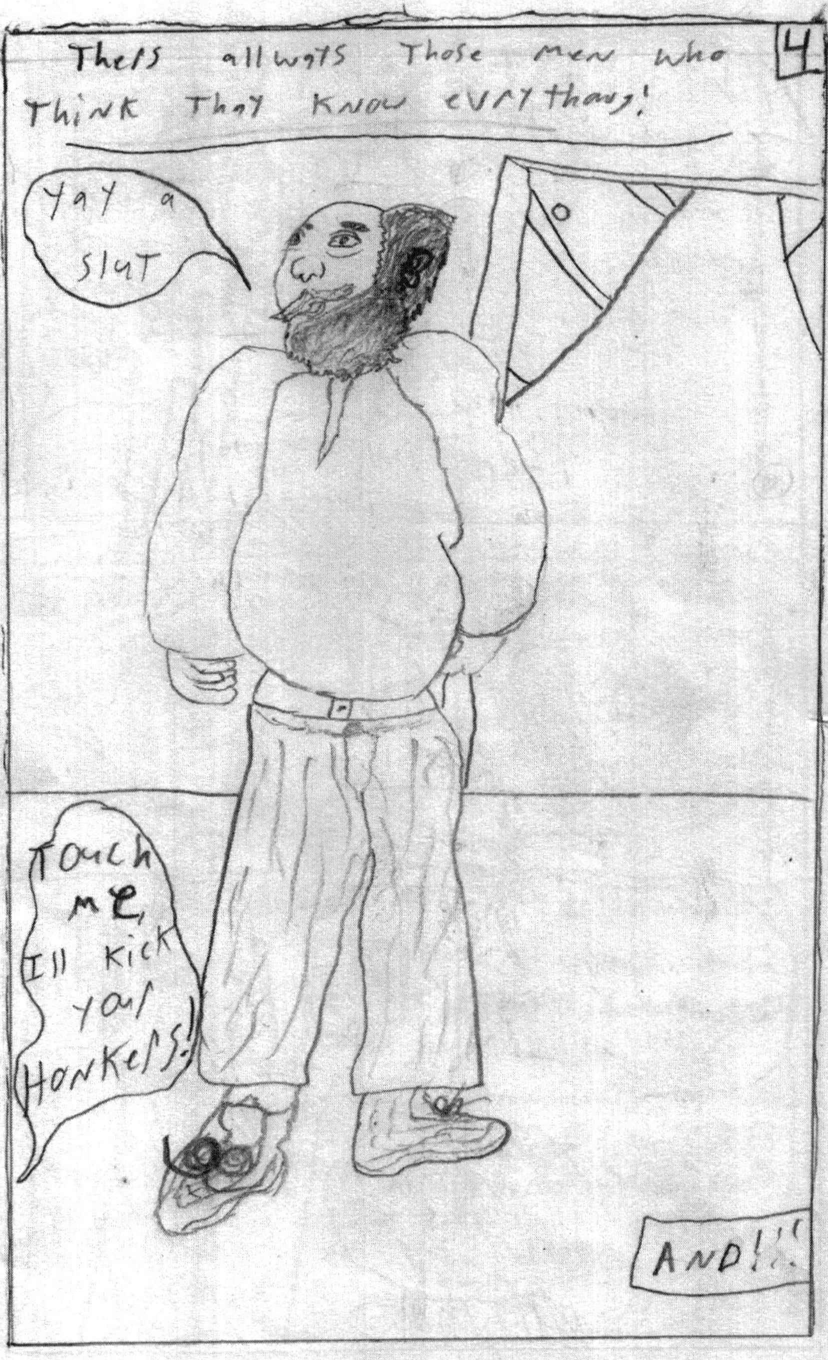
Thers allways Those men who Think Thay Know evryThang!
4
Yay a slut
Touch me, Ill kick your Honkers!
AND!!!

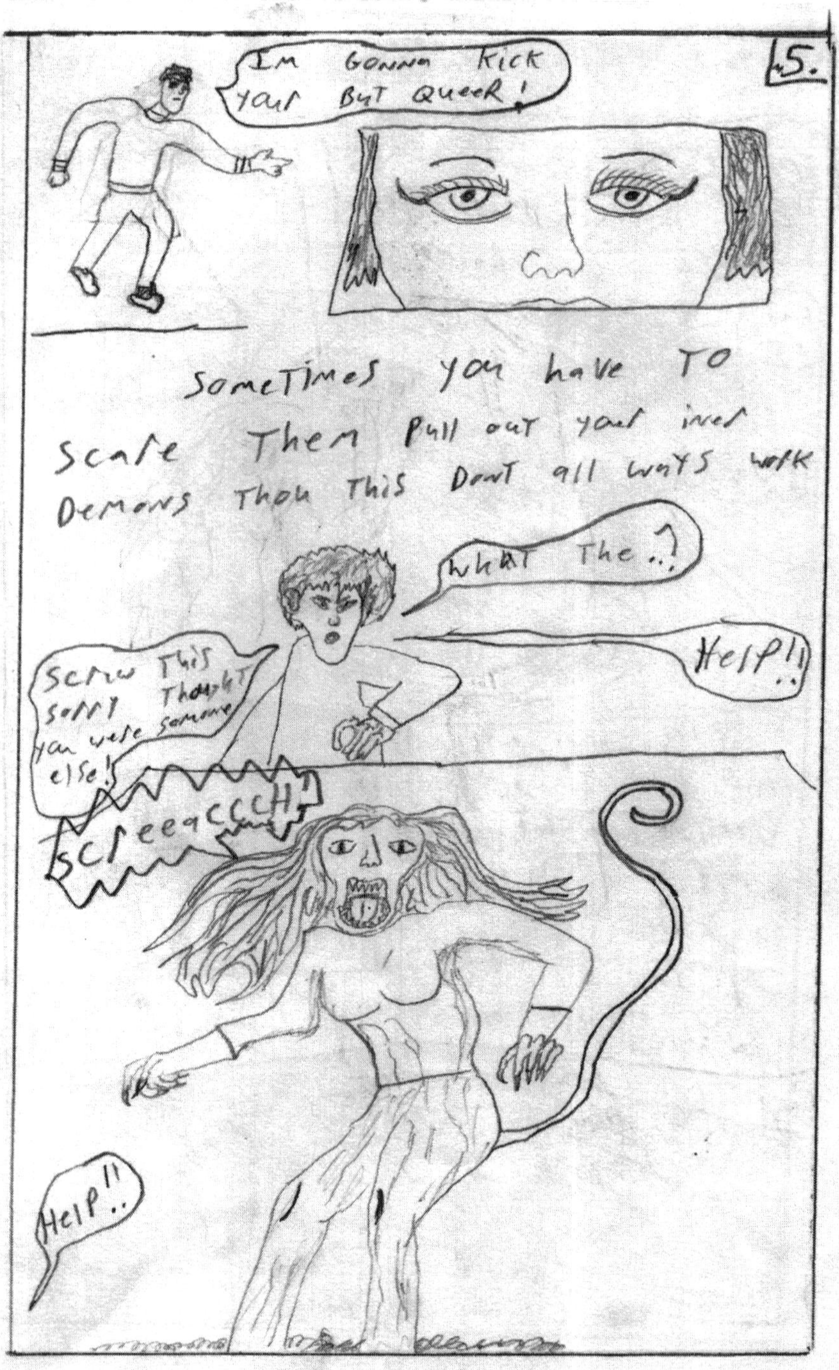
5.
IM GONNA KICK YOUR BUT QUEER!
SomeTimes you have TO Scare Them Pull out your iner Demons Thou This Dont all ways work
WHAT The..?
Help!!..
Screw This sorry Thought you were someone else!
Screeacccch
Help!!..

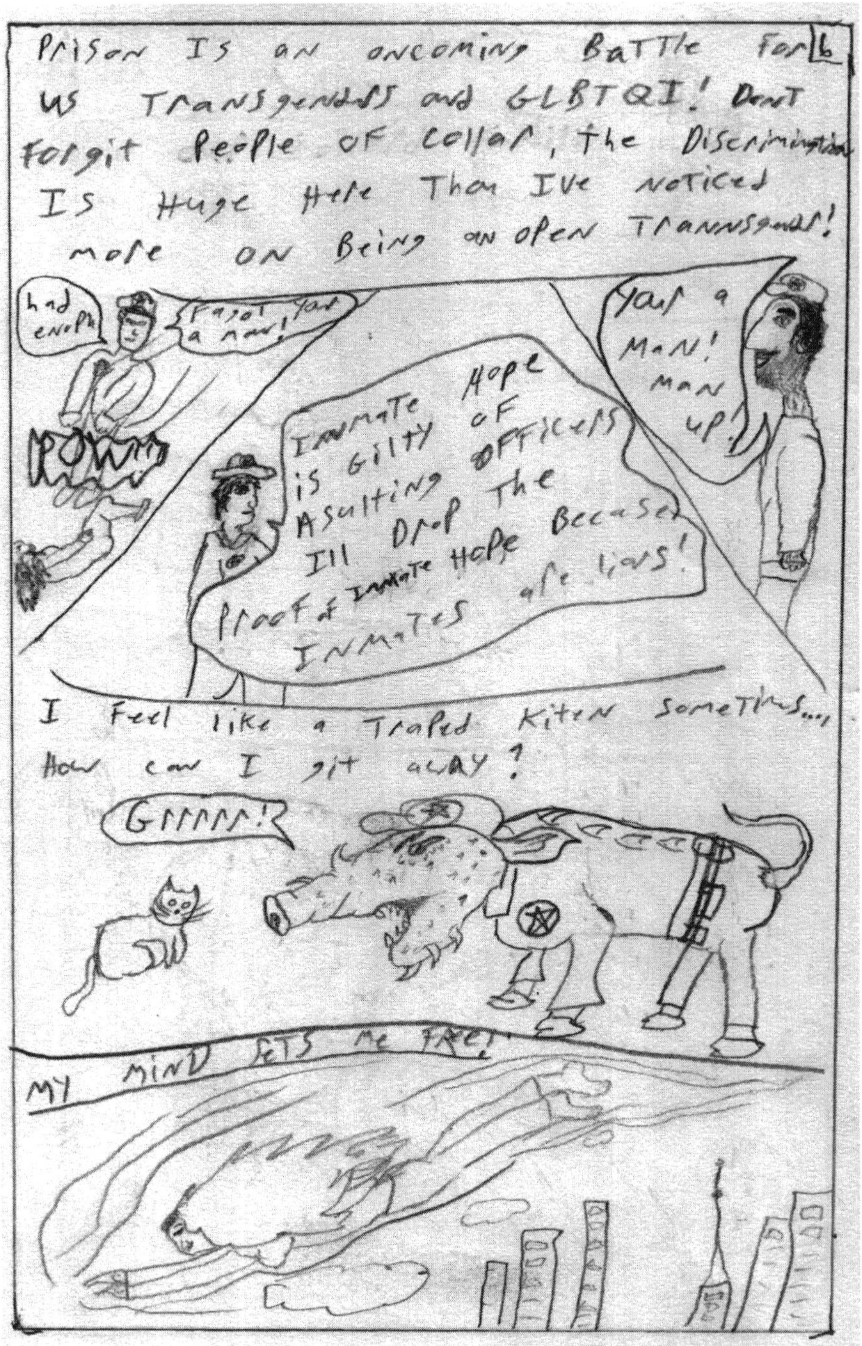
Prison Is an oncoming Battle for 6
us Transgenders and GLBTQI! Don't forgit People of collar, the Discrimination Is Huge Here Than Ive noticed more on Being an open Trannsgender!
had enough
Fagot
Your a man!
POW
Your a Man! man up!
Inmate Hope is gilty of Asulting officers Ill Drop the proof of Inmate Hope Because Inmates are liars!
I Feel like a Traped kiten sometimes...
How can I git away?
Grrrrr!
My mind sets me free!

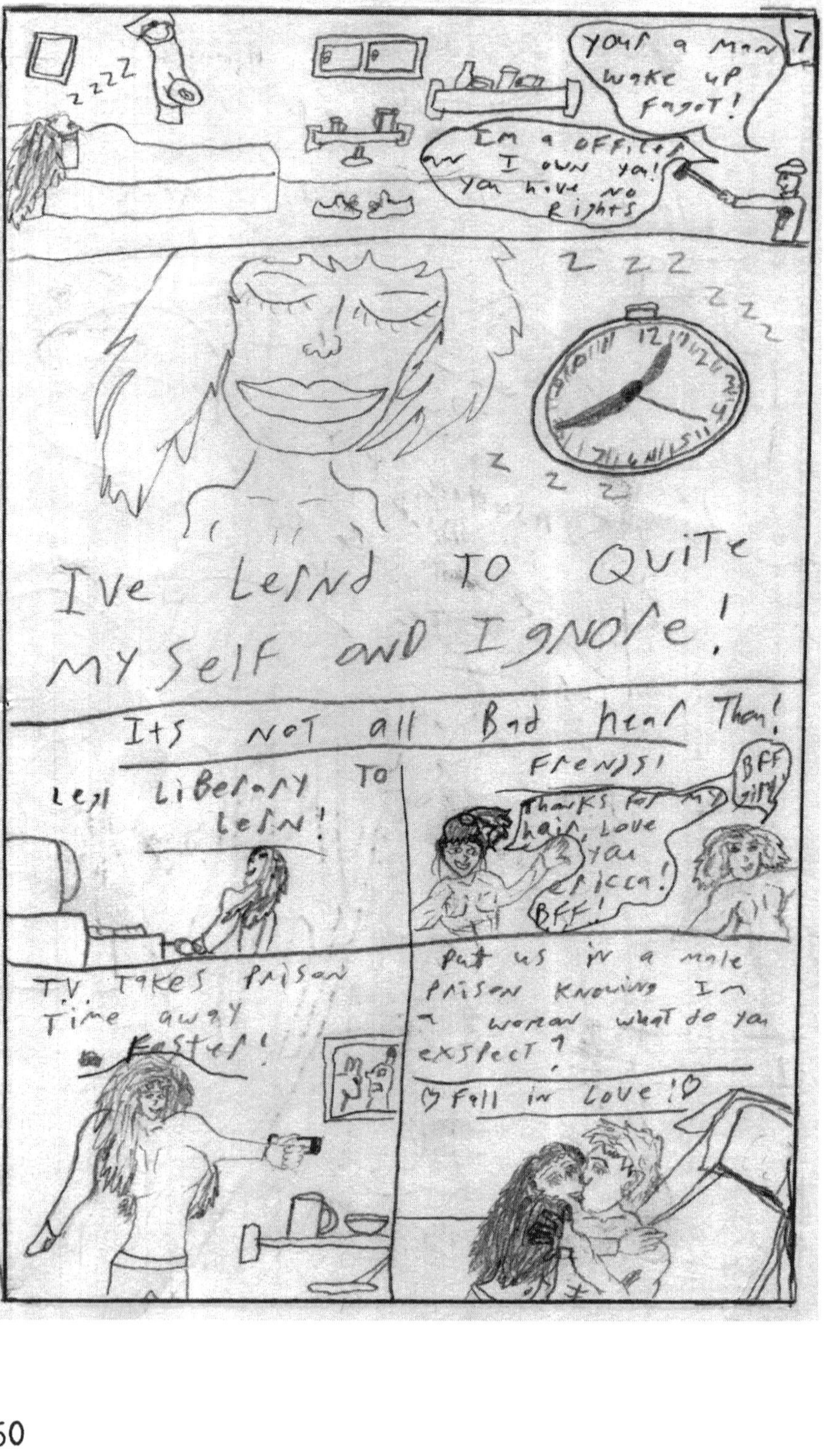
7
zzzZ
your a man wake up Fagot!
Im a officer I own you! you have no rights
z z z
z z z
z z z
Ive Lernd to Quite MySelf and Ignore!
Its not all Bad hear Than!
Lexl Liberary to lern!
Frends!
BFF girl!
Thanks for my hair, Love you Ericca! BFF!
T.V. Takes Prison Time away Faster!
Put us in a male Prison knowing Im a woman what do you exspect?
♡ Fall in Love! ♡

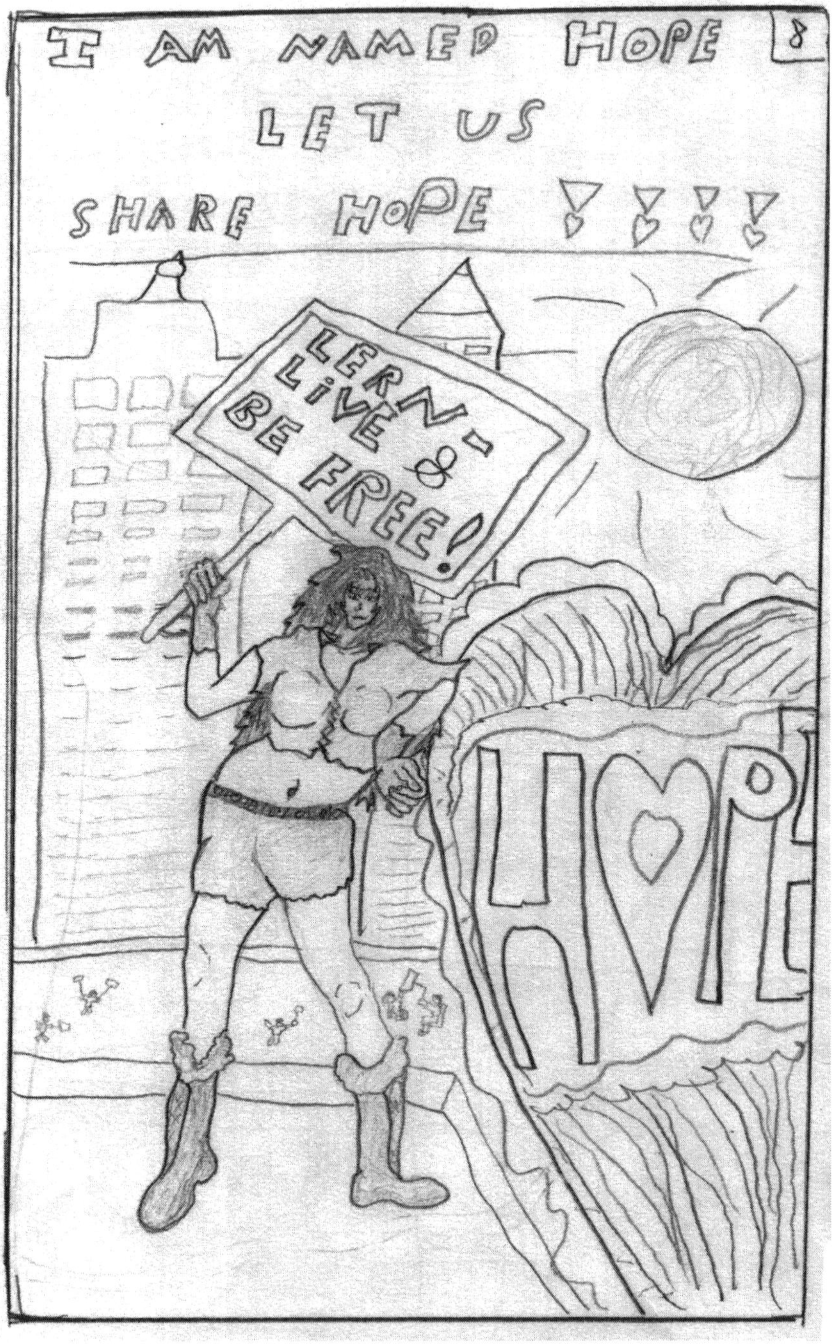
I AM NAMED HOPE
8
LET US
SHARE HOPE
LERN, LIVE & BE FREE!
HOPE

Roman Gaylord
"Queer Crusader"

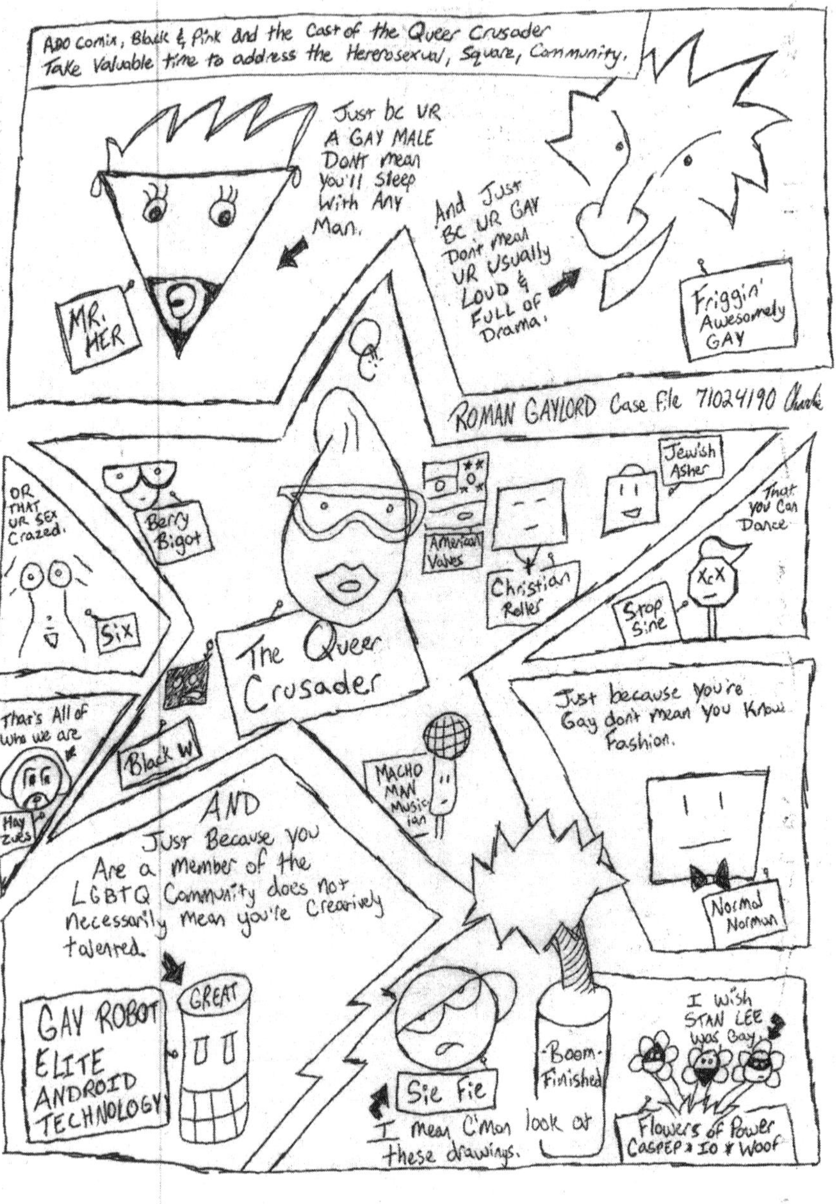

ADO Comix, Black & Pink and the Cast of the Queer Crusader Take Valuable time to address the Hererosexual, Square, Community.
Just bc UR A GAY MALE Dont mean you'll Sleep With Any Man.
MR. HER
And Just bc UR GAY Dont mean UR Usually LOUD & FULL of Drama.
Friggin' Awesomely GAY
ROMAN GAYLORD Case File 71024190
OR THAT UR SEX Crazed.
Six
Berry Bigot
American Values
Christian Roller
Jewish Asher
That you Can Dance
Stop Sine
The Queer Crusader
That's All of who we are
Hay Zues
Black W
MACHO MAN Music ian
Just because you're Gay don't mean you Know Fashion.
Normal Norman
AND Just Because you Are a member of the LGBTQ Community does not necessarily mean you're Creatively talented.
GAY ROBOT ELITE ANDROID TECHNOLOGY
GREAT
Sie Fie
I mean C'Mon look at these drawings.
Boom Finished
I wish STAN LEE Was Gay
Flowers of Power CASPEP * IO * Woof

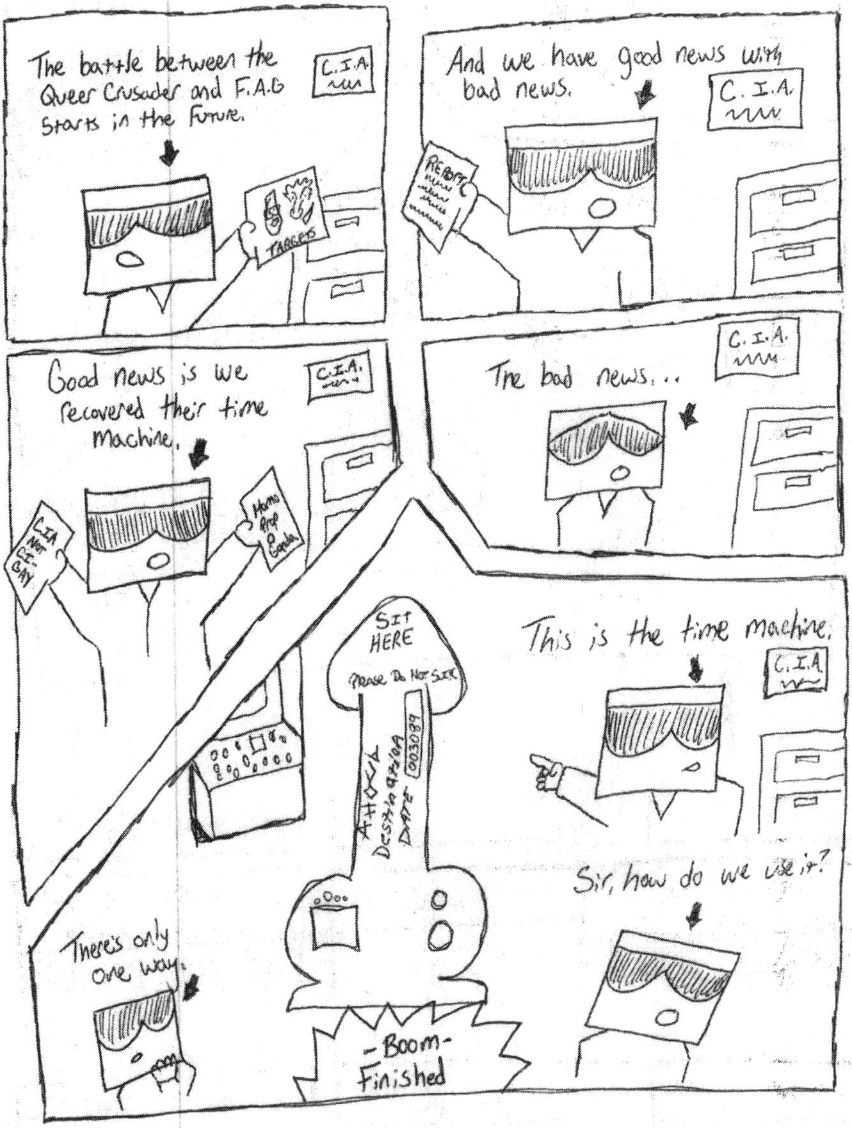
The battle between the Queer Crusader and F.A.G Starts in the Future.
C.I.A.
TARGETS
And we have good news with bad news.
C.I.A.
REPORT
Good news is we recovered their time machine.
C.I.A.
CIA NOT GAY
Homo Prop O Ganda
The bad news...
C.I.A.
This is the time machine.
C.I.A.
SIT HERE
PLEASE DO NOT SIT
DESTINATION DATE
0030B9
Sir, how do we use it?
There's only one way.
-Boom-
Finished

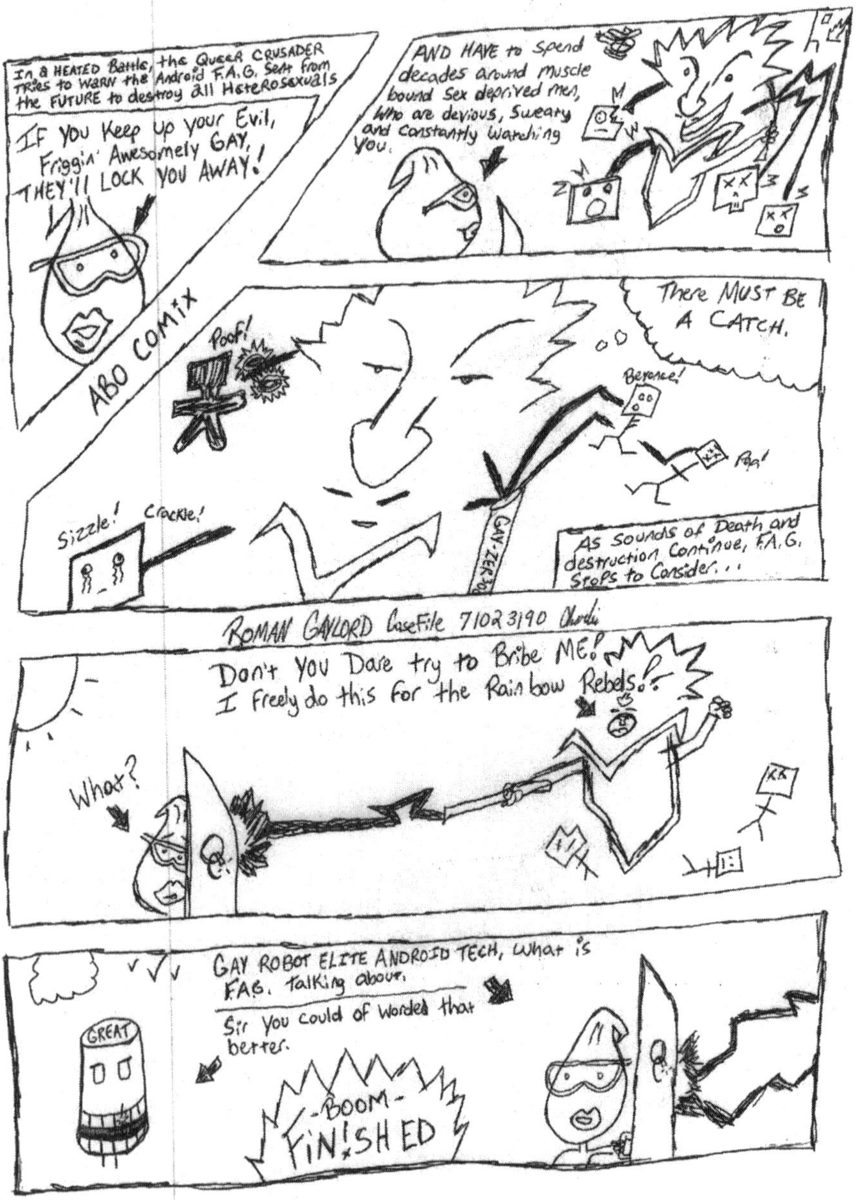
In a HEATED Battle, the QUEER CRUSADER TRIES to WARN the Android F.A.G. Sent from the FUTURE to destroy all HeteRosexuals
IF YOU Keep up your Evil, Friggin' Awesomely GAY, THEY'll LOCK YOU AWAY!
AND HAVE to Spend decades around muscle bound Sex deprived men, Who are devious, Sweary and constantly Watching You.
ABO COMIX
Poof!
There MUST BE A CATCH.
Beyonce!
Pop!
Sizzle!
Crackle!
GAY-ZER
As Sounds of Death and destruction Continue, F.A.G. Stops to Consider...
ROMAN GAYLORD CaseFile 7102 3190
Don't You Dare try to Bribe ME! I Freely do this for the Rainbow Rebels!
What?
GAY ROBOT ELITE ANDROID TECH, What is F.A.G. talking about.
Sir you could of Worded that better.
GREAT
-BOOM-
FIN!SHED

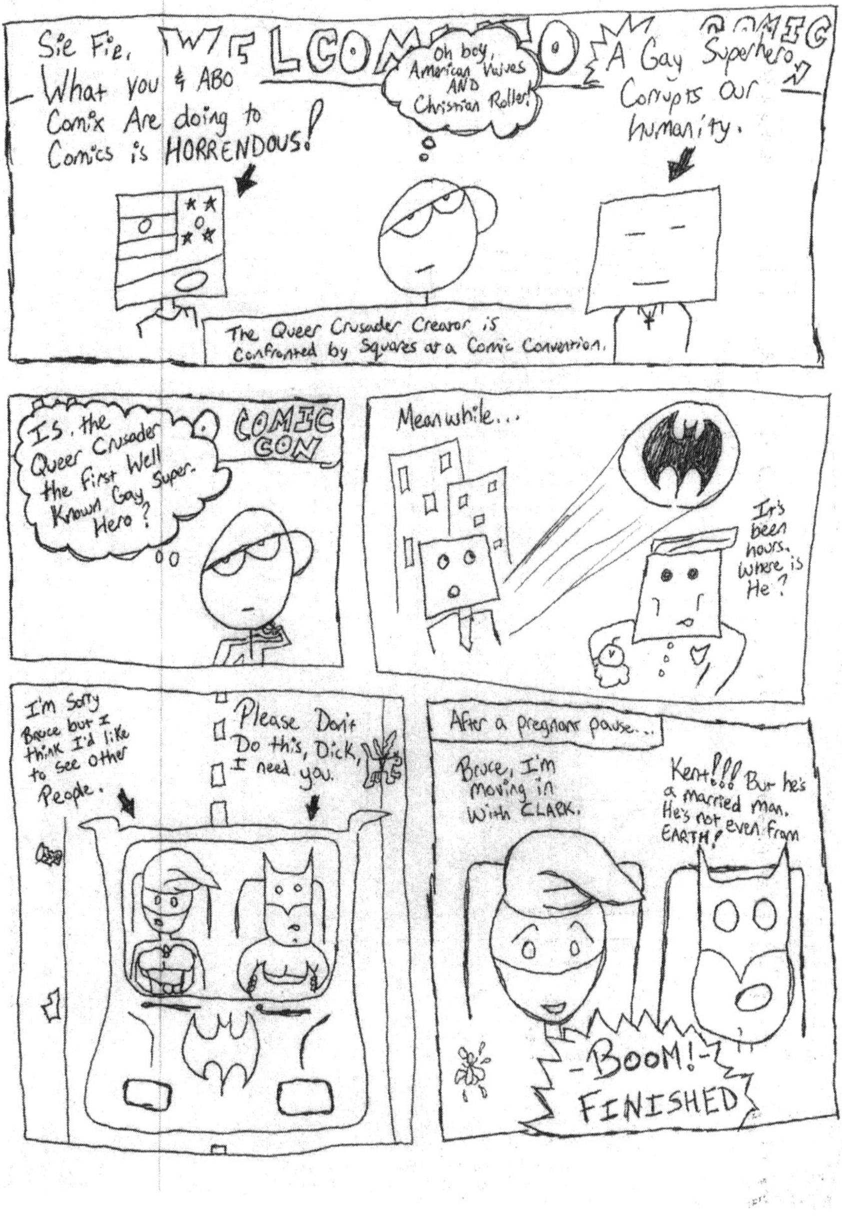
Sie Fie, What you & ABO Comix Are doing to Comics is HORRENDOUS!
Oh boy, American Values AND Christian Rollers!
A Gay Superhero Corrupts our humanity.
The Queer Crusader Creator is confronted by Squares at a Comic Convention.
Is the Queer Crusader the First Well Known Gay Super-Hero?
COMIC CON
Meanwhile...
It's been hours. Where is He?
I'm Sorry Bruce but I think I'd like to see other People.
Please Don't Do this, Dick, I need you.
After a pregnant pause...
Bruce, I'm moving in With CLARK.
Kent!!! But he's a married man. He's not even from EARTH!
-BOOM!-
FINISHED

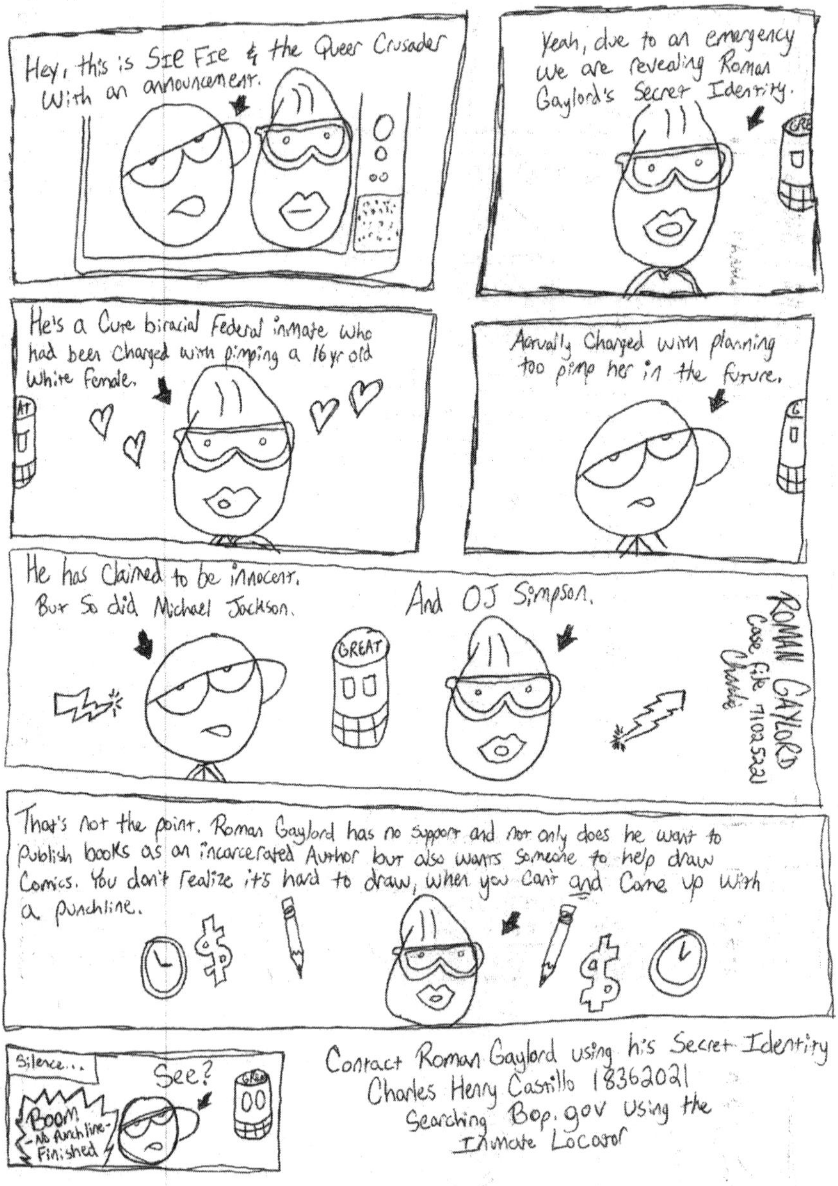
Hey, this is SIE FIE & the Queer Crusader With an announcement.
Yeah, due to an emergency we are revealing Roman Gaylord's Secret Identity.
He's a Cute biracial Federal inmate who had been Charged with pimping a 16yr old White Female.
Actually Charged with planning too pimp her in the future.
He has Claimed to be innocent. But So did Michael Jackson.
And OJ Simpson.
GREAT
ROMAN GAYLORD
Case file 71025221
That's not the point. Roman Gaylord has no support and not only does he want to publish books as an incarcerated Author but also wants someone to help draw Comics. You don't realize it's hard to draw, when you can't and Come up with a punchline.
Silence...
Boom! - No Punchline - Finished
See?
Contact Roman Gaylord using his Secret Identity Charles Henry Castillo 18362021 Searching Bop.gov Using the Inmate Locator

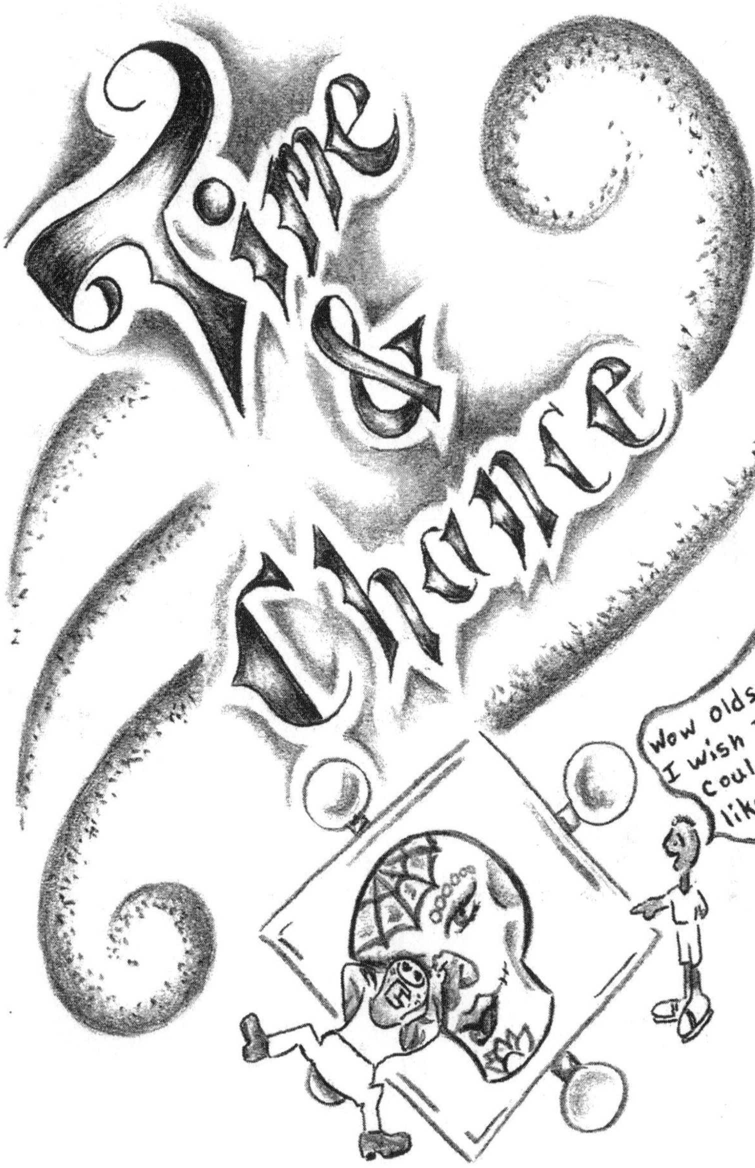
Time & Chance
Wow oldschool! I wish I could Draw like that

by E.L. TEDANA

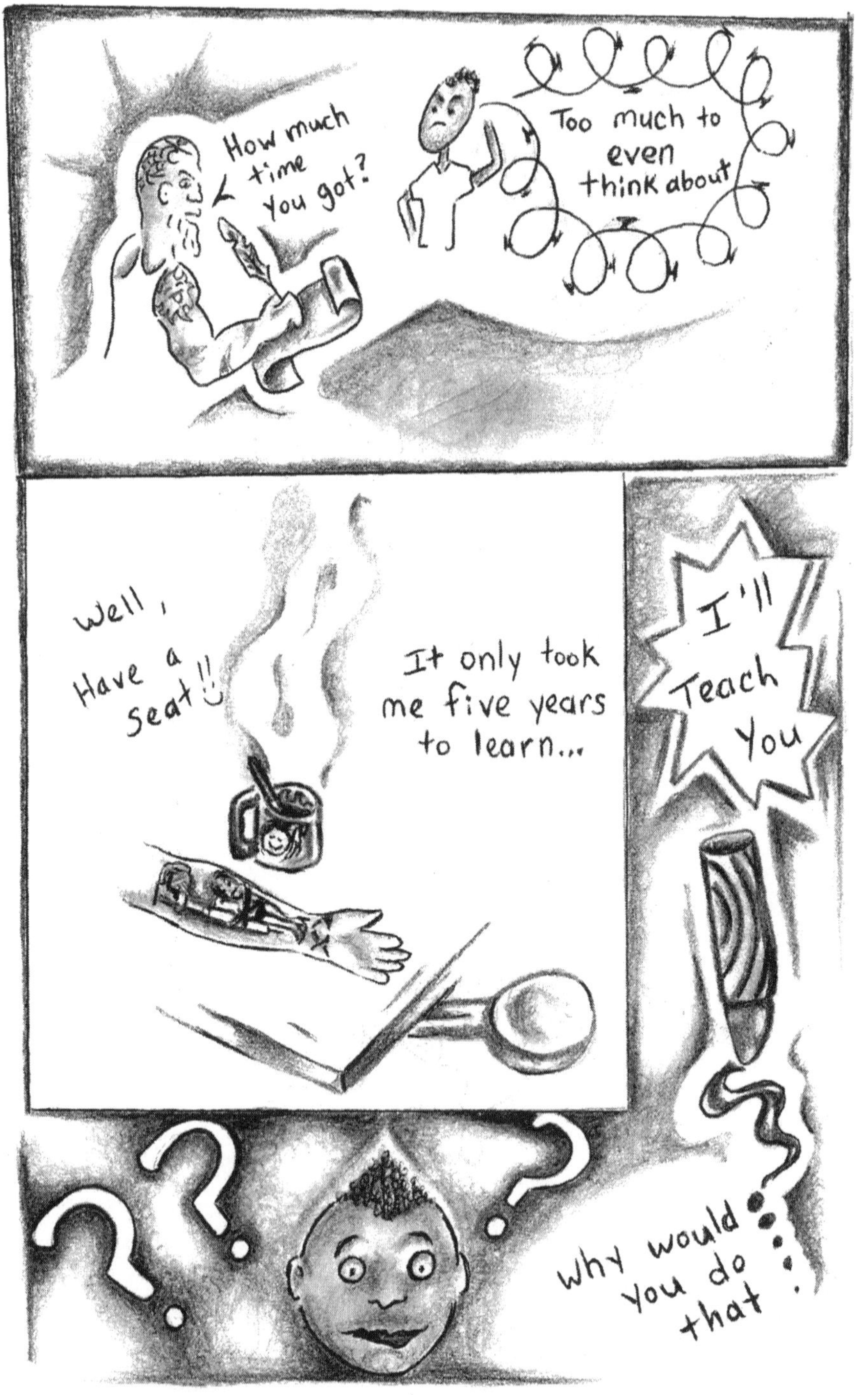
How much time you got?
Too much to even think about
Well, Have a seat!!
It only took me five years to learn...
I'll Teach You
why would you do that

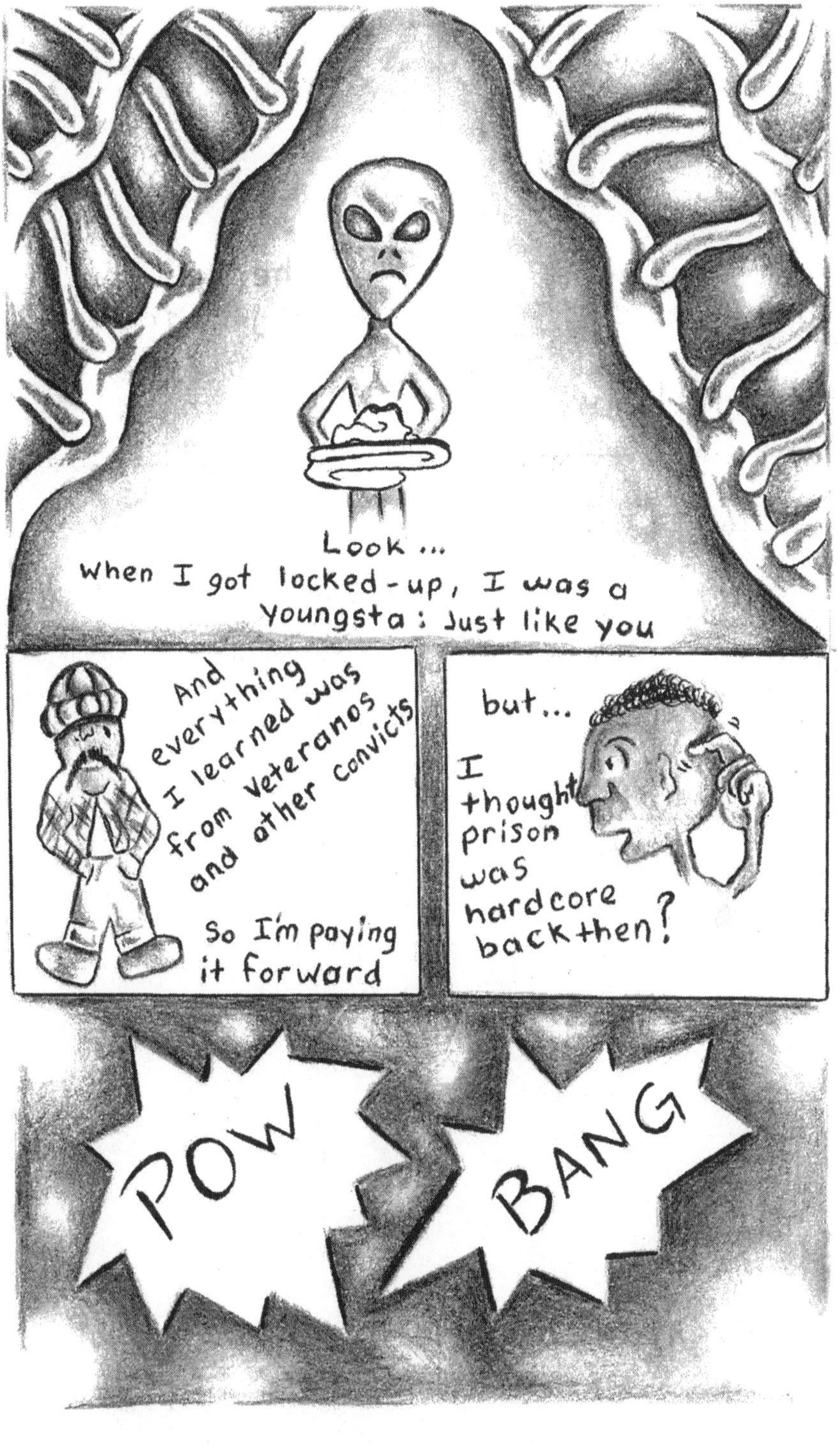
Look ...
When I got locked-up, I was a youngsta: Just like you
And everything I learned was from veteranos and other convicts
So I'm paying it forward
but...
I thought prison was hardcore back then?
POW
BANG

Some actually wanted to

help...

others,
were just tryin'
to show off

Either way, I learned their styles

And

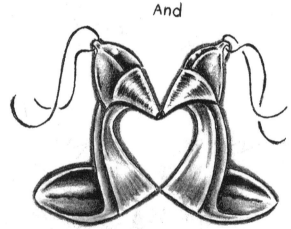

Eventually came up with my own

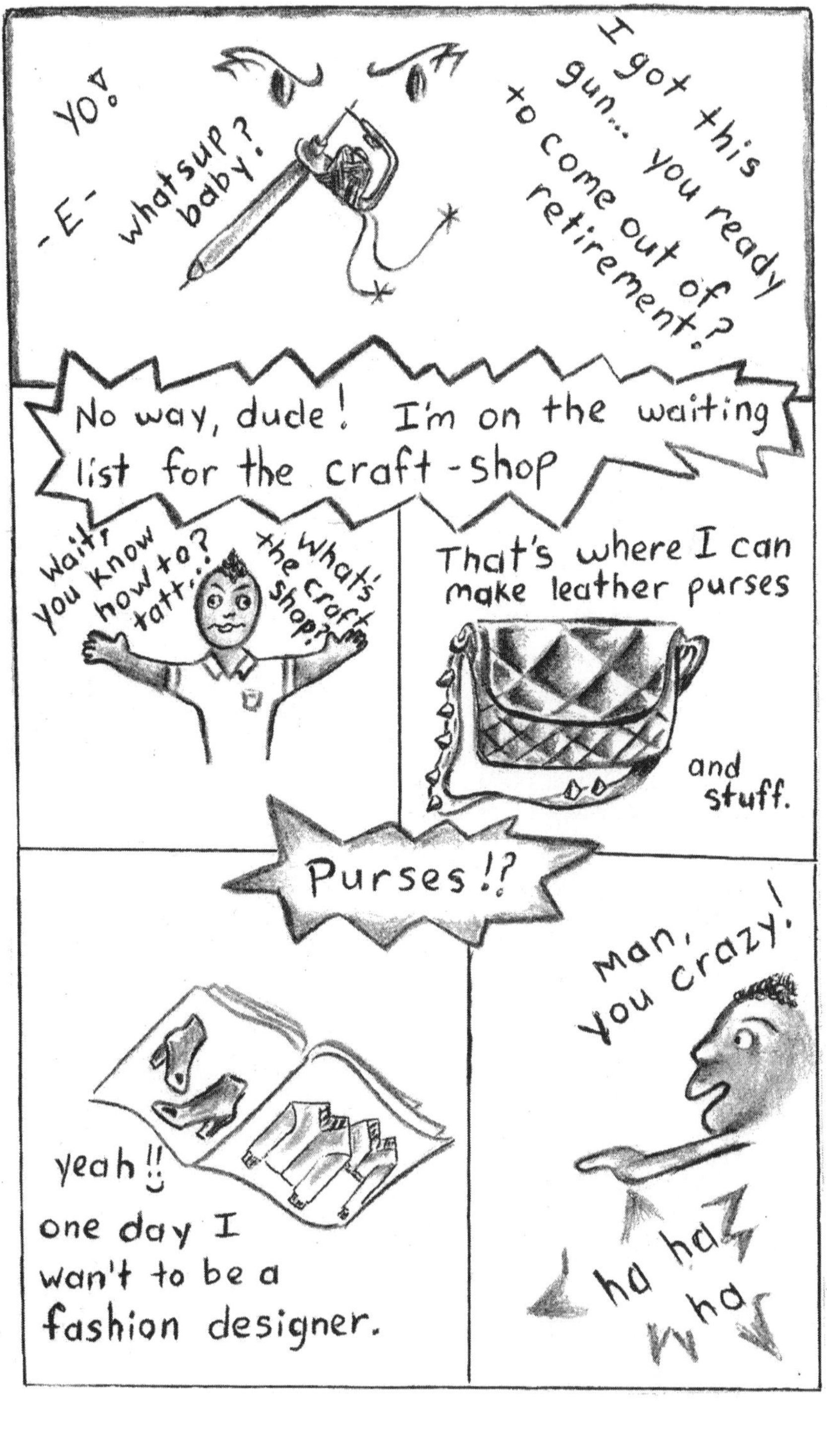
YO!
-E- whatsup? baby!
I got this gun... you ready to come out of retirement?
No way, dude! I'm on the waiting list for the craft-shop
Wait, you know how to? tatt...
What's the craft shop?
That's where I can make leather purses
and stuff.
Purses!?
yeah!!
one day I wan't to be a fashion designer.
Man, you crazy!
ha ha ha

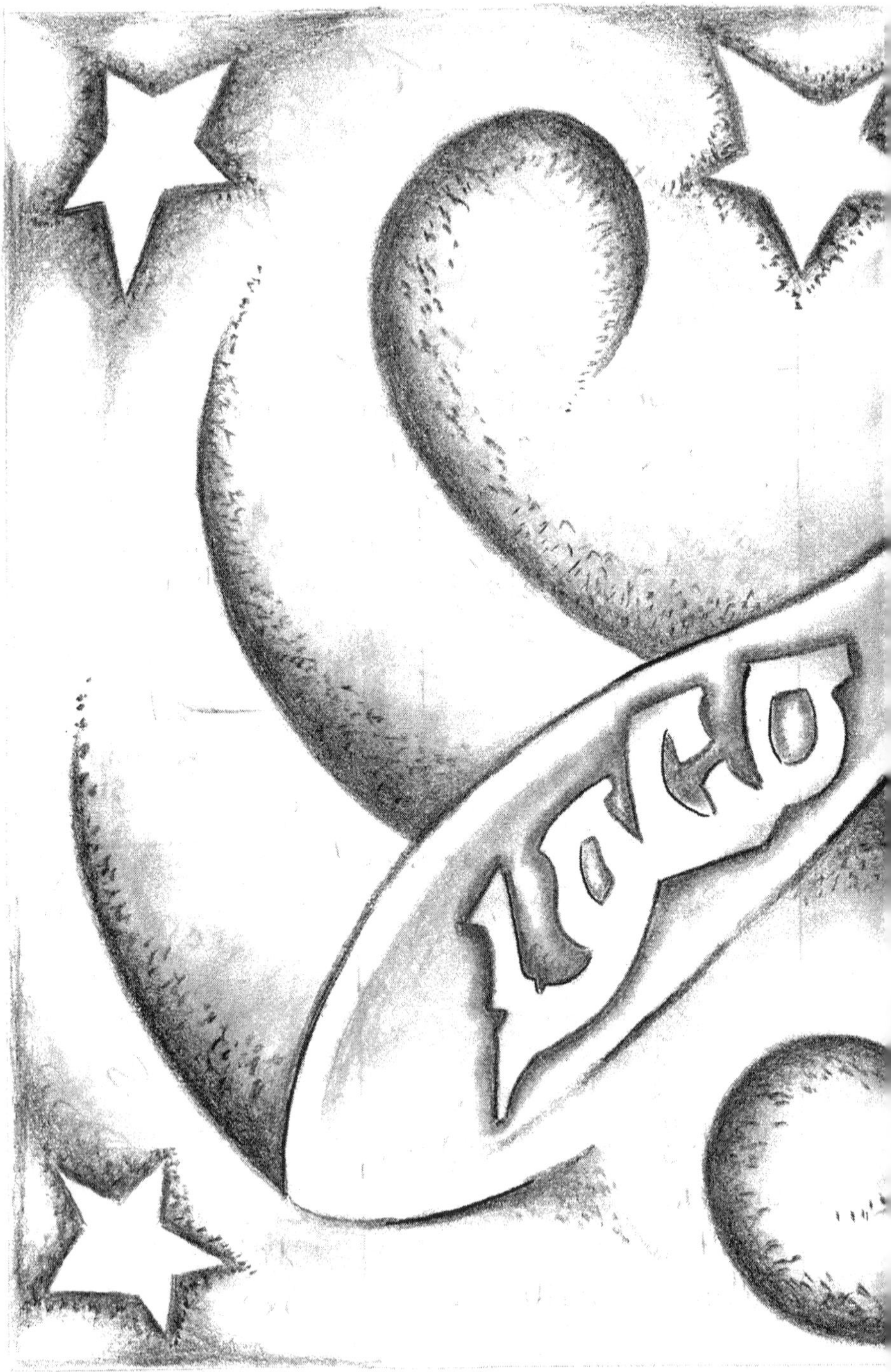

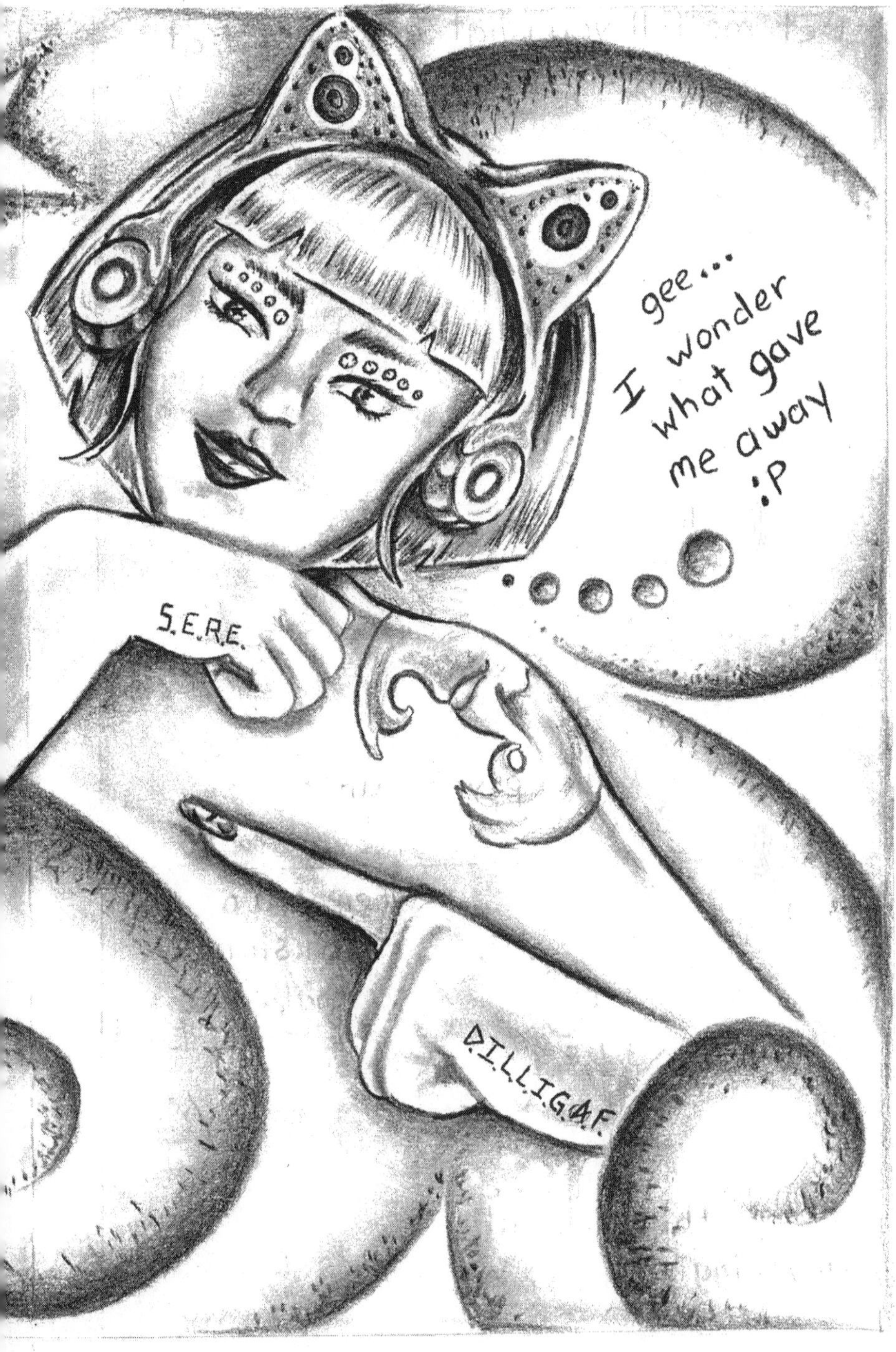
gee...
I wonder
what gave
me away
:P
S.E.R.E.
D.I.L.L.I.G.4.F.

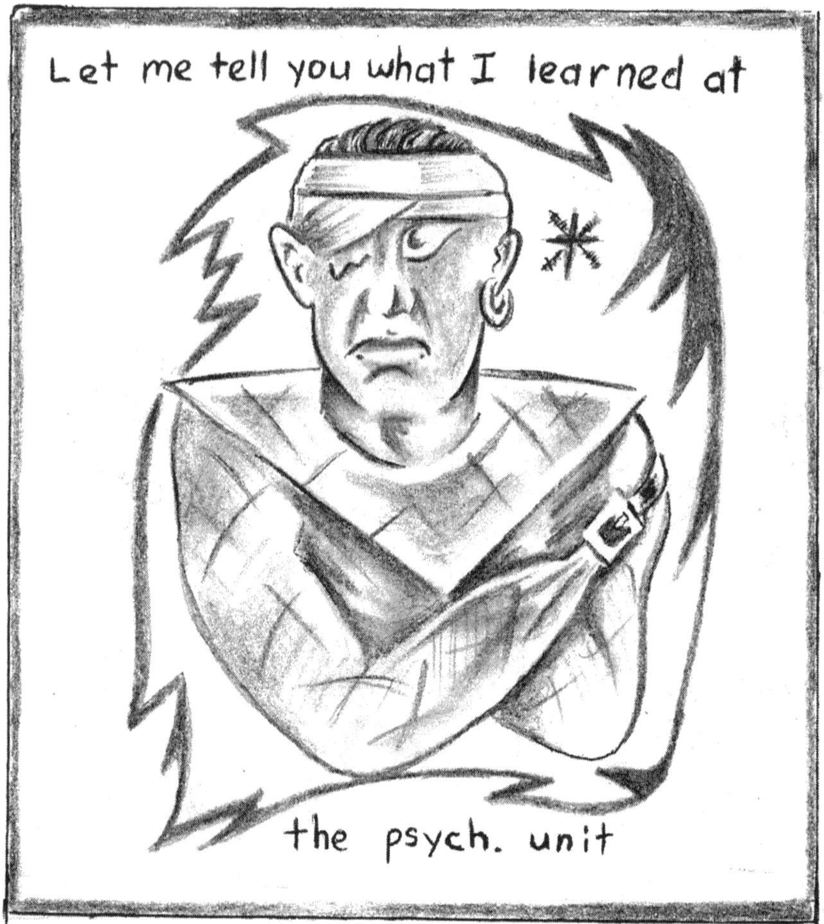
Let me tell you what I learned at
the psych. unit

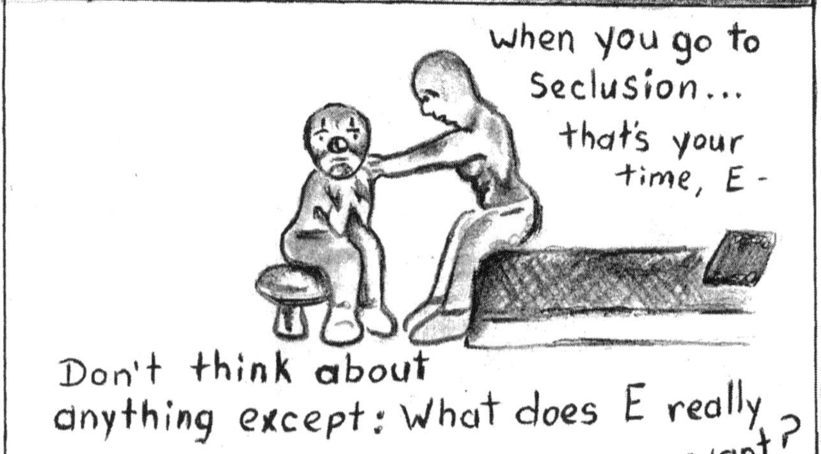
when you go to Seclusion...
that's your time, E-
Don't think about anything except: What does E really want?

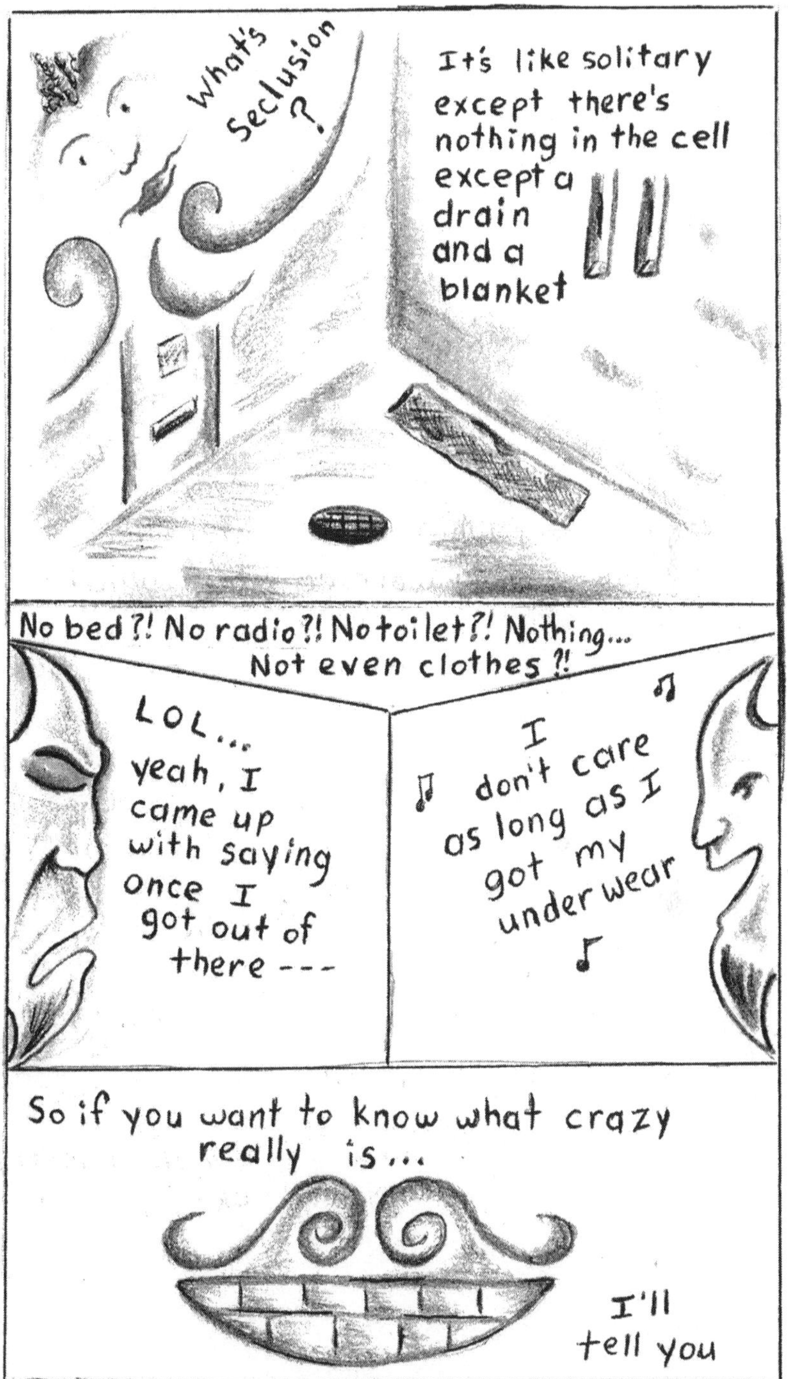
What's Seclusion ?
It's like solitary except there's nothing in the cell except a drain and a blanket
No bed?! No radio?! No toilet?! Nothing... Not even clothes?!
LOL... yeah, I came up with saying once I got out of there ---
I don't care as long as I got my under wear
So if you want to know what crazy really is...
I'll tell you

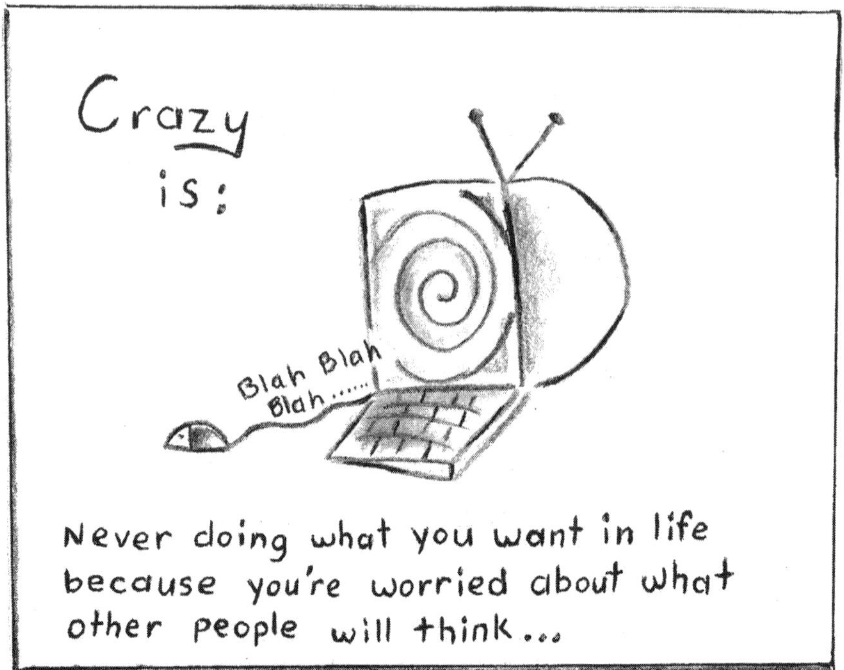
Crazy is:
Blah Blah Blah......
Never doing what you want in life because you're worried about what other people will think...

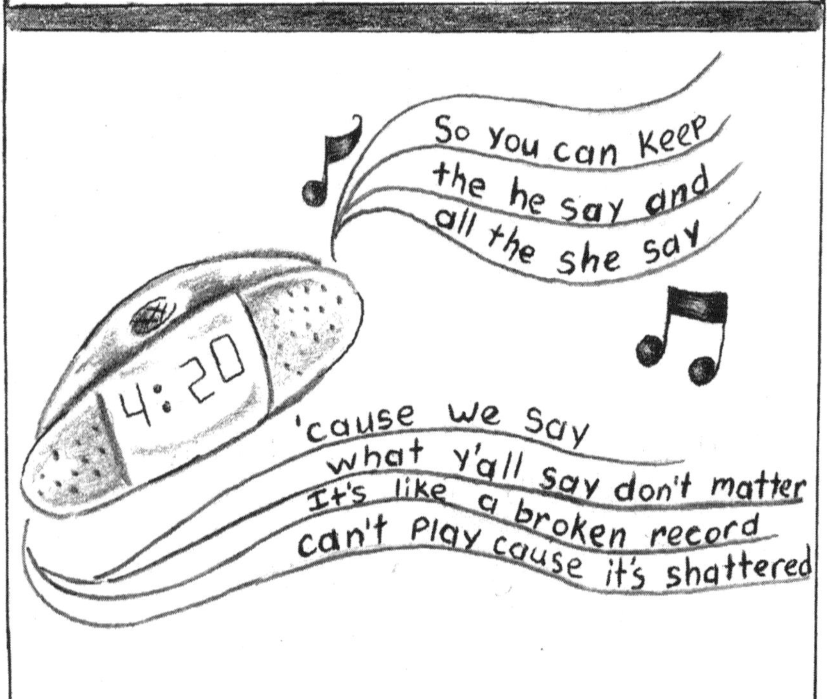
So you can keep the he say and all the she say
4:20
'cause we say what y'all say don't matter
It's like a broken record can't play cause it's shattered

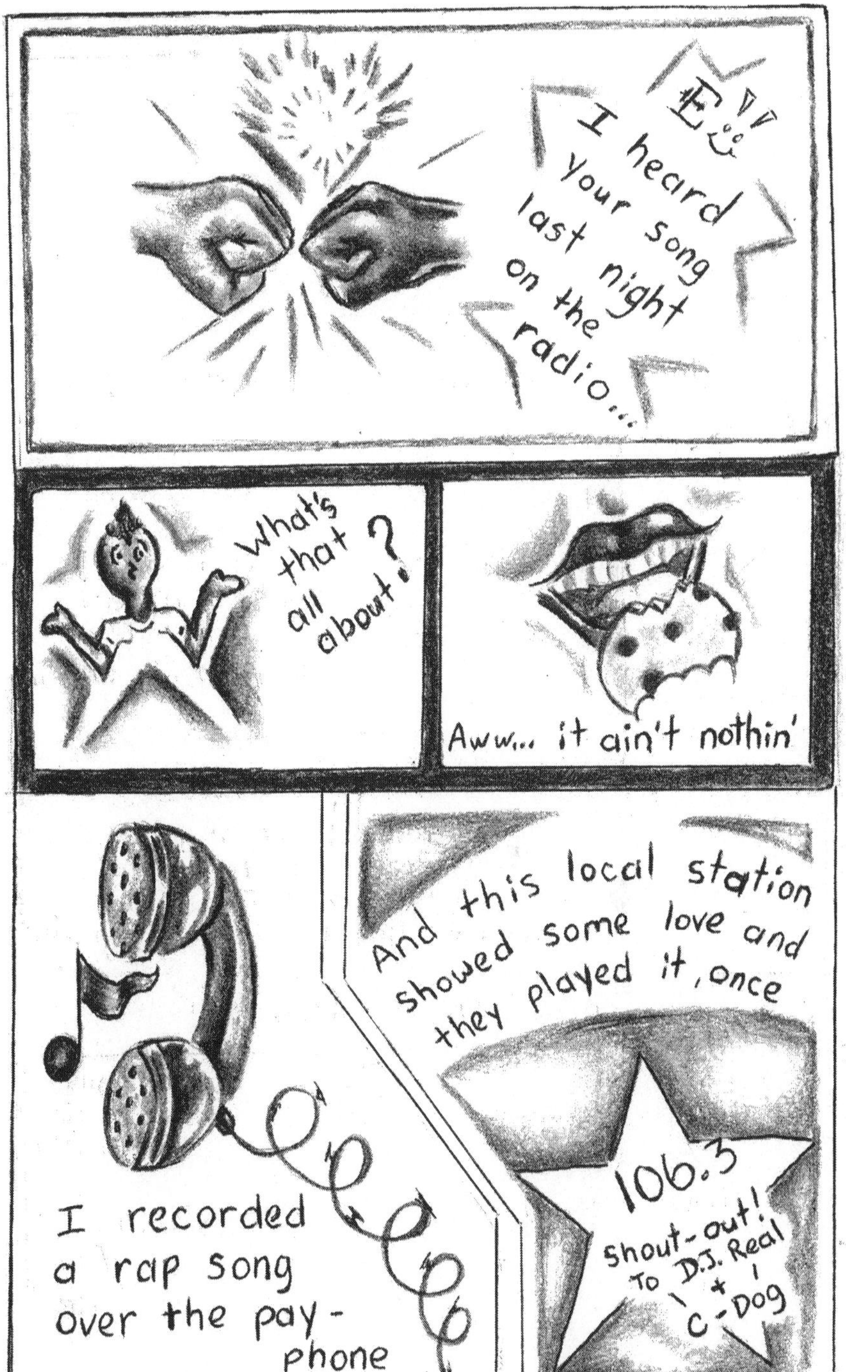
E! I heard your song last night on the radio...
What's that all about?
Aww... it ain't nothin'
I recorded a rap song over the pay-phone
And this local station showed some love and they played it, once
106.3
Shout-out! To D.J. Real + C-Dog

You? rap!

Yeah, I sing and write poetry too

How do you get all these ideas ???

Just because we live in a box... Doesn't mean we have to think inside one...

Have you ever read Ecclesiastes CH. 9 vs. 11 ?

It says,... the race is not to the swift, nor the battle to the strong... but Time and Chance happeneth to them all.

What's that mean ???

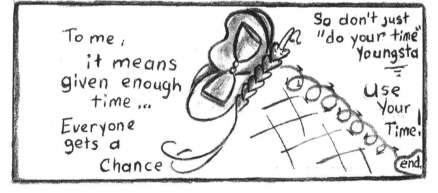

To me, it means given enough time... Everyone gets a Chance

So don't just "do your time" Youngsta

Use Your Time.

end.

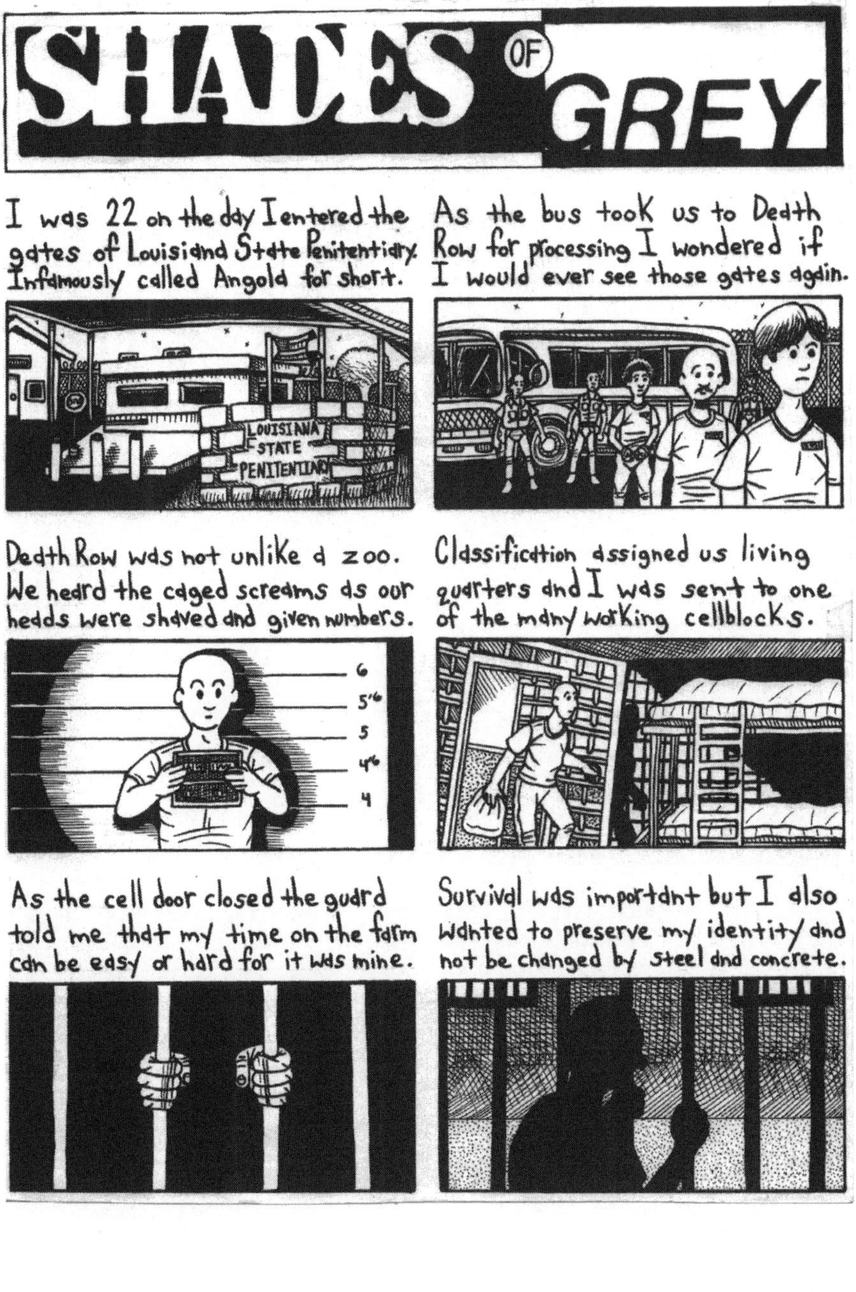
SHADES OF GREY
I was 22 on the day I entered the gates of Louisiana State Penitentiary. Infamously called Angola for short.
LOUISIANA
STATE
PENITENTIARY
As the bus took us to Death Row for processing I wondered if I would ever see those gates again.
Death Row was not unlike a zoo. We heard the caged screams as our heads were shaved and given numbers.
6
5'6
5
4'6
4
Classification assigned us living quarters and I was sent to one of the many working cellblocks.
As the cell door closed the guard told me that my time on the farm can be easy or hard for it was mine.
Survival was important but I also wanted to preserve my identity and not be changed by steel and concrete.

Before the lights went out I wrote my mom a letter. I let her know A-Block is my new residence.

She is not to blame for how I turned out or where I ended up. She did the best she could by me.

Mom raised three kids all by herself. Her hands were full just keeping us under a roof and food on the table.

By the age of fourteen I was an alcoholic, drug addict and trying to be with as many girls as possible.

I never thought the party would end. It did though, with me in handcuffs for a murder charge.

Until my death I will carry an enormous amount of guilt and shame on my shoulders.

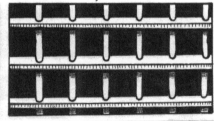

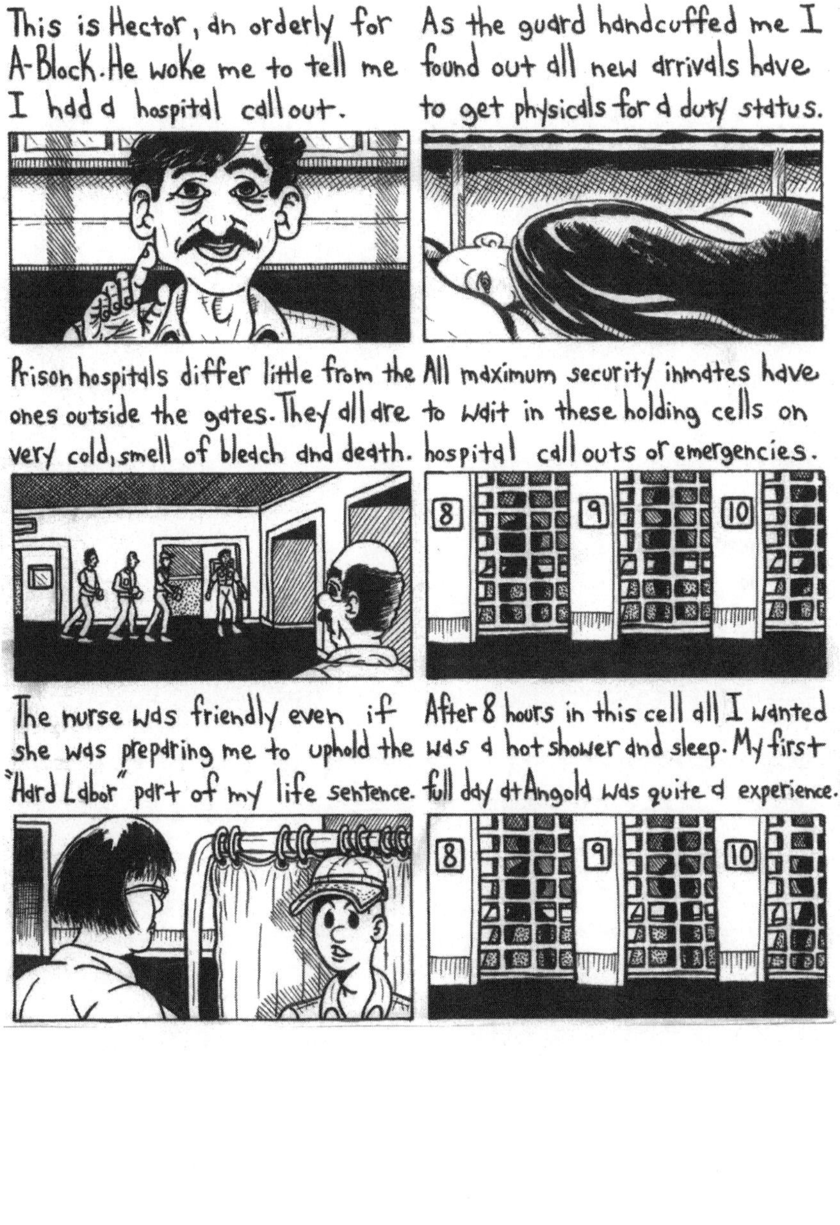
This is Hector, an orderly for A-Block. He woke me to tell me I had a hospital callout.
As the guard handcuffed me I found out all new arrivals have to get physicals for a duty status.
Prison hospitals differ little from the ones outside the gates. They all are very cold, smell of bleach and death.
All maximum security inmates have to wait in these holding cells on hospital callouts or emergencies.
8
9
10
The nurse was friendly even if she was preparing me to uphold the "Hard Labor" part of my life sentence.
After 8 hours in this cell all I wanted was a hot shower and sleep. My first full day at Angola was quite a experience.
8
9
10

Bio Info

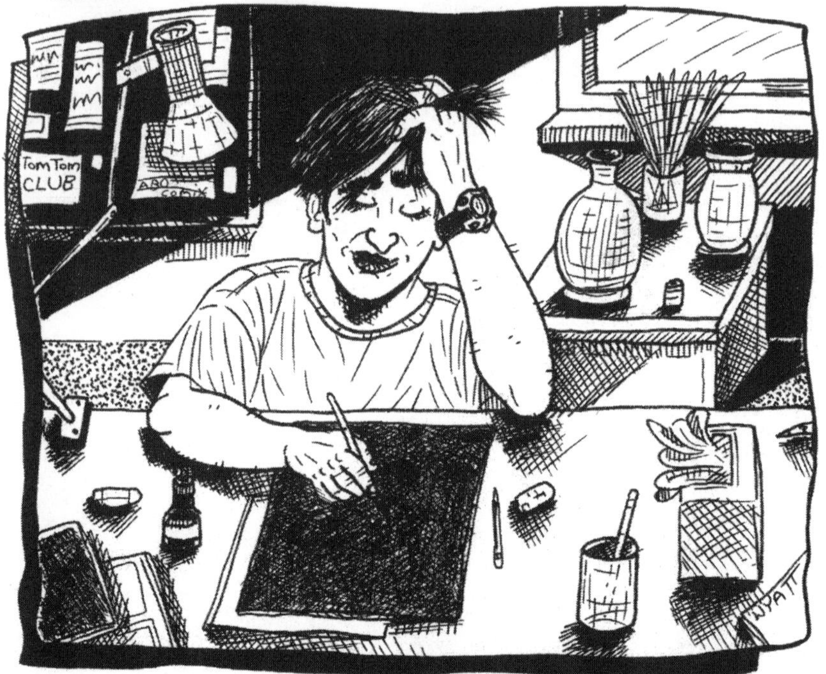
Tom Tom
CLUB
WYATT

GabeWyatt is a self-taught artist from Monroe, LA. He has quite a few "habits"....., but making his own comics is one of the healthier ones. The artist has been busy producing these underground comics for two decades now and has no plans to quit.....

WYATT

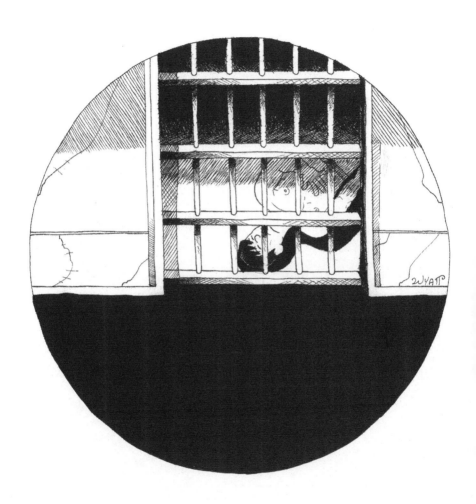

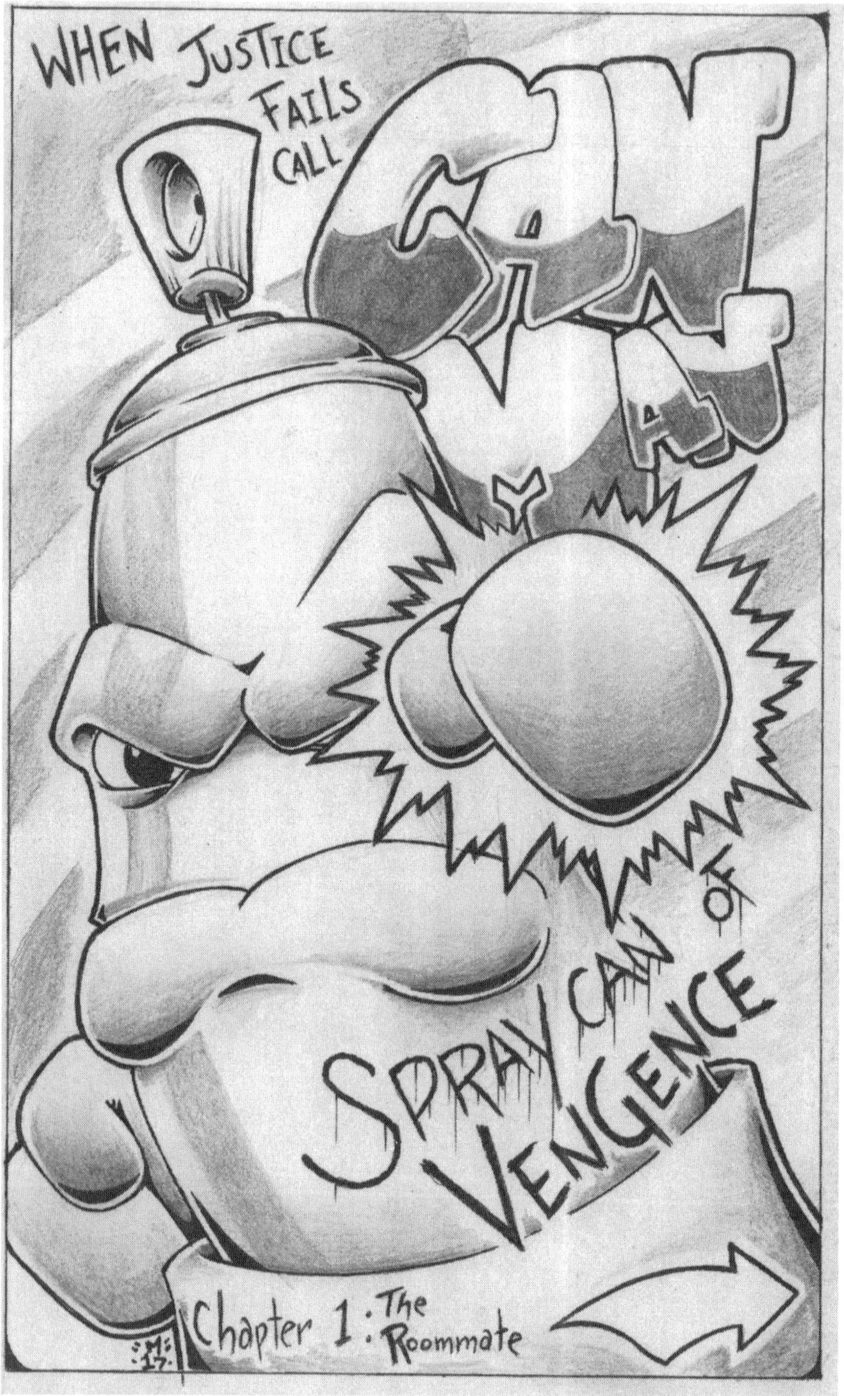
WHEN JUSTICE FAILS CALL
SPRAY CAN OF VENGENCE
Chapter 1: The Roommate

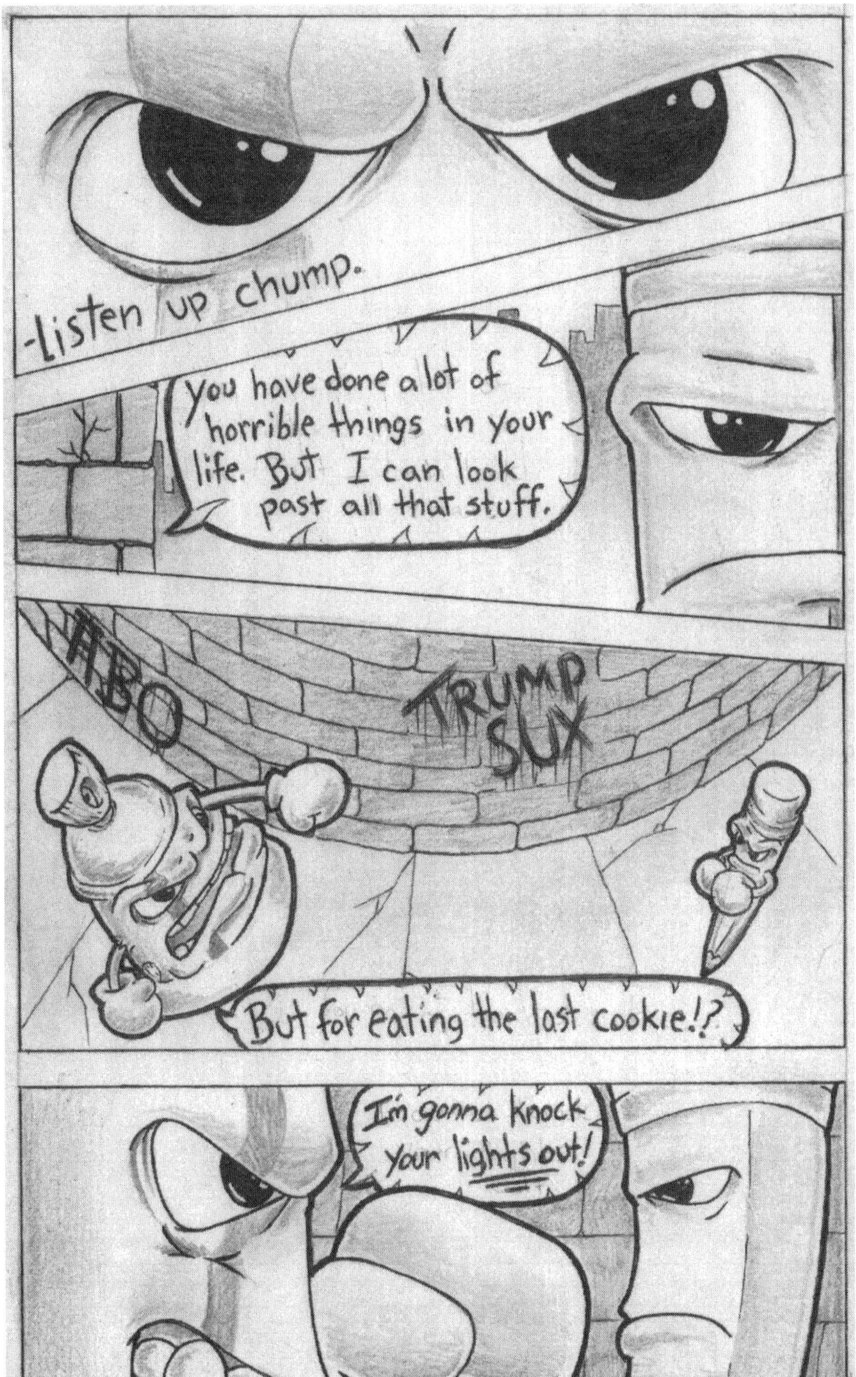
-listen up chump.
You have done a lot of horrible things in your life. But I can look past all that stuff.
HBO
TRUMP SUX
But for eating the last cookie!?
I'm gonna knock your lights out!

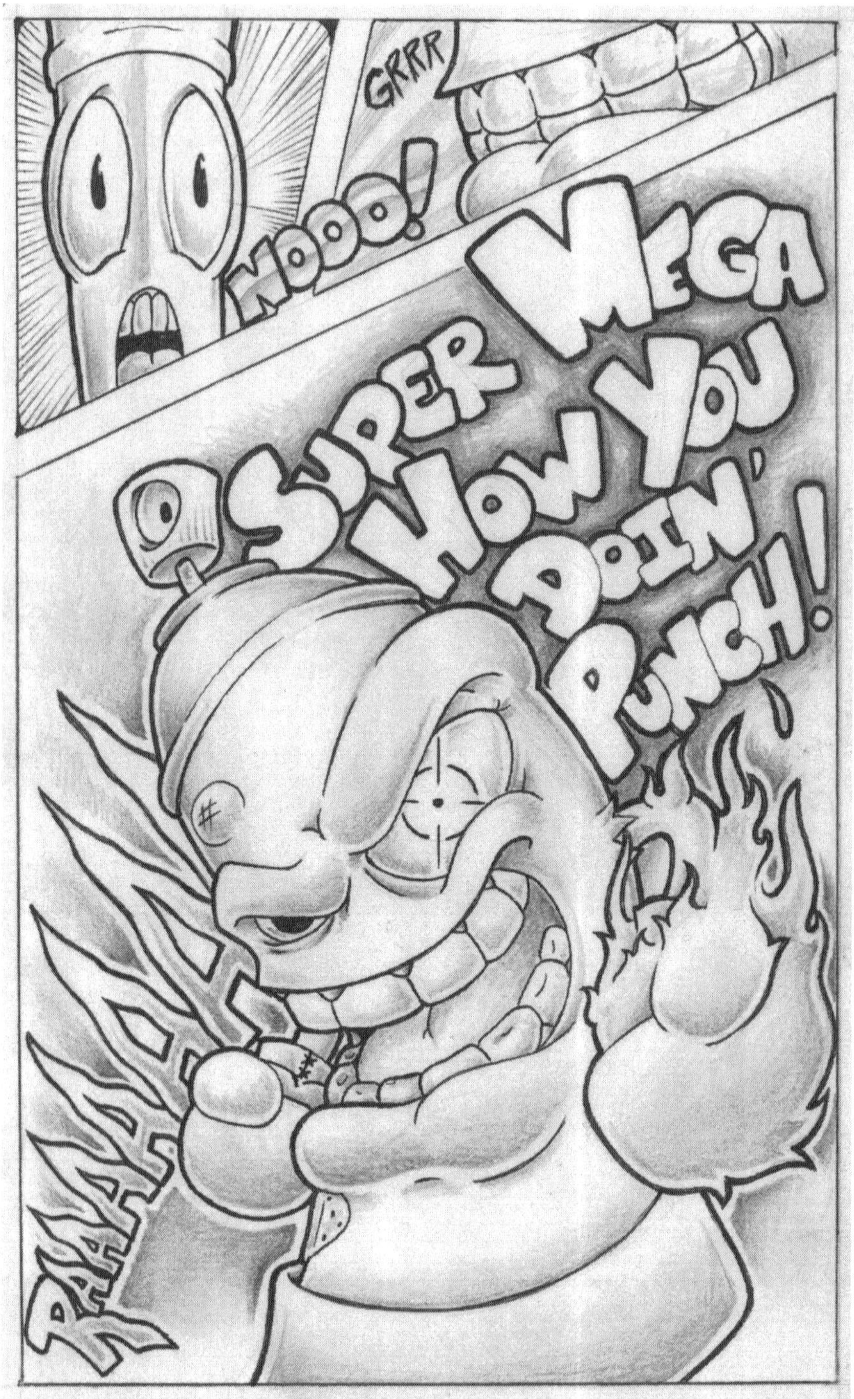
GRRR
NOOO!
SUPER MEGA HOW YOU DOIN' PUNCH!

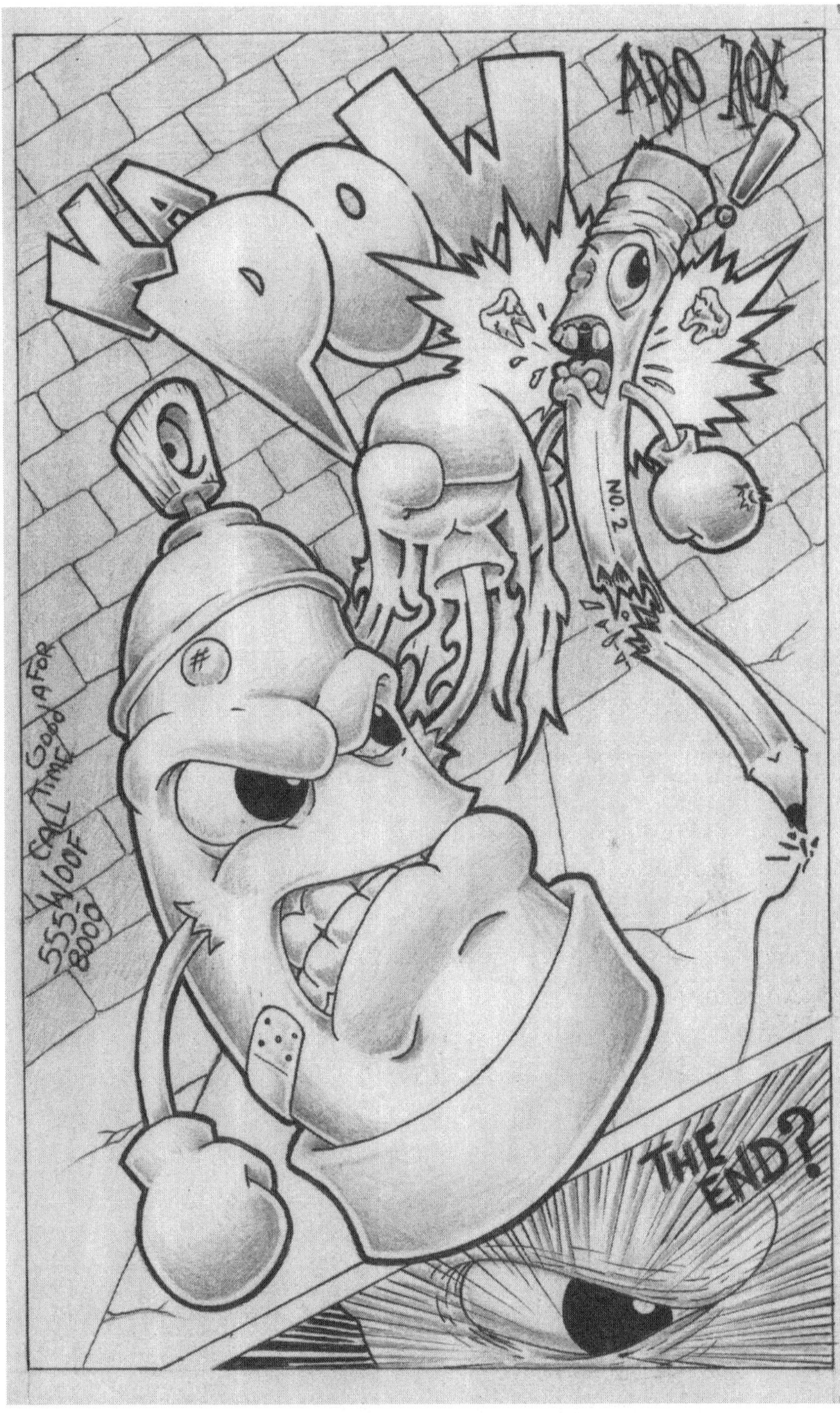

NO. 2
FOR A Good TIME CALL 555-WOOF 8000
THE END?

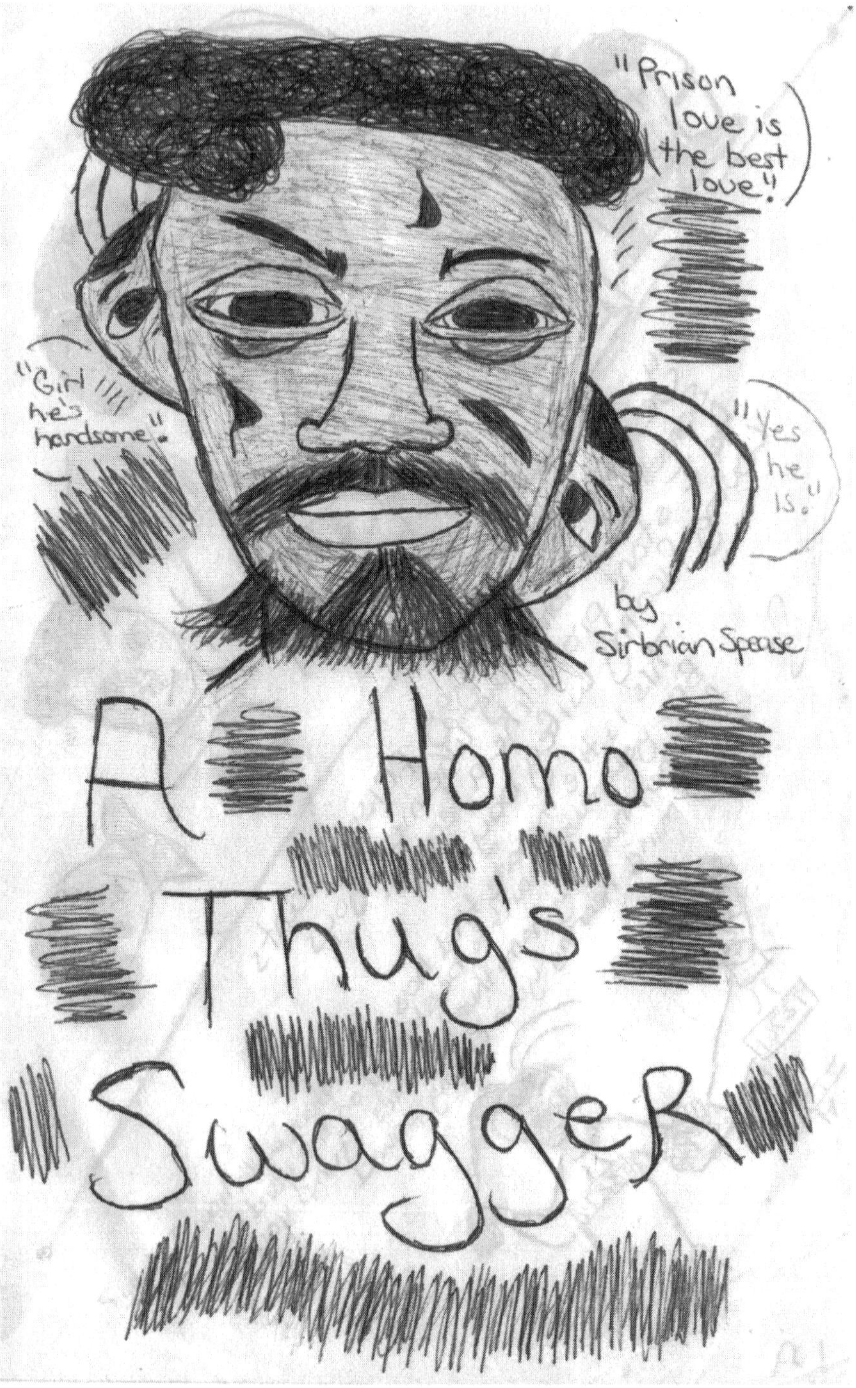
"Prison love is the best love!!
"Girl he's handsome!!
"Yes he is."
by Sirbrian Spease
A Homo Thug's Swagger

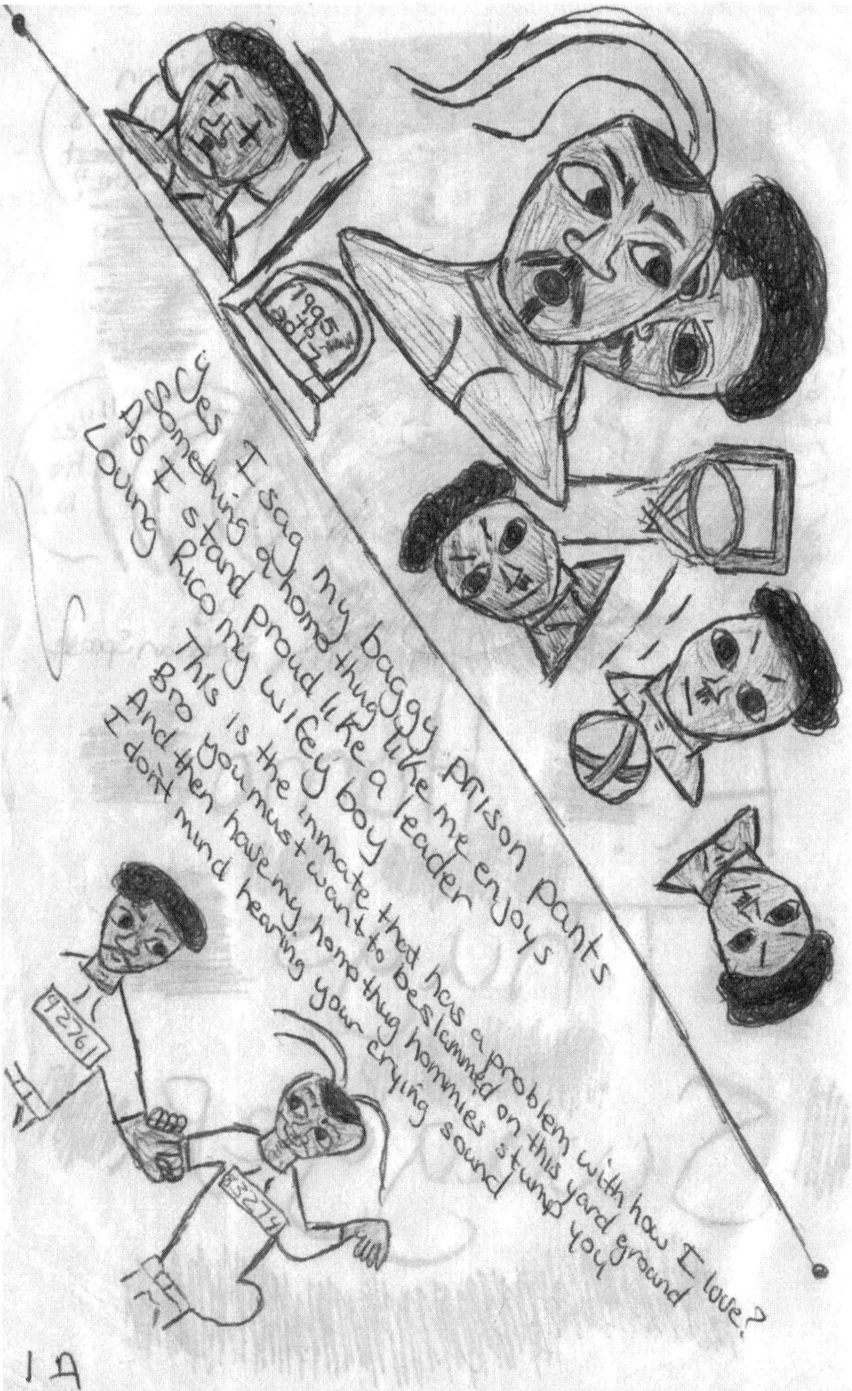
Yes I sag my baggy prison pants
Something a homo thug like me enjoys
As I stand proud like a leader
Loving Rico my wifey boy
This is the inmate that has a problem with how I love?
Bro you must want to be slammed on this yard ground
And then have my homo thug hommies stump you
I don't mind hearing your crying sound

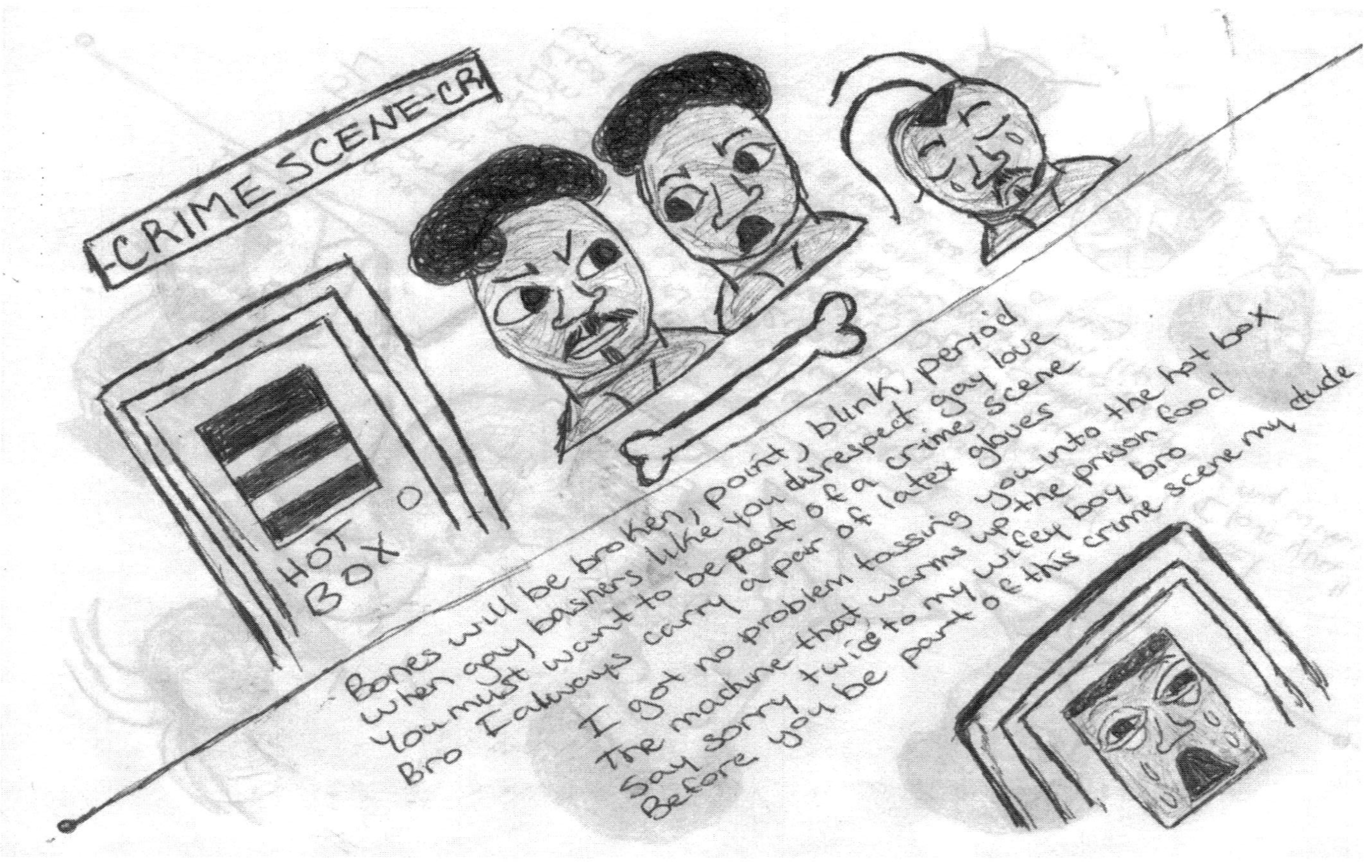
CRIME SCENE-CR
HOT BOX
Bones will be broken, point, blink, period
When gay bashers like you disrespect gay love
You must want to be part of a crime scene
Bro I always carry a pair of latex gloves
I got no problem tossing you into the hot box
The machine that warms up the prison food
Say sorry twice to my wifey boy bro
Before you be part of this crime scene my dude

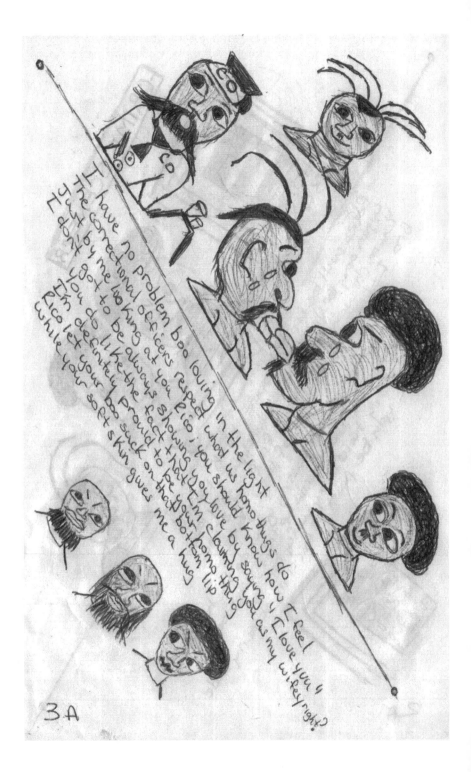

I have no problem boo loving in the light
The correctional officers respect when we homo thugs do
Just by me looking at you Rico you should know how I feel
I don't got to be always showing you love by saying I love you 4
You do like the fact that I'm clowning you as my wifey right?
I'm definitely proud to be your homo thug
Rico let your boo suck on that bottom lip
while your soft skin gives me a hug

3A

91

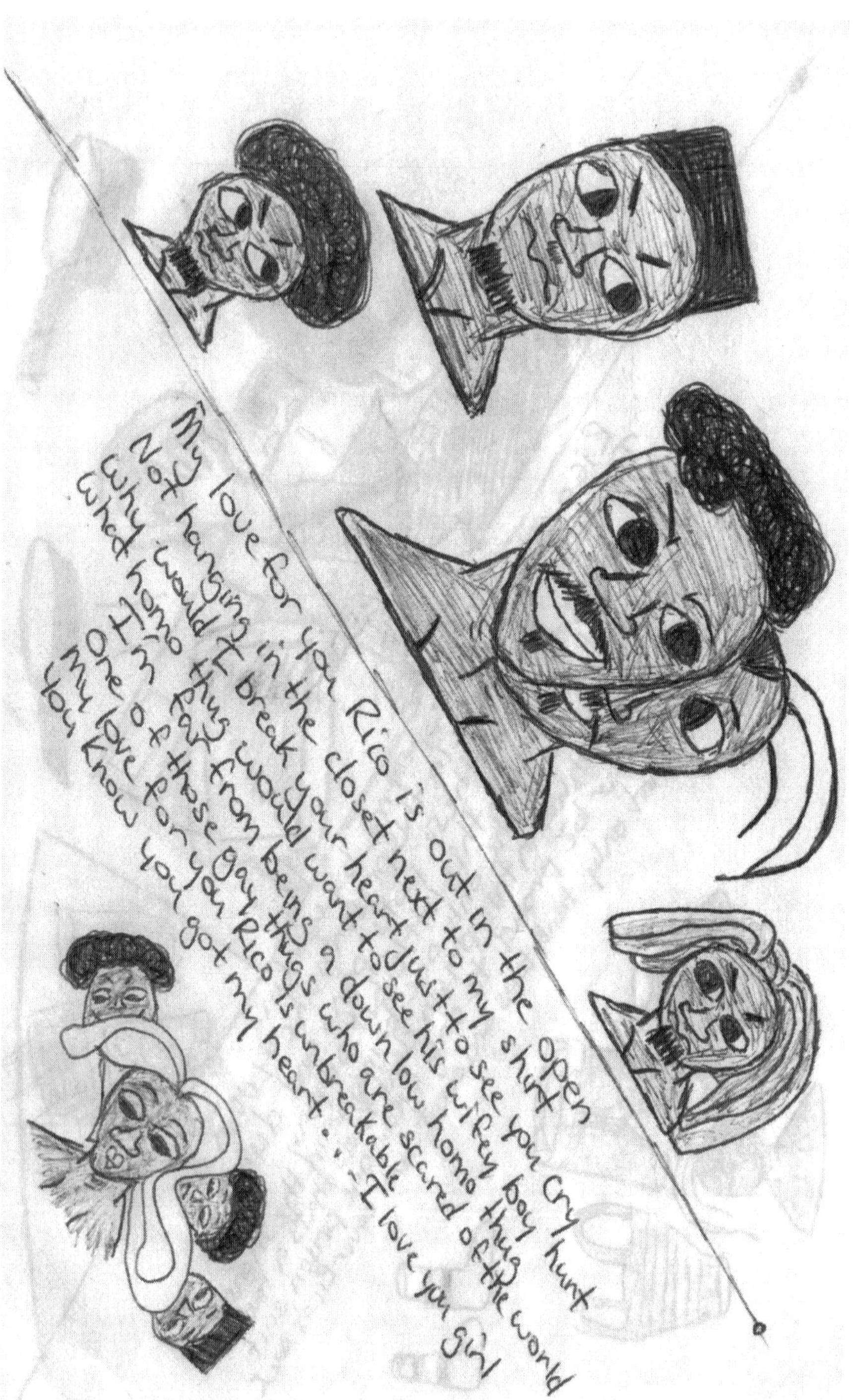
My love for you Rico is out in the open
Not hanging in the closet next to my shirt
why would I break your heart just to see you cry
what homo thug would want to see his wifey boy hurt
I'm far from being a down low homo thug
One of those gay thugs who are scared of the world
my love for you Rico is unbreakable
You know you got my heart... -I love you girl

Rico will not disrespect me by working $4.00 a day
I do over time here in this prison make
1+1=3 My job is to wash these pots pans and dishes
1+1=3 I'm proud to make this little bit of pay money
I determine to be the only one bringing in the money
What home thug in this prison don't know that's a rasty
Rico will never be proud to only wear one prison suit
I make sure that only tank tops and sweat shirts cover Rico's back

INMATE

93

The prisoners know Rico's stomach don't crave for prison slop only the street food he'll swallow that I bought from the prison store Rico was proud to cook it behind the cell door you better believe that hell only be allowed to eat good tasting food you could cook in the cell hot water was given to us so we could cook in the cell don't spill that hot water on your hand hot water definitely hurts to know that Rico was in the cell cooking for us forced my mind and heart to never flirt

SOAPS

SOUPS

CRACKERS

WIFEY BOY

HOME THUG

TUNA

94

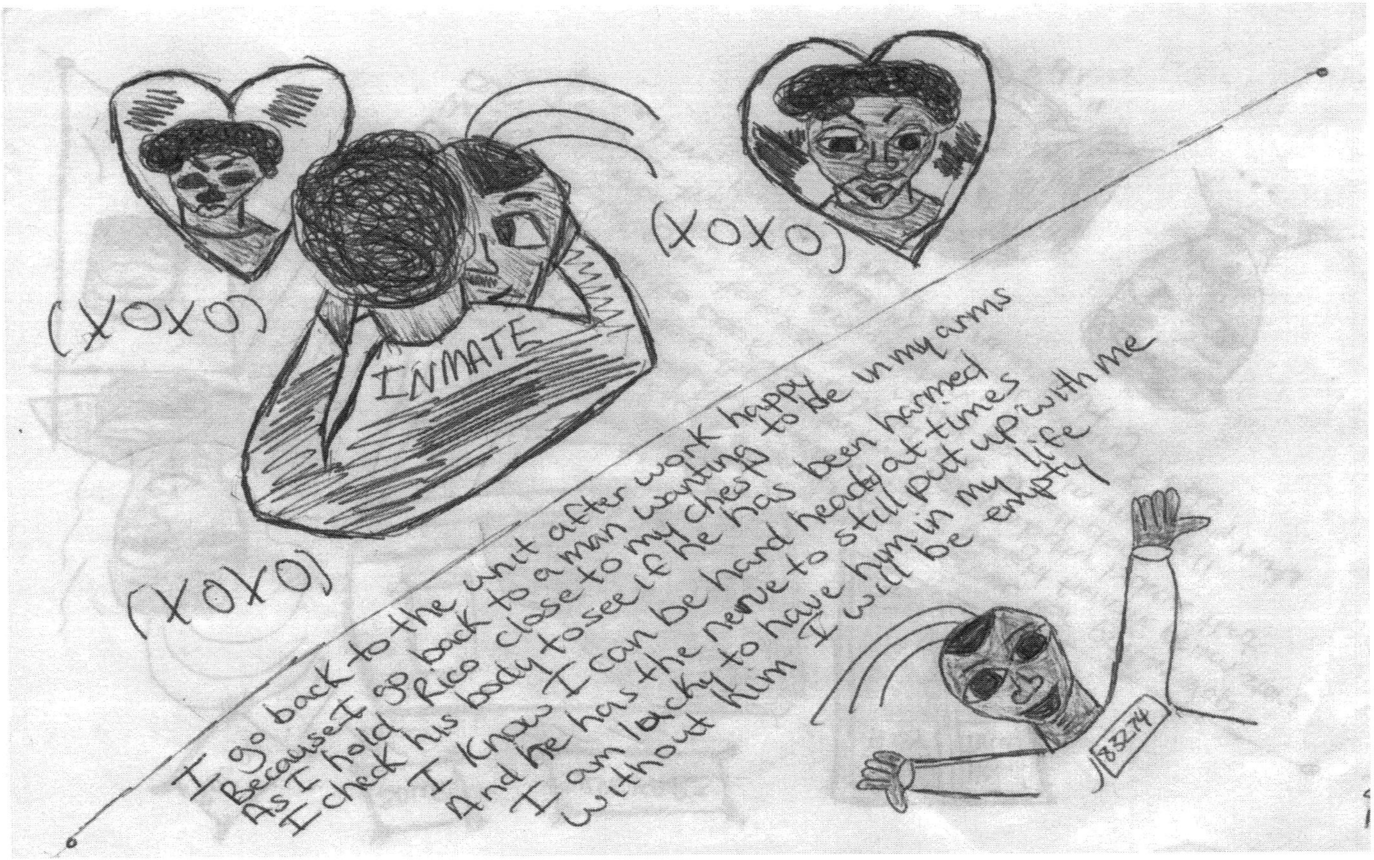
(XOXO)
INMATE
(XOXO)
(XOXO)
I go back to the unit after work happy
Because I go back to a man wanting to be in my arms
As I hold Rico close to my chest
I check his body to see if he has been harmed
I know I can be hard headed at times
And he has the nerve to still put up with me
I am lucky to have him in my life
without him I will be empty
832.74

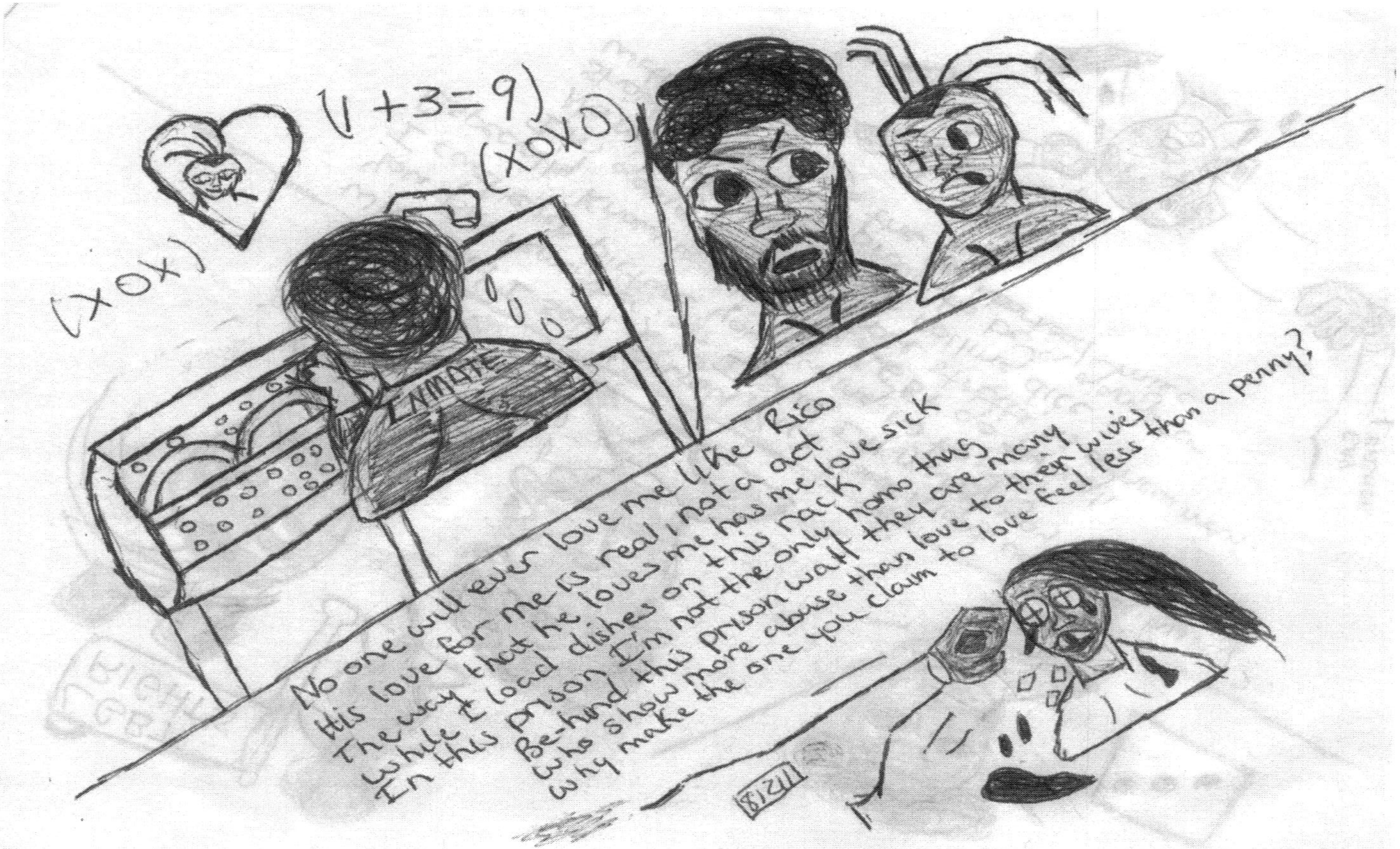
(XOX)
(1+3=9)
(XOXO)
INMATE
No one will ever love me like Rico
His love for me is real, not a act
The way that he loves me has me love sick
While I load dishes on this rack
In this prison I'm not the only homo thug
Be-hind this prison wall they are many
Who show more abuse than love to their wives
Why make the one you claim to love feel less than a penny?

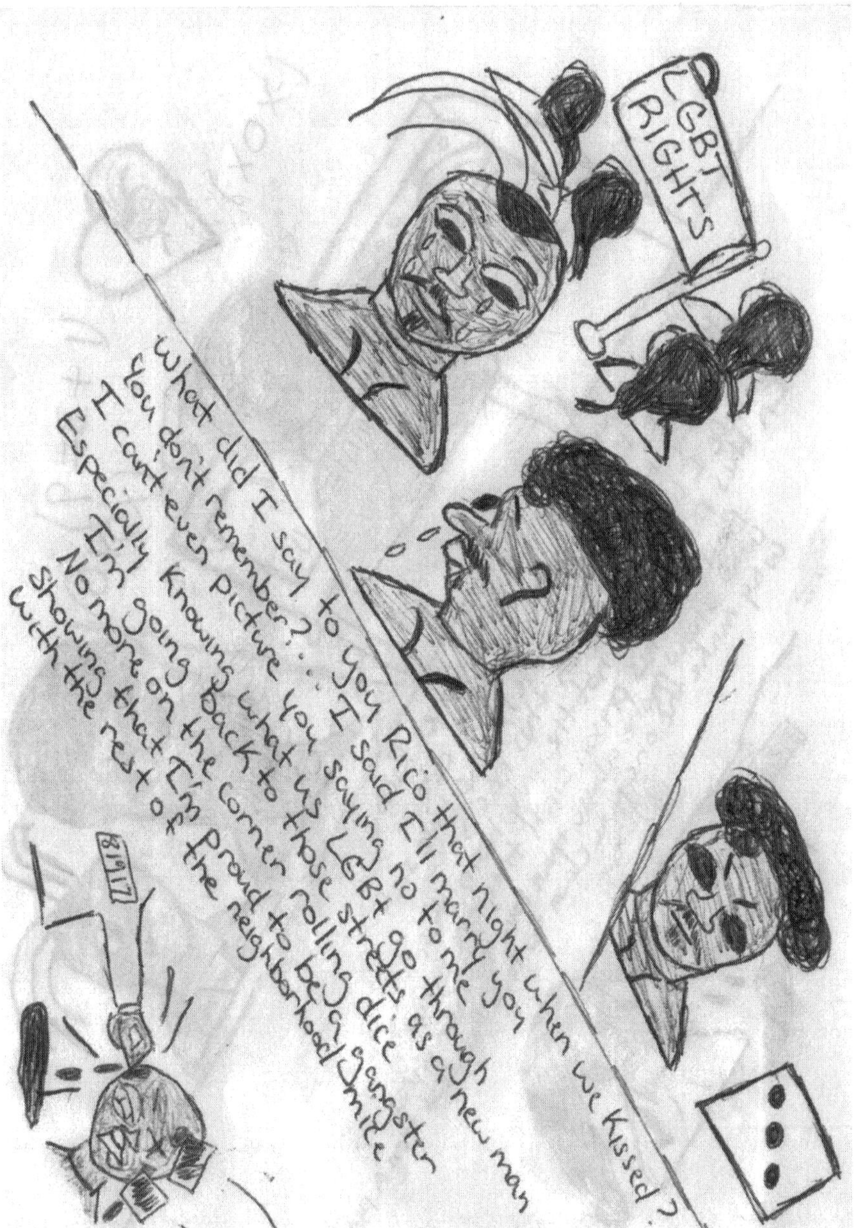
LGBT RIGHTS
What did I say to you Rico that night when we Kissed?
You don't remember?... I said I'll marry you
I can't even picture you saying no to me
Especially Knowing what us LGBt go through
I'm going back to those streets as a new man
No more on the corner rolling dice
Showing that I'm proud to be a gangster
with the rest of the neighborhood Smile
81917
GAY BASHER

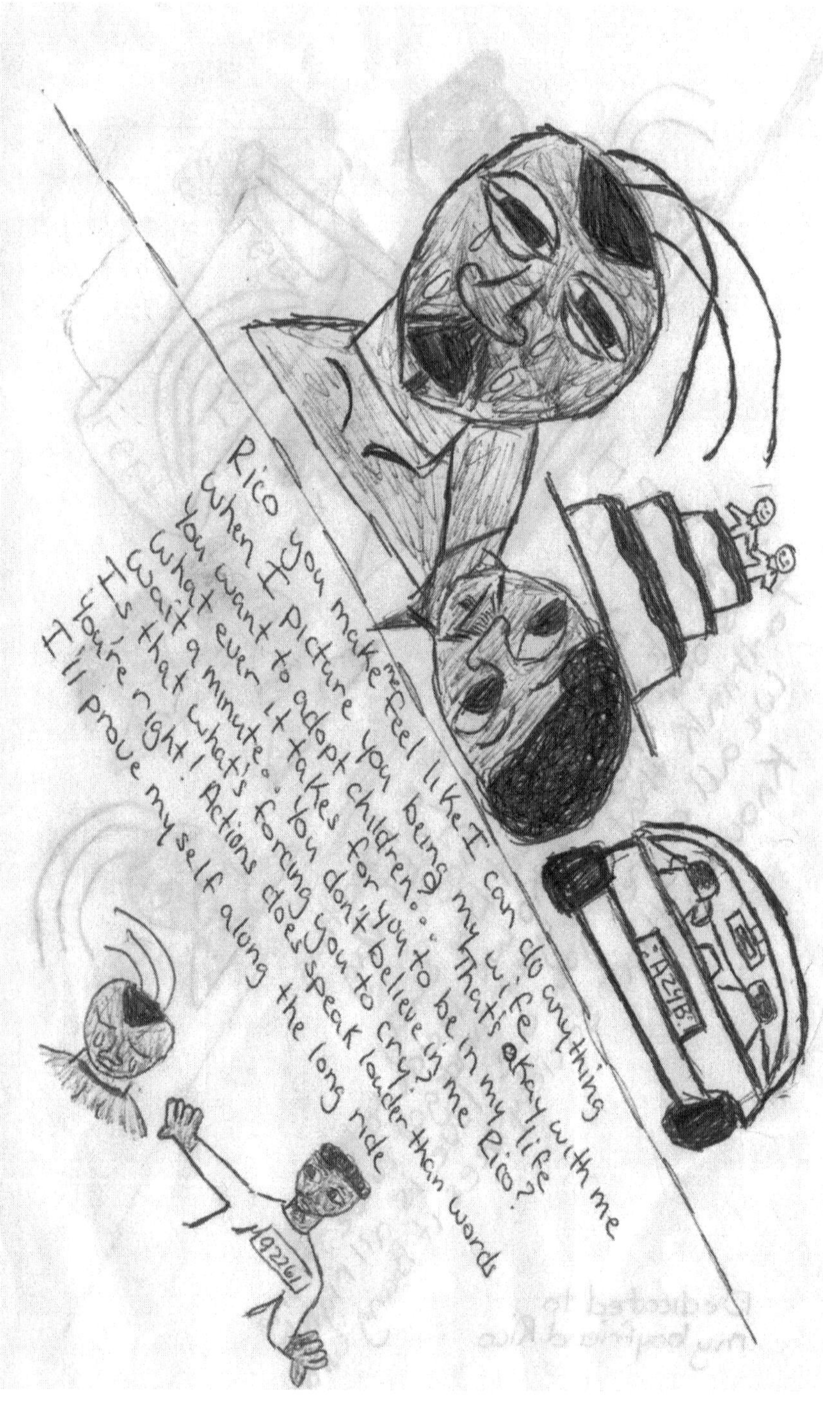
Rico you make me feel like I can do anything
When I picture you being my wife
You want to adopt children... That's okay with me
What ever it takes for you to be in my life
Wait a minute.. You don't believe in me Rico?
Is that what's forcing you to cry?
You're right! Actions does speak louder than words
I'll prove myself along the long ride

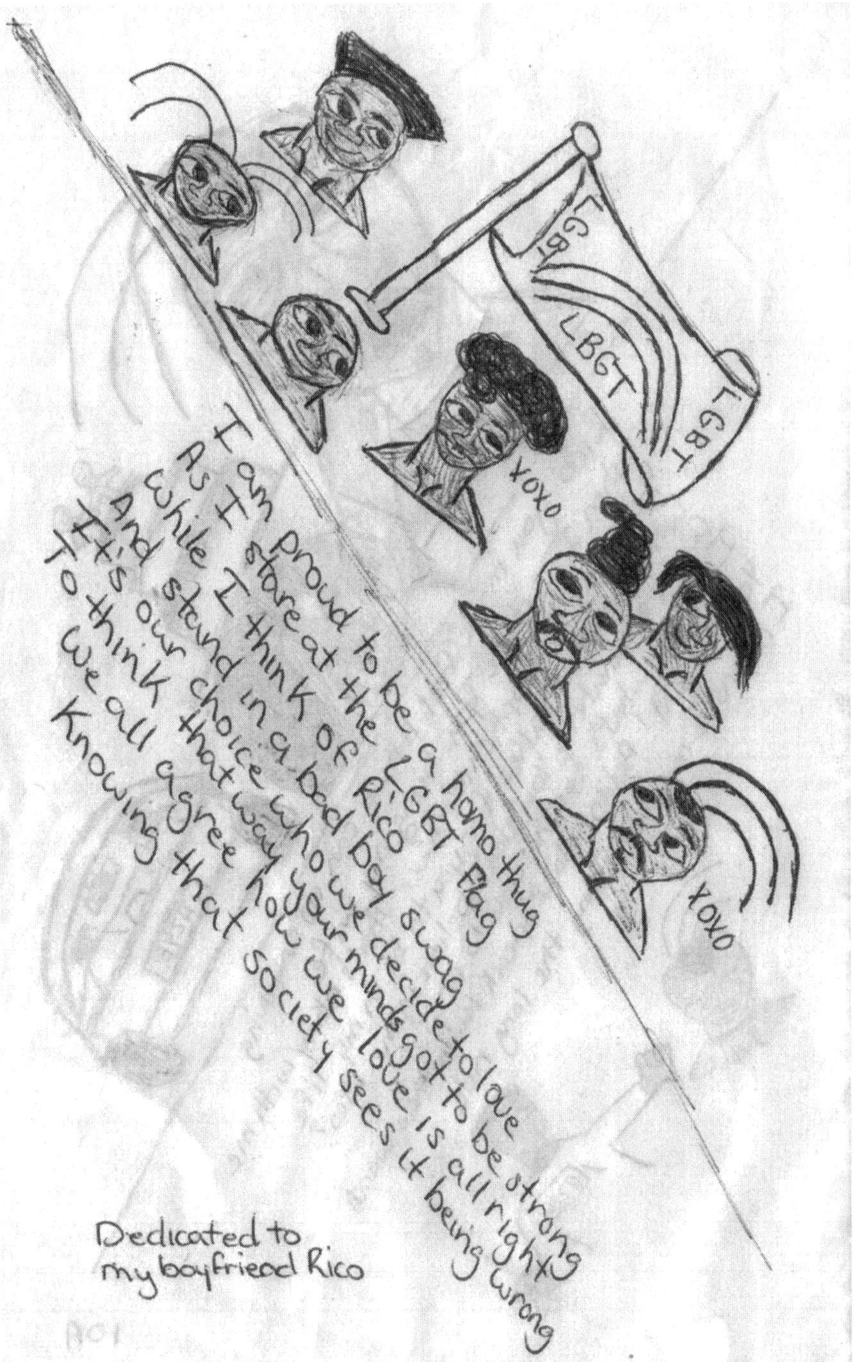
LGBT
LBGT
LGBT
XOXO
XOXO

I am proud to be a homo thug
As I stare at the LGBT flag
While I think of Rico
And stand in a bad boy swag
It's our choice who we decide to love
To think that way your minds got to be strong
We all agree how we love is all right
Knowing that society sees it being wrong

Dedicated to
my boyfriend Rico

Dumb Ass Nixon

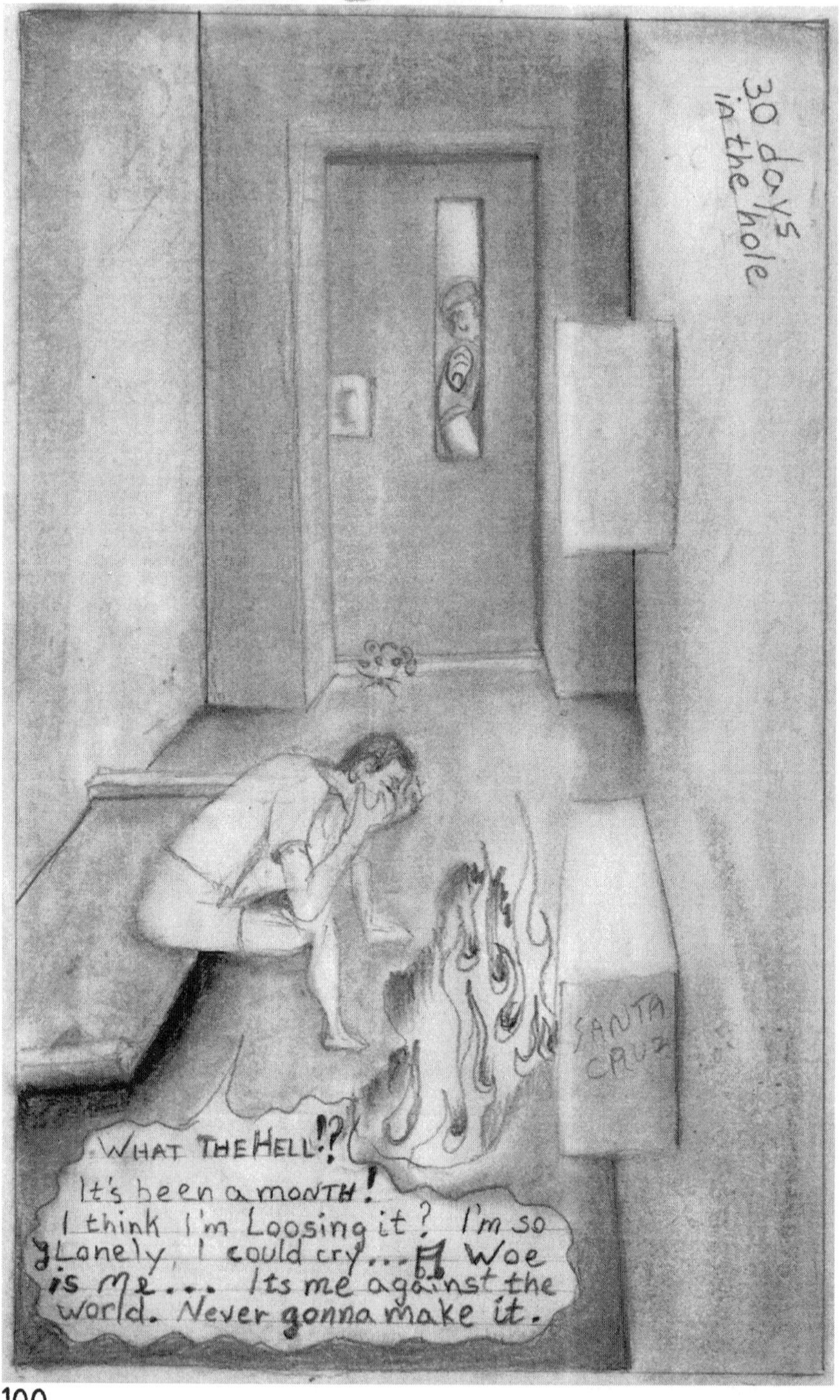
30 days in the hole
SANTA CRUZ
WHAT THE HELL!?
It's been a MONTH!
I think I'm Loosing it? I'm so Lonely, I could cry... ♫ Woe is Me... Its me against the world. Never gonna make it.

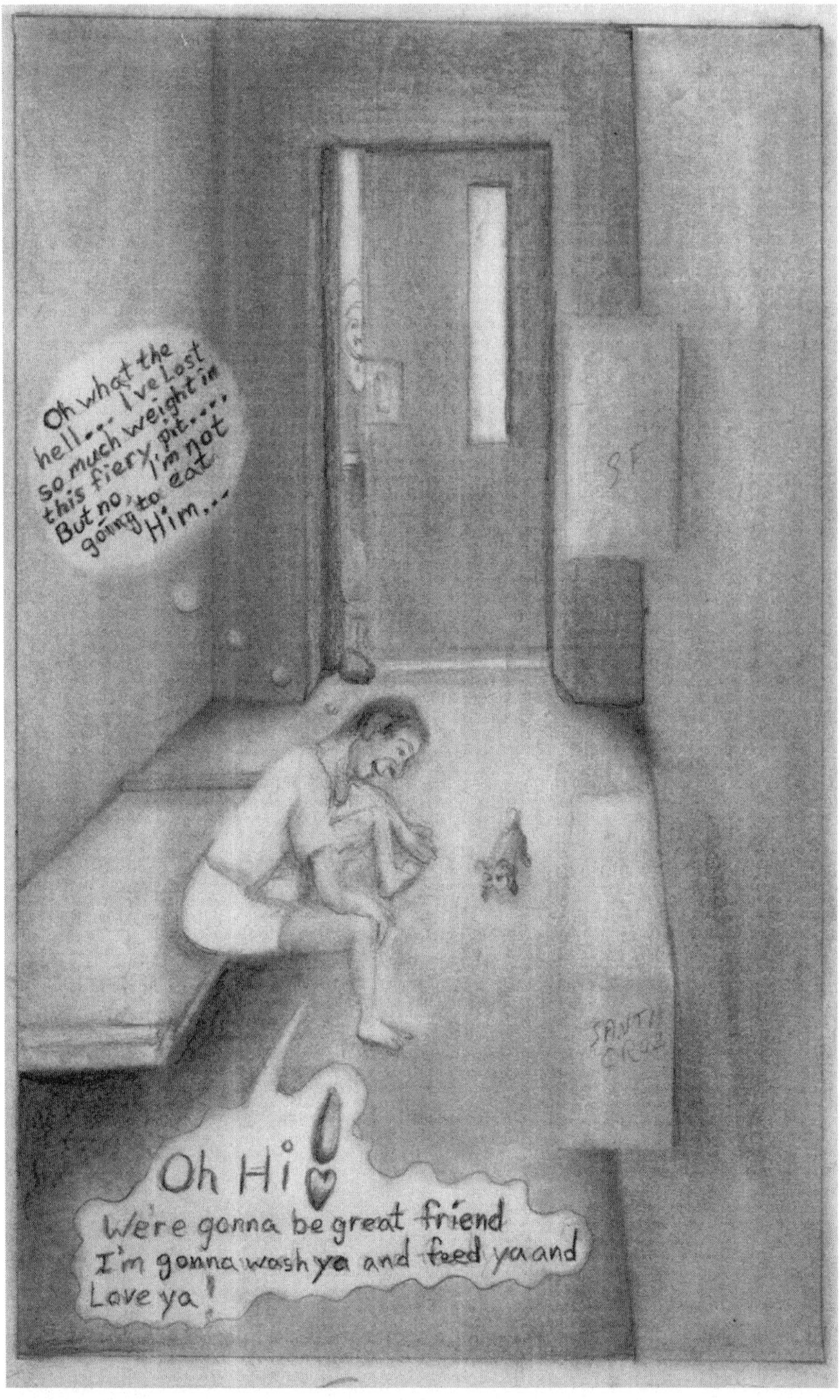
Oh what the hell... I've Lost so much weight in this fiery pit.... But no, I'm not going to eat Him...
Oh Hi
We're gonna be great friend I'm gonna wash ya and feed ya and Love ya!

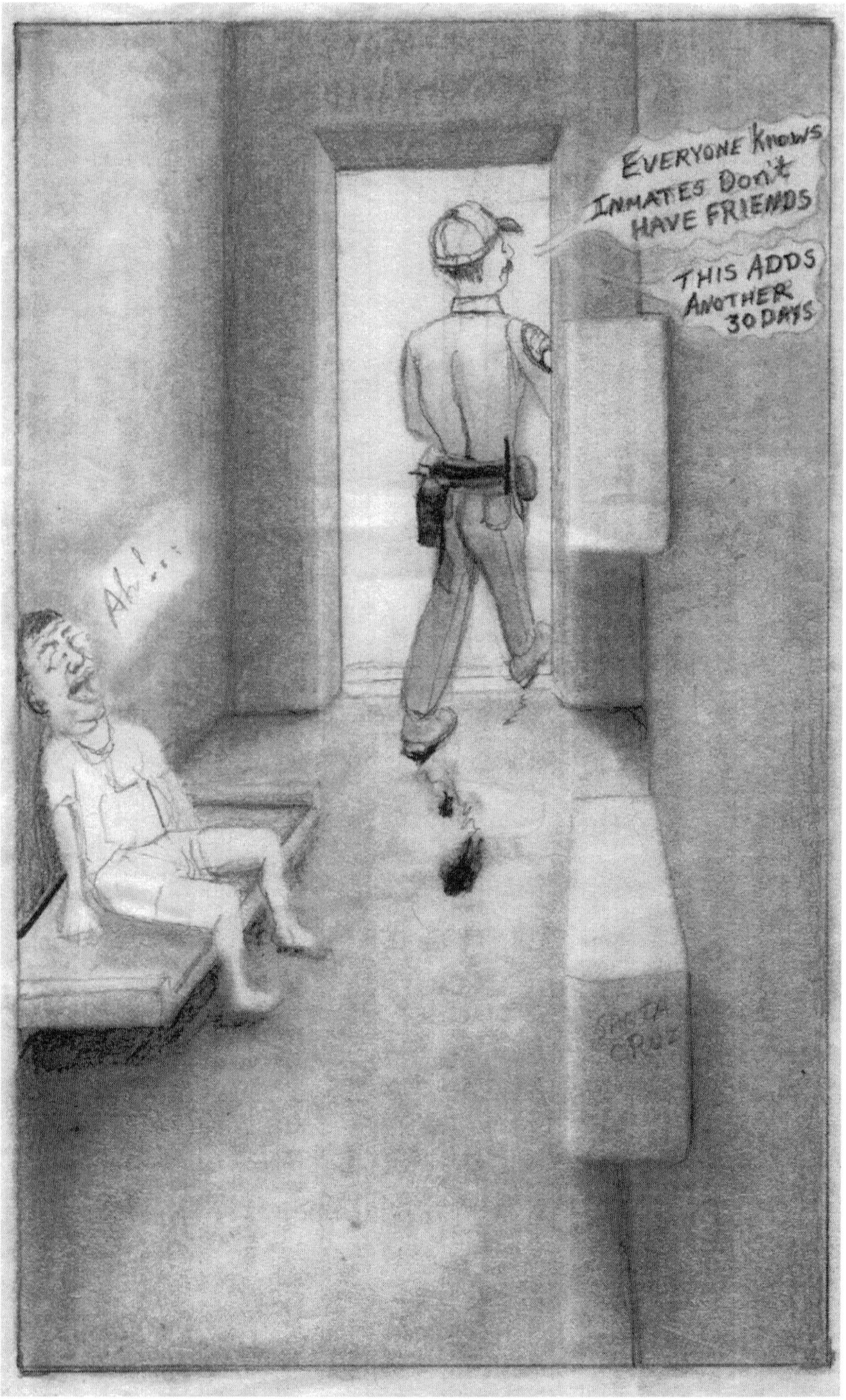
EVERYONE KNOWS INMATES DON'T HAVE FRIENDS
THIS ADDS ANOTHER 30 DAYS
Ah!...

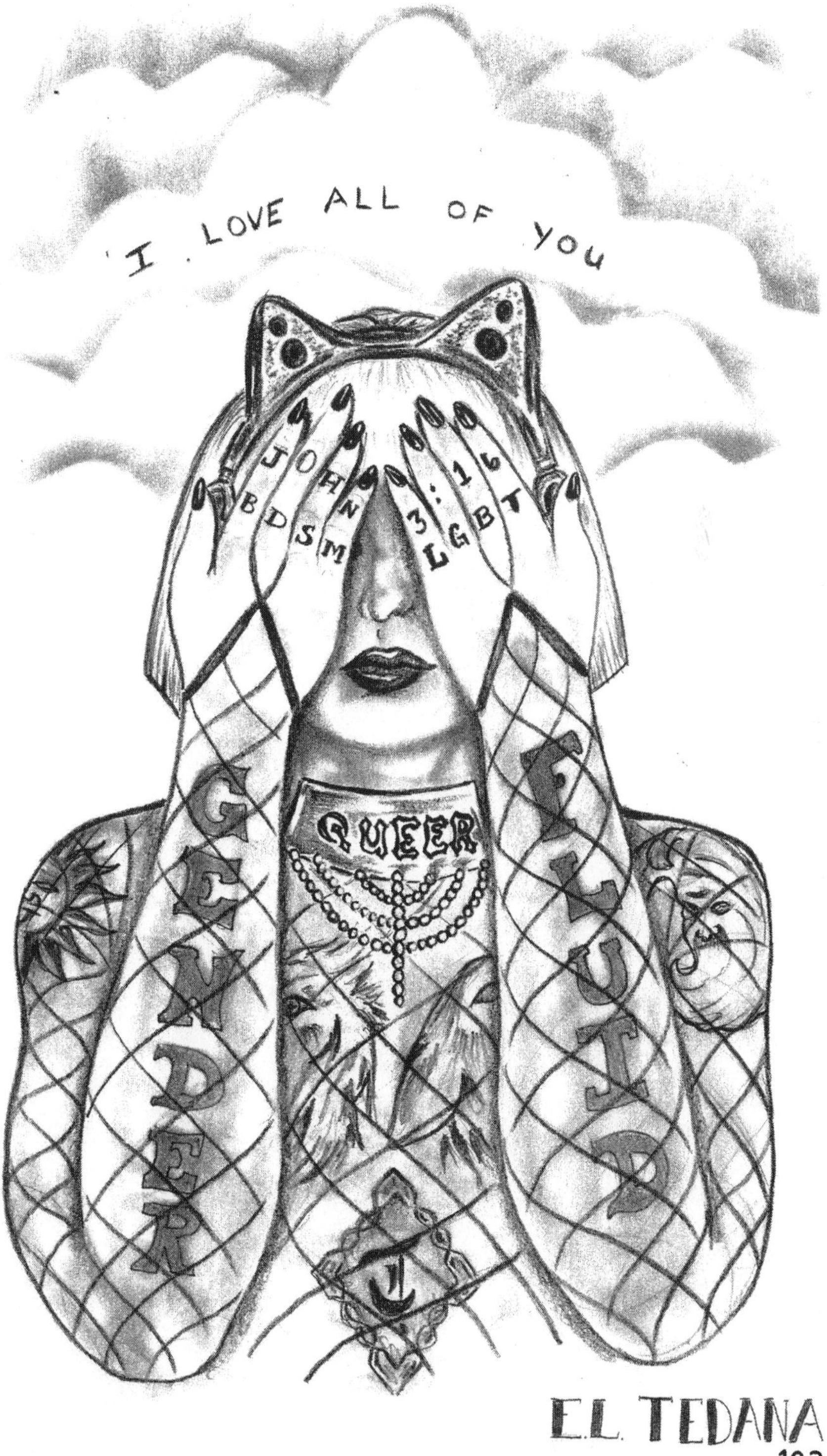
I LOVE ALL OF YOU
JOHN 3:16
BDSM
LGBT
QUEER

E.L. TEDANA

Kay Johnson

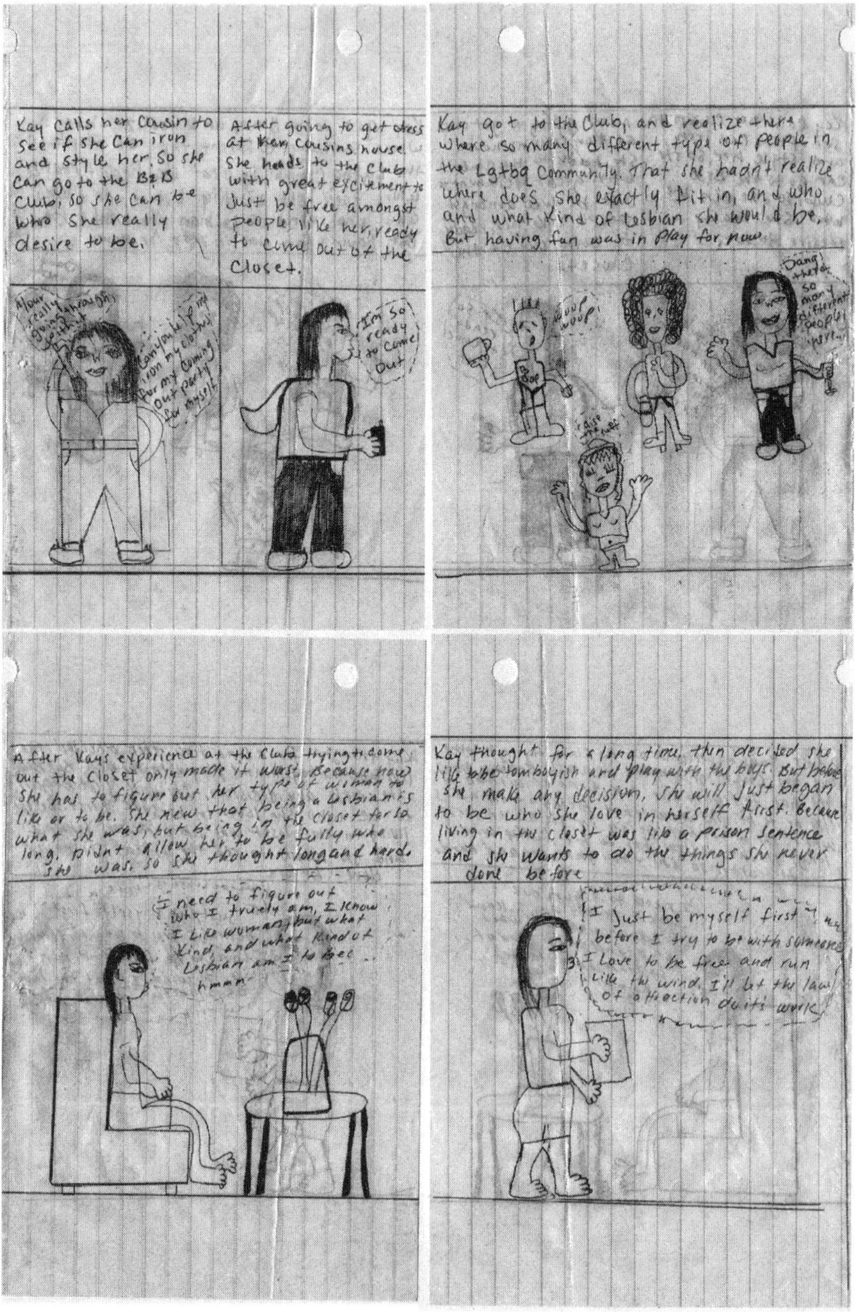
Kay Calls her Cousin to see if she Can iron and style her, so she Can go to the B&B Club, so she can be who she really desire to be.
Your really going through with it
Can you help me iron my clothes for my Coming out party for myself
After going to get dress at them Cousins house She heads to the Club with great excitement to Just be free amongst people like her, ready to Come out of the Closet.
I'm so ready to Come Out
Kay got to the Club, and realize there where so many different type of people in the Lgtbq Community. That she hadn't realize where does she exactly fit in, and who and what Kind of Lesbian she would be, But having fun was in Play for now.
Woof Woof
Dang! there so many different people here...
After Kays experience at the Club trying to come out the Closet only made it worst. Because now She has to figure out her type of woman to like or to be. She new that being a Lesbian is what she was, but being in the closet for so long, Didnt allow her to be fully who she was. So she thought long and hard.
I need to figure out who I truely am, I Know I like womans, but what Kind, and what Kind of Lesbian am I to bee.. hmmm
Kay thought for a long time, then decided she like to be tomboyish and play with the boys. But before she make any decision, she will Just began to be who she love in herself first. Because living in the closet was like a prison sentence and she wants to do the things she never done before
I Just be myself first before I try to be with someone I Love to be free and run like the wind. I'll let the law of attraction do it's work

this comic strip was me
trying to figure out how to come out
the closet, and be who I wanted to
be a lesbian, I boy kind who likes
girls. The transition was extremely
hard because. my family and
friends was againgst it. After I thought
about it after going to the bench and bar
in Oakland. I realize that people
were free in so many ways, I got
confuse cause I never been that
free in my sexuality. Today it is still
and unspoken curse to my family.
Being in prison with a lot of women.
you think would be easy it is still
a living in the closet experience.

Jay Shandy II
"Prison Frog"

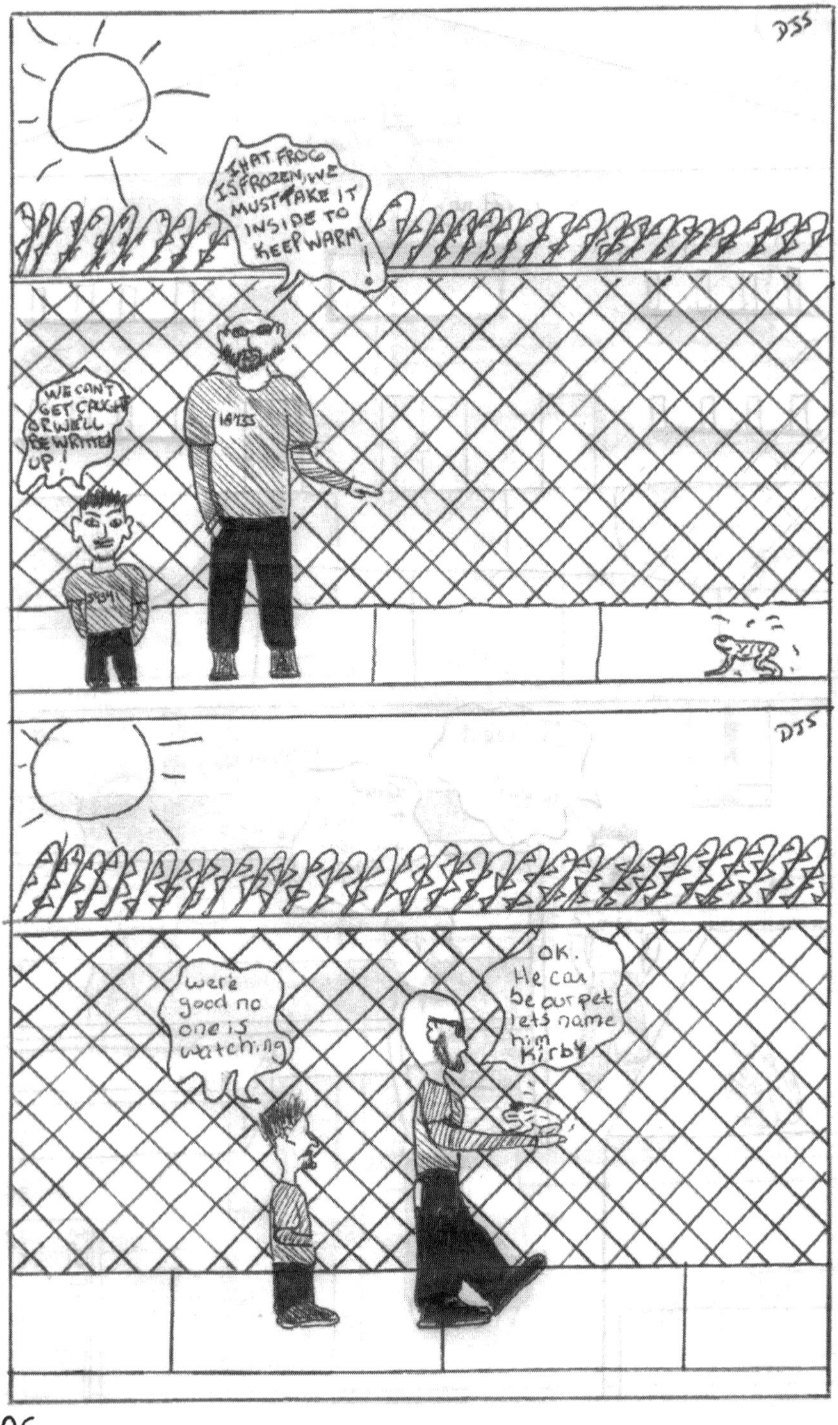
DJS
THAT FROG IS FROZEN, WE MUST TAKE IT INSIDE TO KEEP WARM !
WE CAN'T GET CAUGHT OR WE'LL BE WRITTEN UP !
DJS
We're good no one is watching
OK. He can be our pet lets name him Kirby

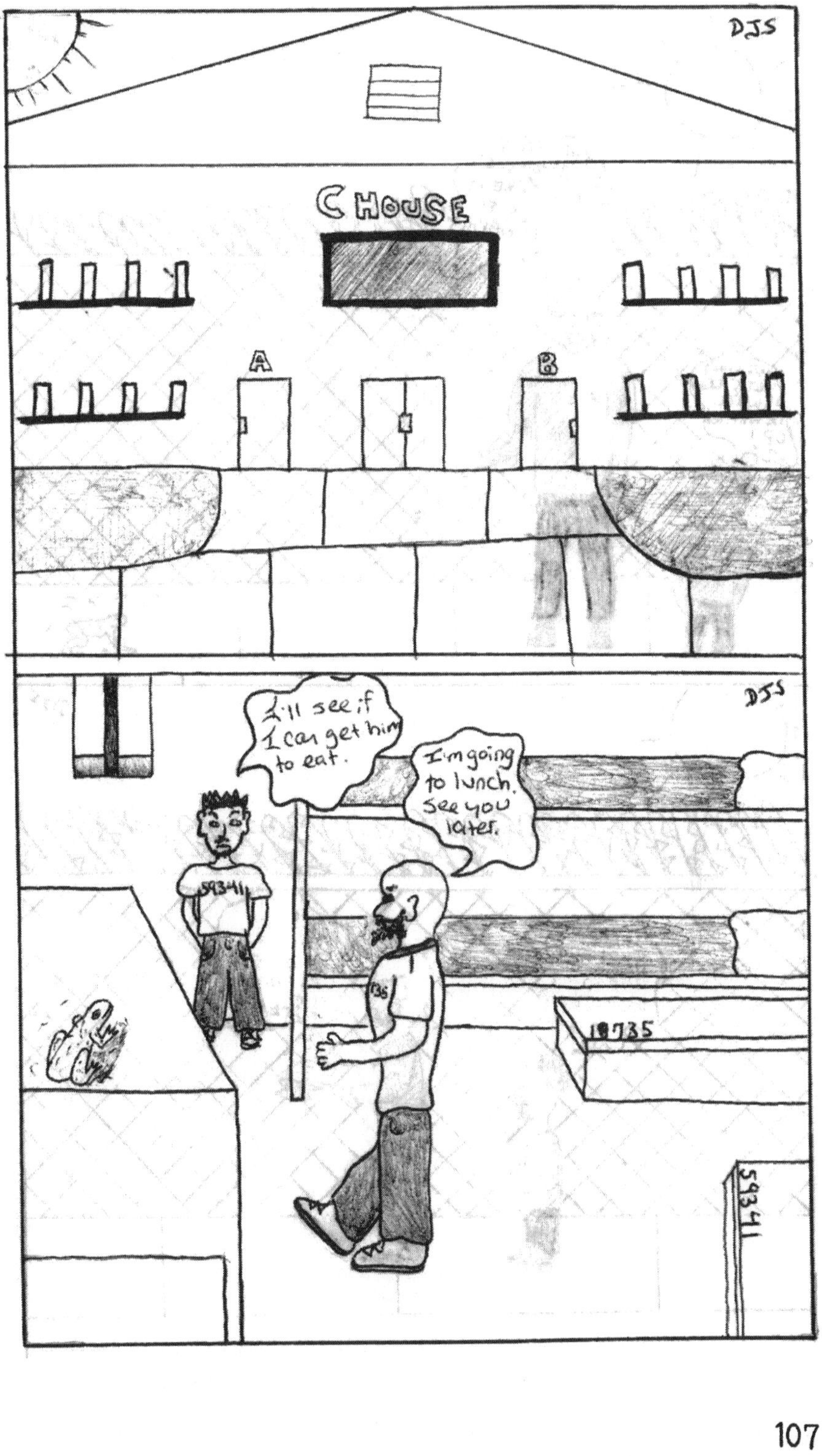
DJS
C HOUSE
A
B
DJS
I'll see if I can get him to eat.
I'm going to lunch. See you later.
59341
59341

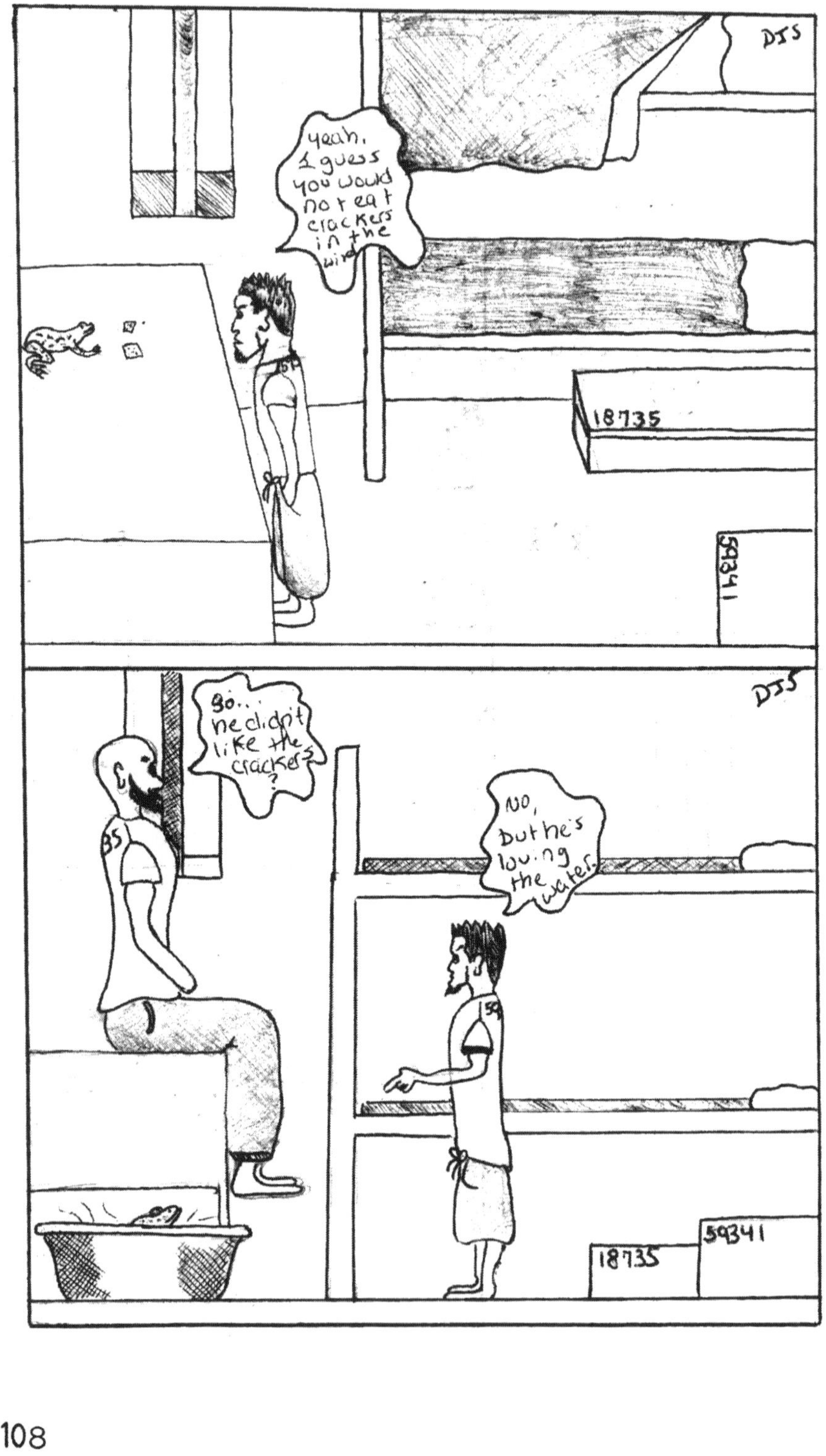
DJS
yeah, I guess you would not eat crackers in the wild
18735
59341
DJS
So... he didn't like the crackers?
No, but he's loving the water.
18735
59341

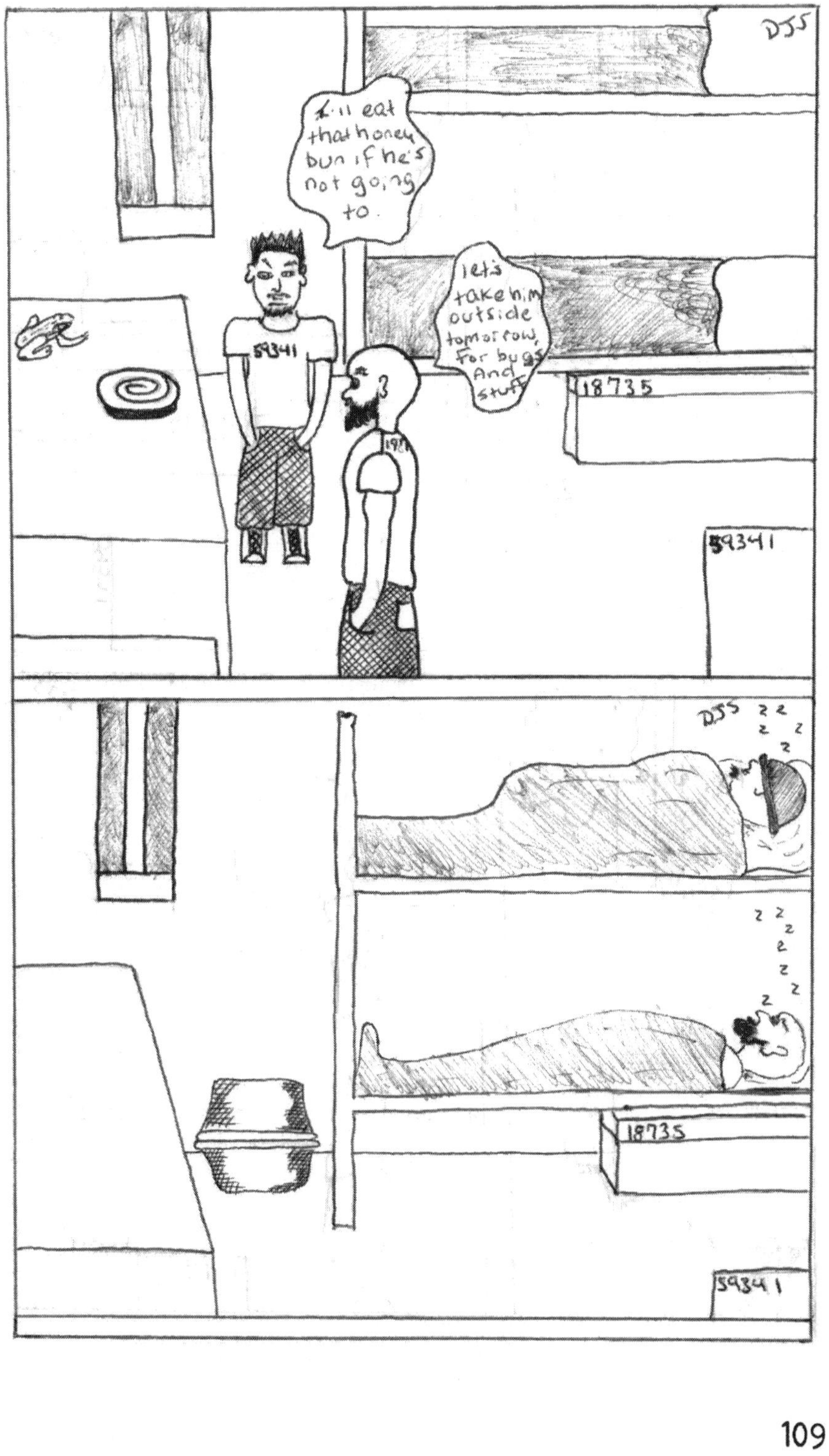
I'll eat that honey bun if he's not going to.
let's take him outside tomorrow, For bugs And stuff

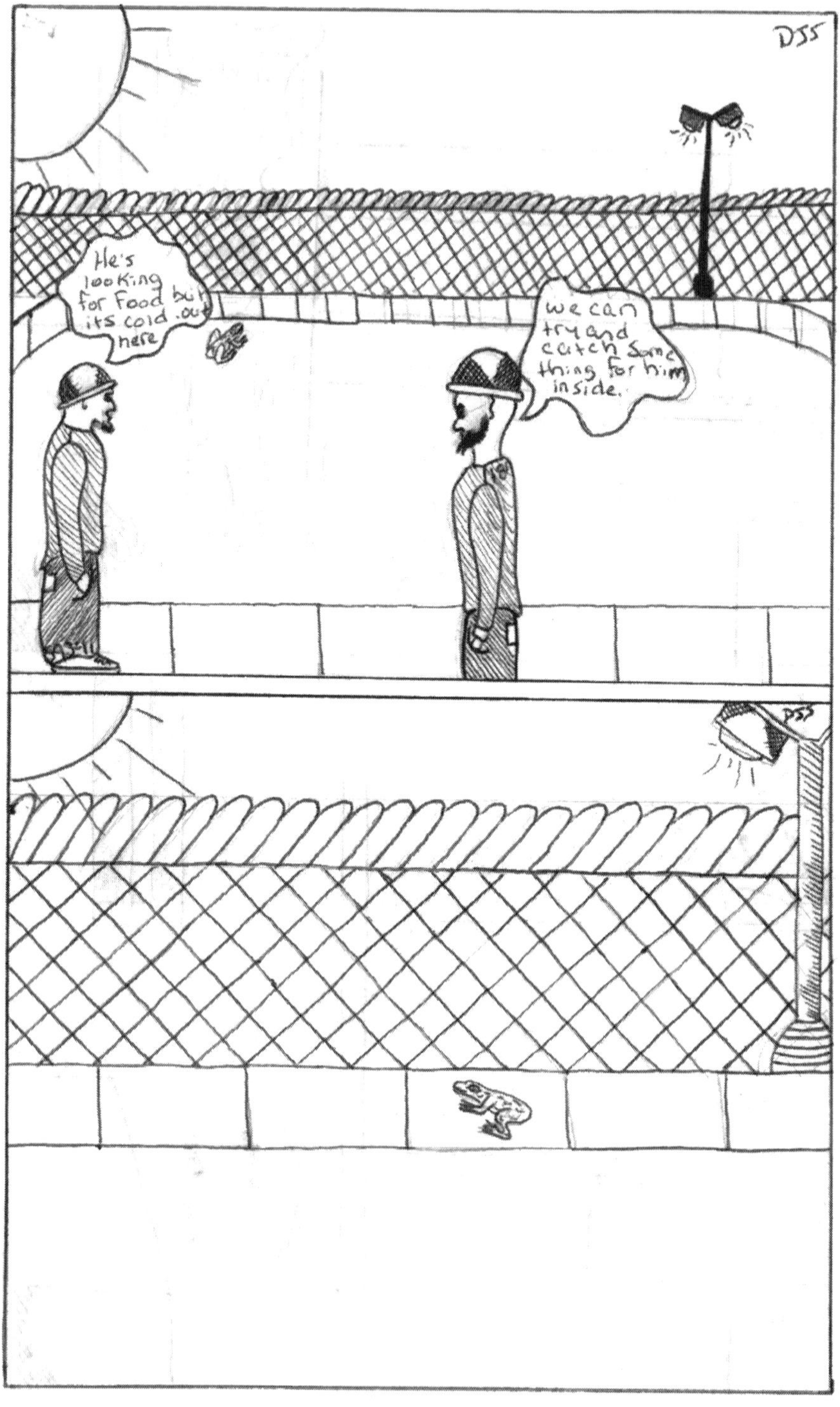
DJ5
He's looking for Food but its cold out here
we can try and catch Some thing for him inside.
DJ5

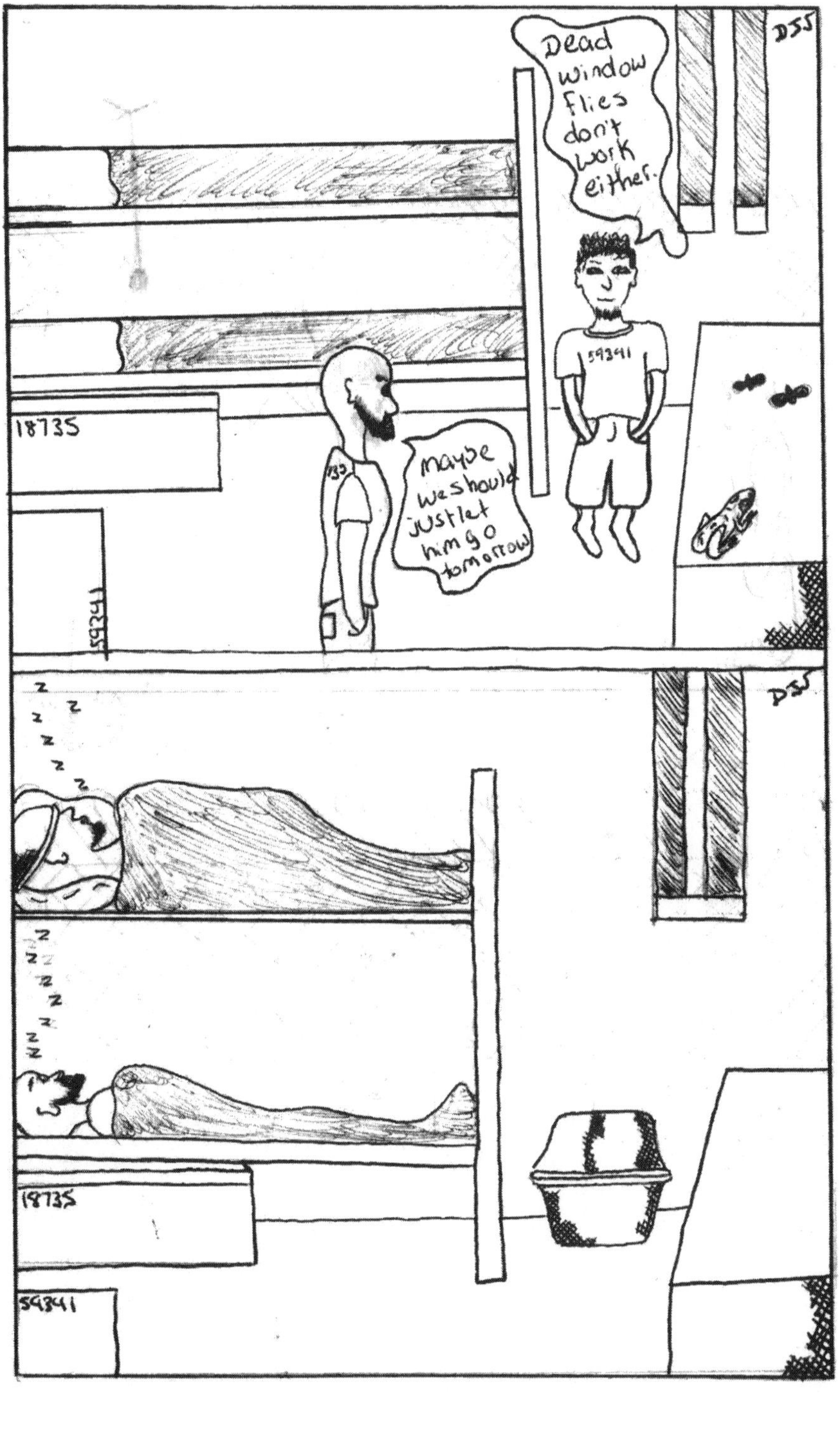
DJS
Dead window flies don't work either.
18735
59341
maybe we should just let him go tomorrow
DJS
18735
59341

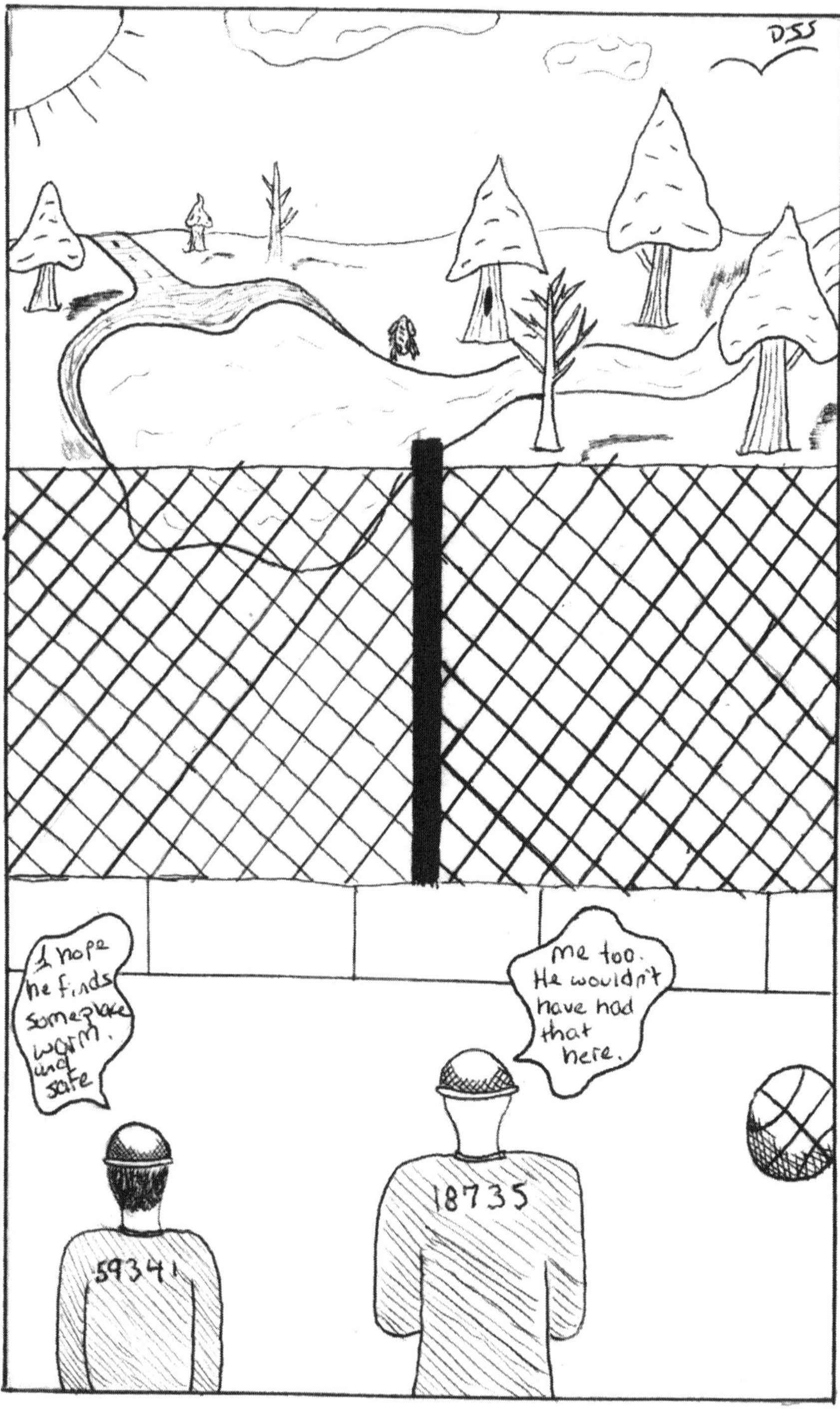
DJS
I hope he finds someplace warm and safe
me too. He wouldn't have had that here.
18735
59341

Prison Frog

Bubbles and words by: Shane M. Stevens
Illustration and story By: Daniel J. Schaffer.

We experienced exactly this two
Summers ago, and this last winter.
This Comic is based on that winter.

Shane M. Stevens #1113824
and
Daniel J. Schaffer #1161082

are

Jay Shandy II

CRoss Roads Correctional Center
Cameron. MO

Oct. 2017

Tony Gentry

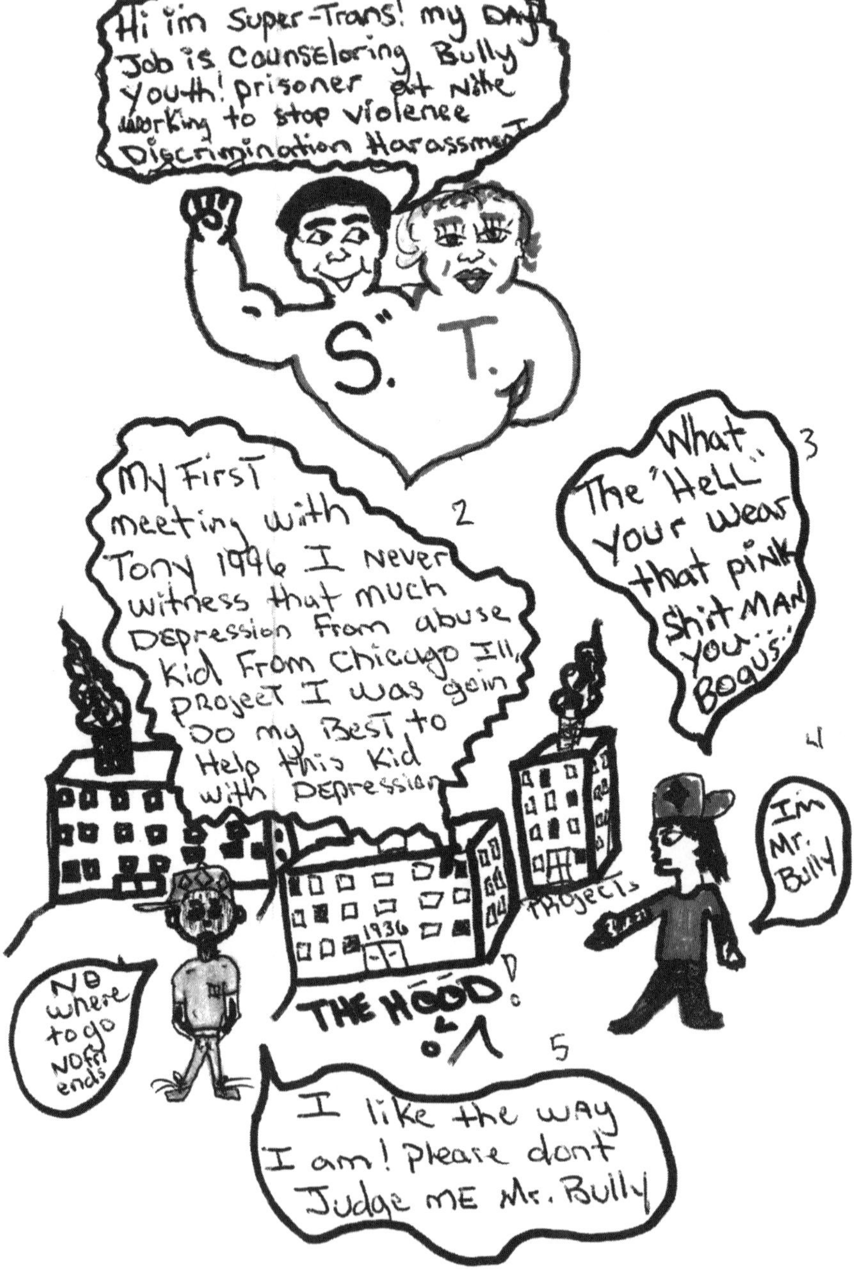

Hi im Super-Trans! my DAY Job is Counseloring Bully youth! prisoner at Nite working to stop violence Discrimination Harassment
S."T.
My First meeting with Tony 1996 I Never witness that much Depression From abuse Kid From Chicago Ill, project I was goin Do my Best to Help this Kid with Depression
2
What The "HELL" Your wear that pink Shit MAN You.. Bogus..
3
4
Im Mr. Bully
PROJECTS
1936
THE HOOD!
No where to go NOfri ends
1
5
I like the WAY I am! please dont Judge ME Mr. Bully

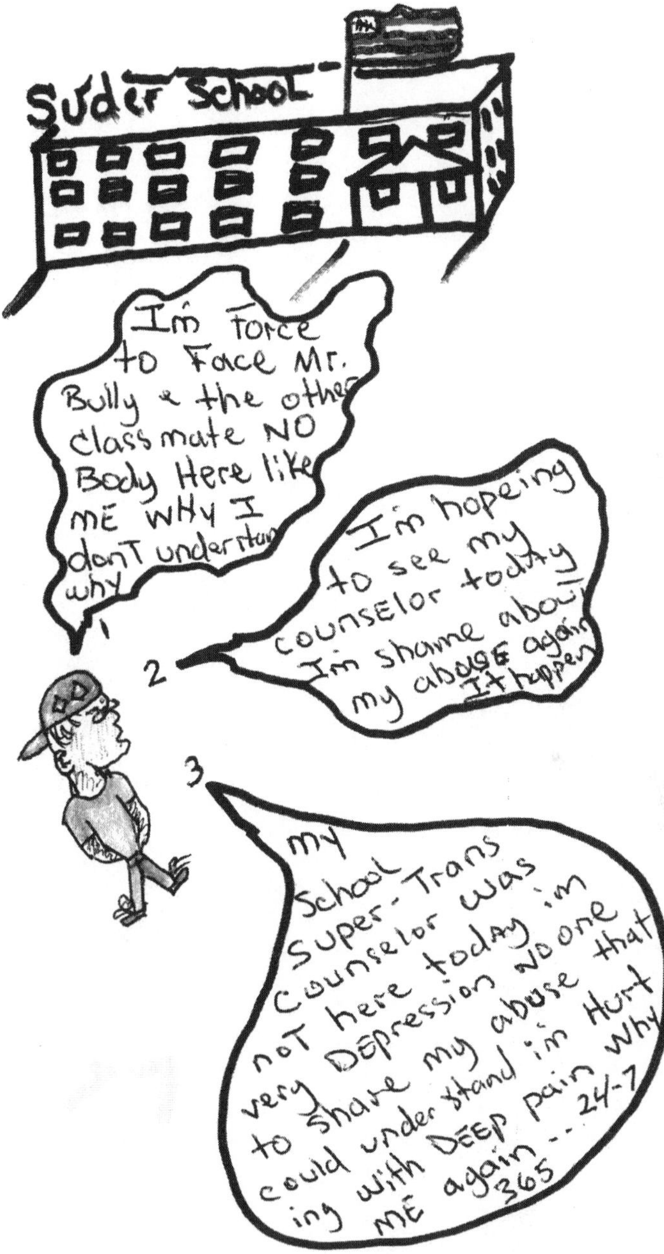
Suder School
I'm Force to Face Mr. Bully & the other classmate NO Body Here like ME WHY I donT understan why
1
2
I'm hopeing to see my counselor today I'm shame about my abuse again It happen
3
my School Super-Trans counselor was noT here today im very Depression no one to share my abuse that could understand im Hurting with DEEP pain Why ME again .. 24-7 365

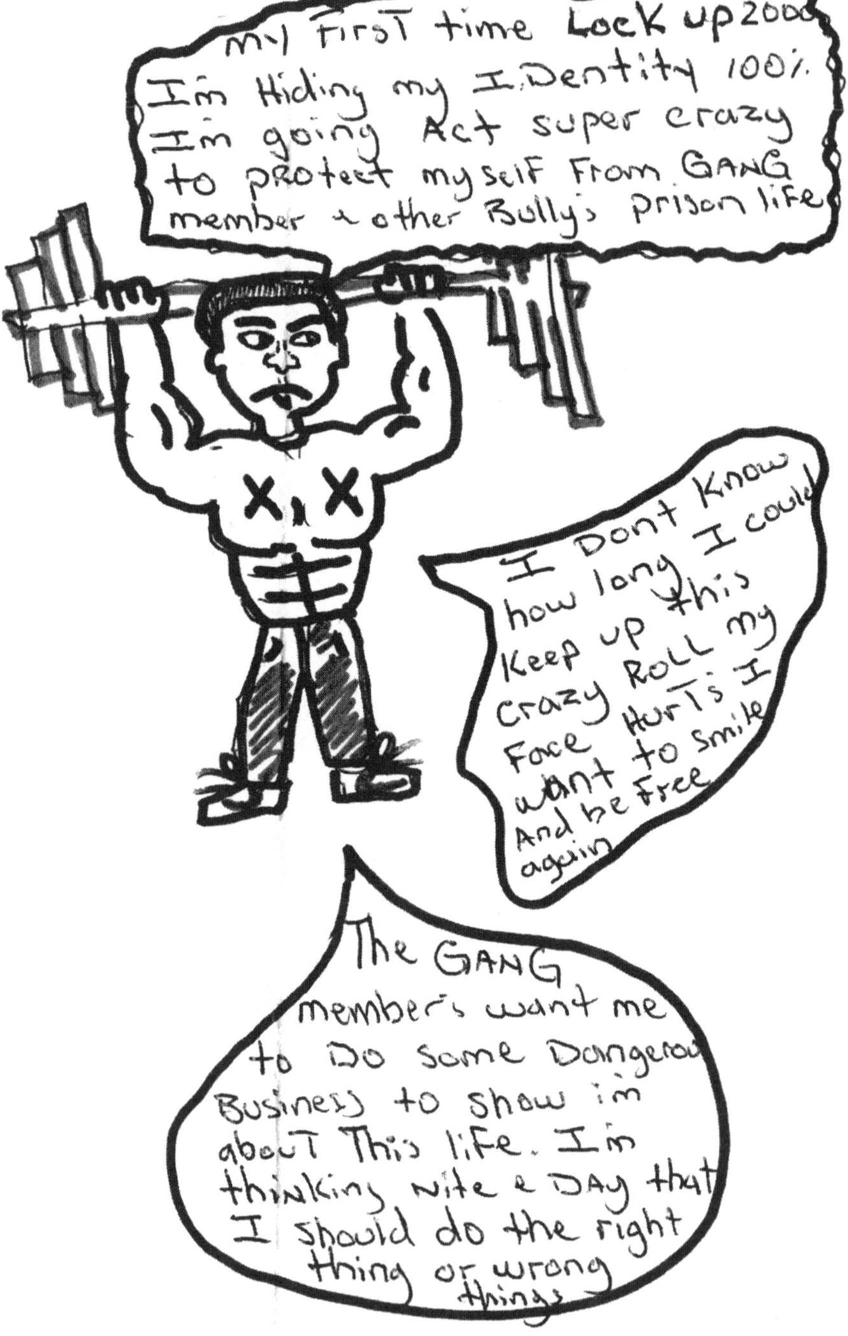
My first time Lock up 2000 I'm Hiding my I.Dentity 100% I'm going Act super crazy to protect myself From GANG member & other Bully's prison life
I Dont Know how long I could keep up this crazy Roll my Face Hurts I want to smile And be Free again
The GANG member's want me to Do some Dangerous Business to show im about This life. I'm thinking nite & DAY that I should do the right thing or wrong things

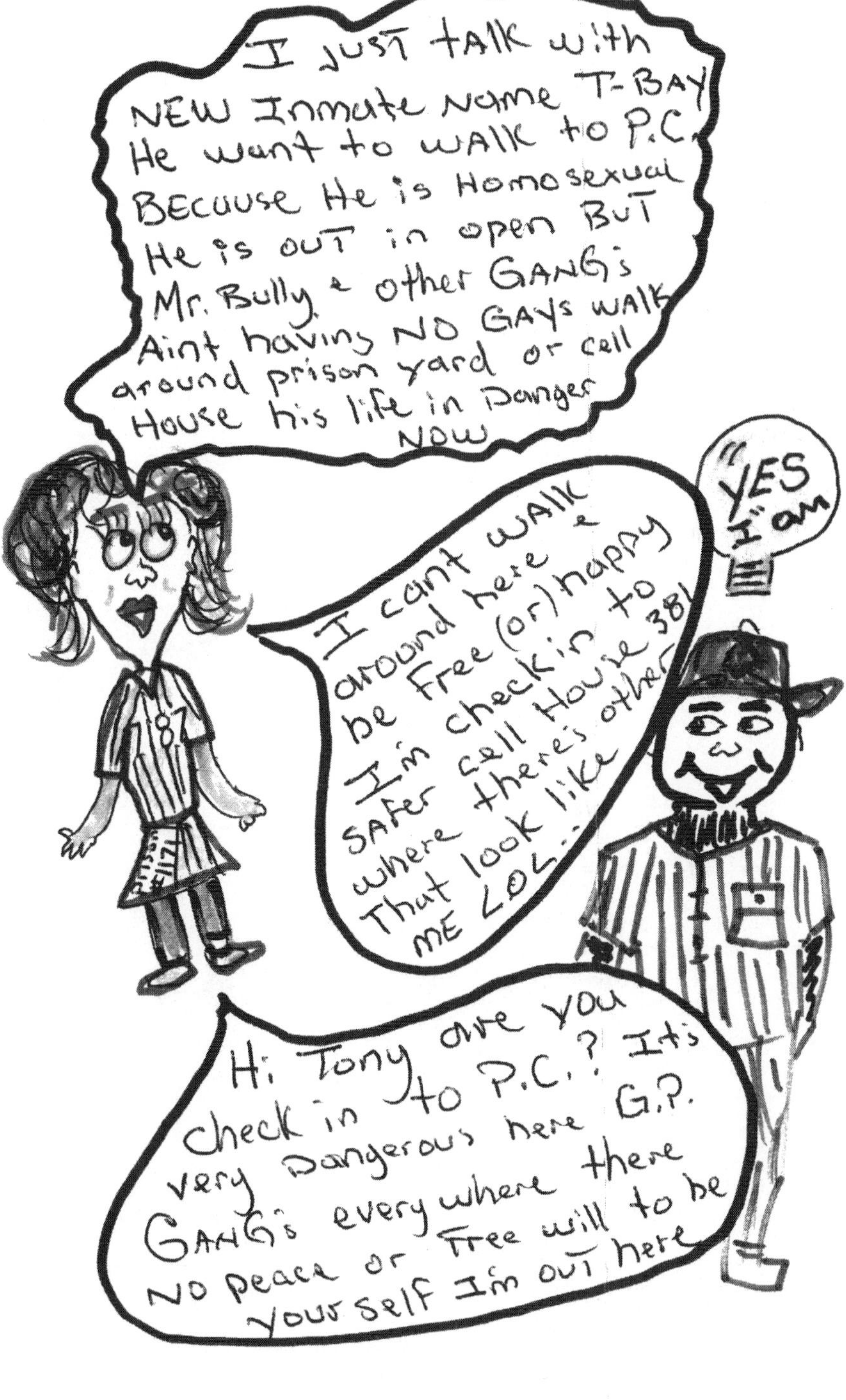
I JUST TALK with NEW Inmate Name T-BAY He want to WALK to P.C. BEcause He is Homosexual He is OUT in open BUT Mr. Bully & other GANG's Aint having NO GAYS WALK around prison yard or cell House his life in Danger NOW
YES I am
I cant WALK around here & be Free (or) happy I'm check in to safer cell House 381 where there's other That look like ME LOL...
187
Hi Tony are YOU check in to P.C.? It's very Dangerous here G.P. GANG's every where there No peace or Free will to be your self I'm out here

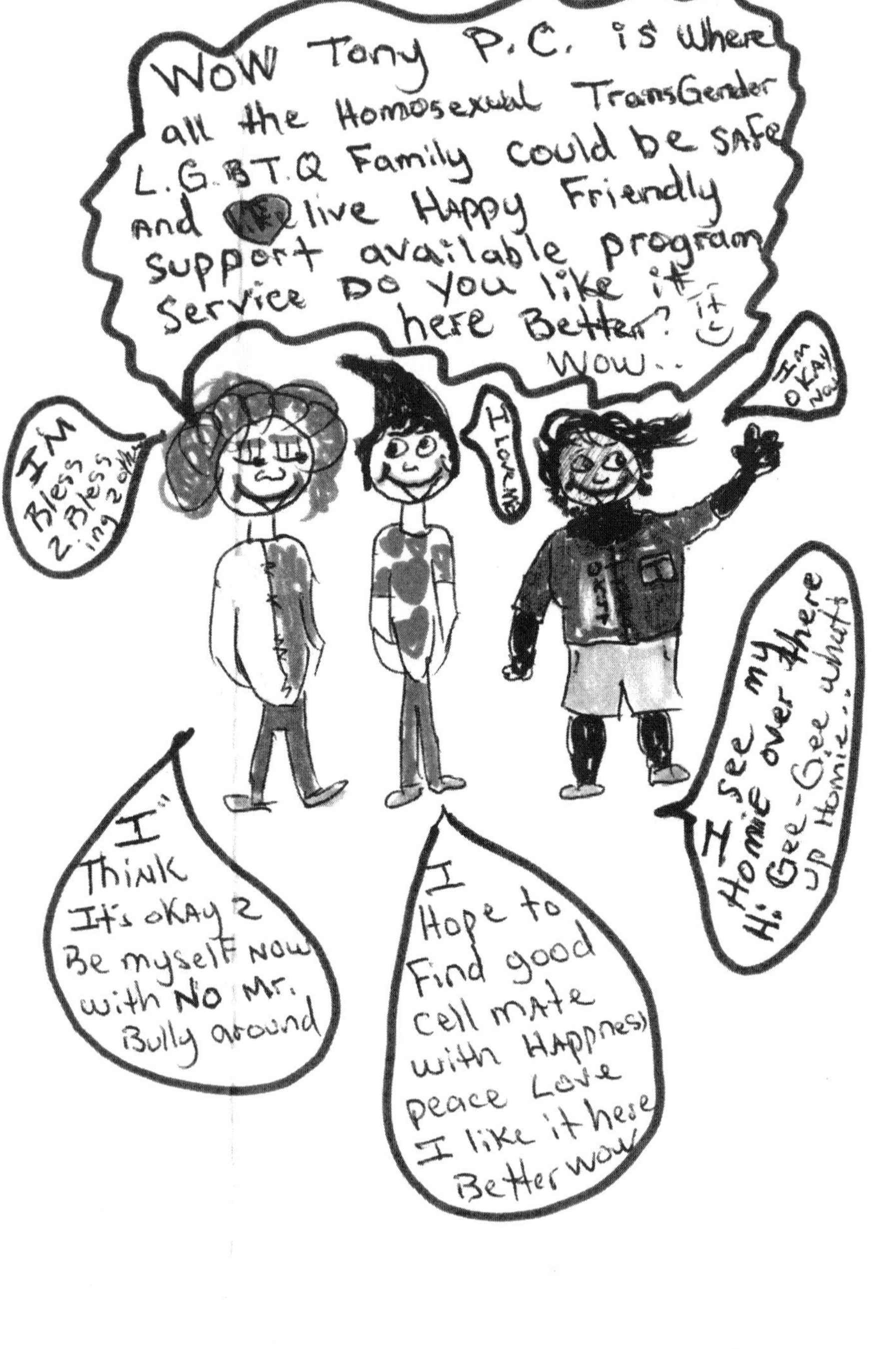
WOW Tony P.C. is Where all the Homosexual TransGender L.G.B.T.Q Family could be safe and live Happy Friendly support available program Service Do you like it here Better? It WOW..
I'M Bless 2 Blessing 2 others
Hi Love Me
I'm OKAY Now
I see my Homie over there Hi Gee-Gee what's up Homie..
I" Think It's OKAY 2 Be myself Now with No Mr. Bully around
I Hope to Find good cell mate with Happness peace Love I like it here Better wow

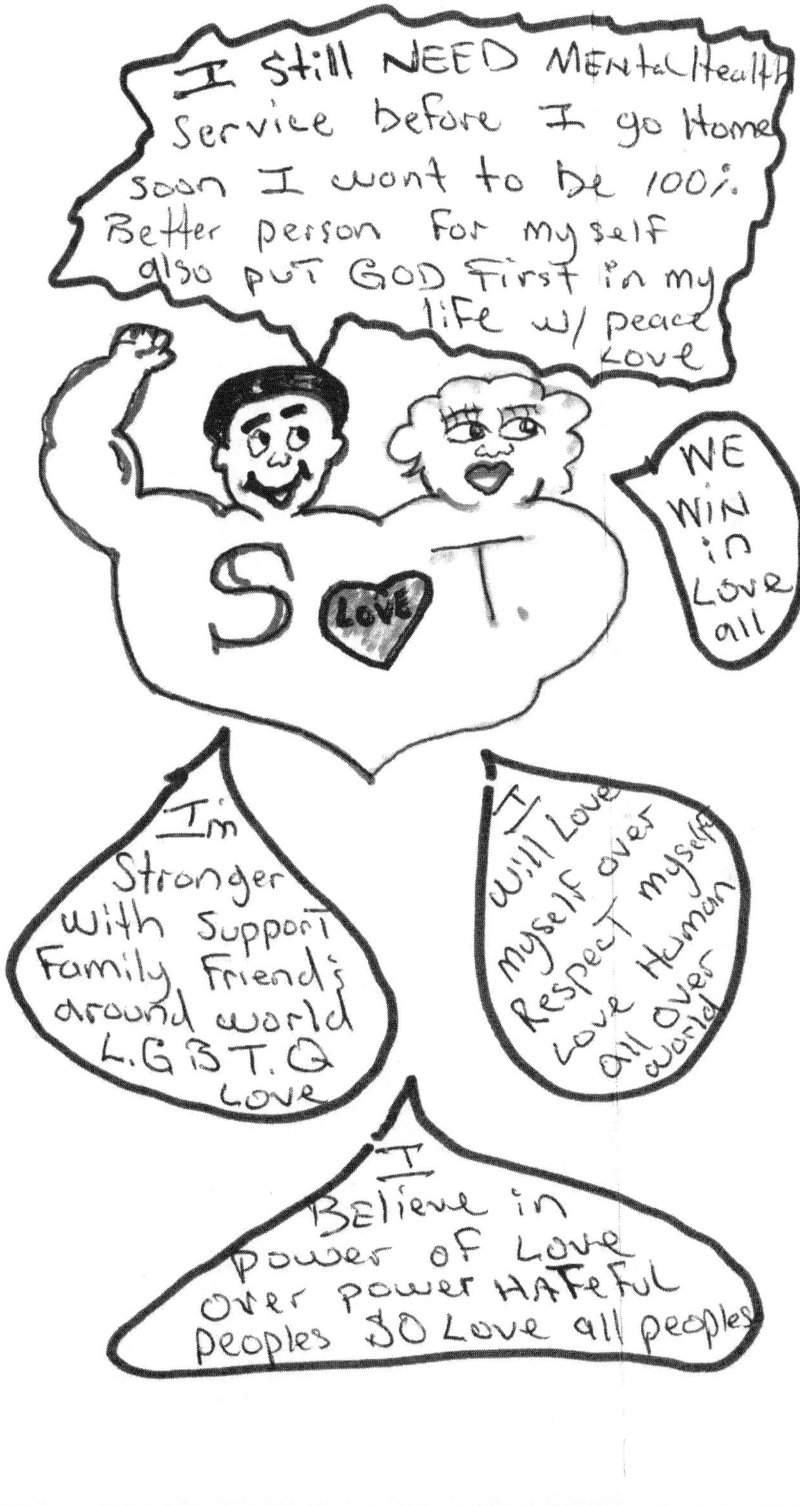
I still NEED MENtal Health Service before I go Home soon I wont to be 100% Better person for myself also puT GOD First in my life w/ peace Love
WE WIN in Love all
S LOVE T.
I'm Stronger with SupporT Family Friend's around world L.G.B.T.Q LOVE
I Will Love myself over Respect myself Love Human all over world
I Believe in power of Love over power HAFeFul peoples $O Love all peoples

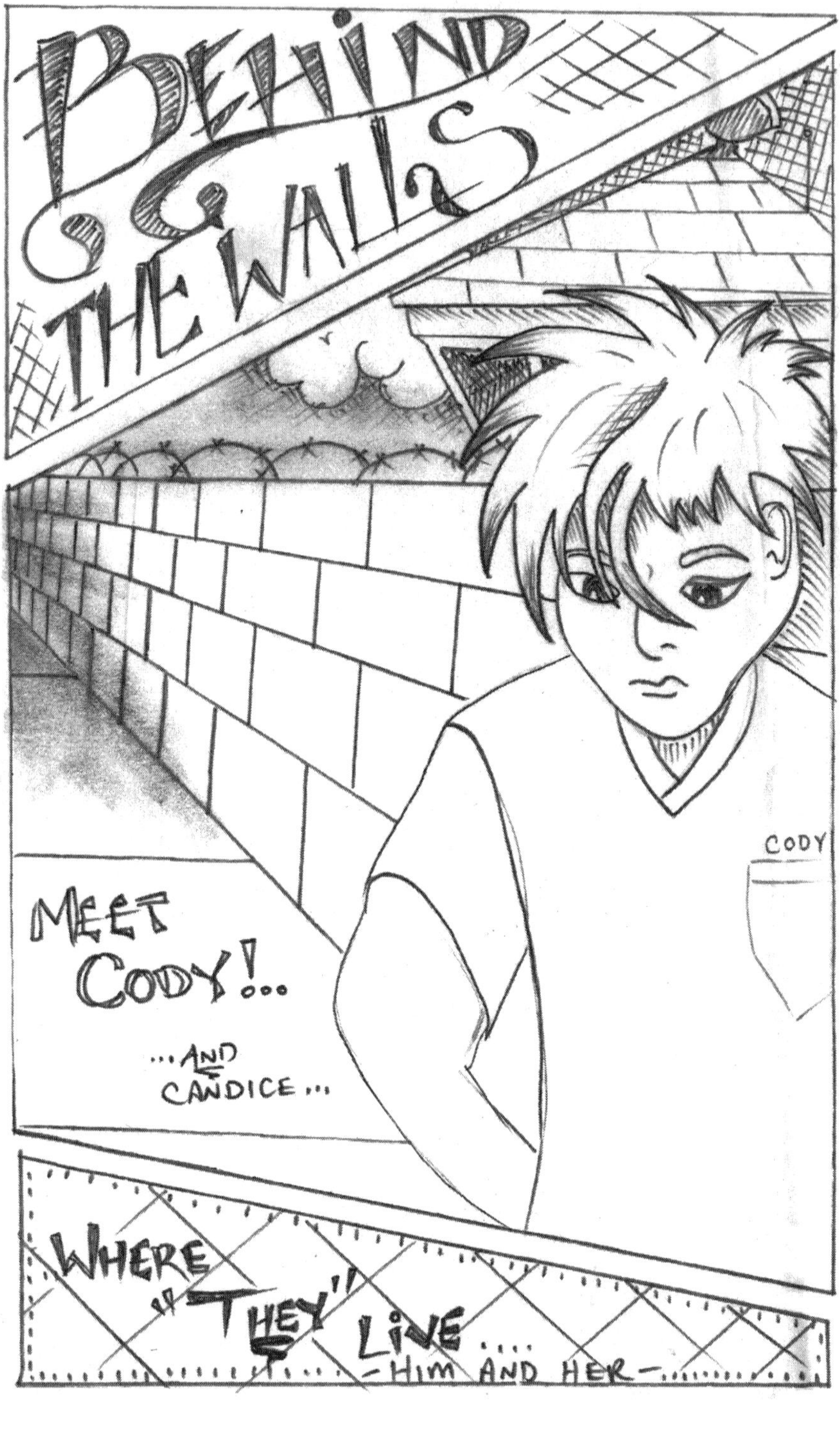

BEHIND THE WALLS
CODY
MEET CODY!...
...AND CANDICE...
WHERE "THEY" LIVE....
-HIM AND HER-

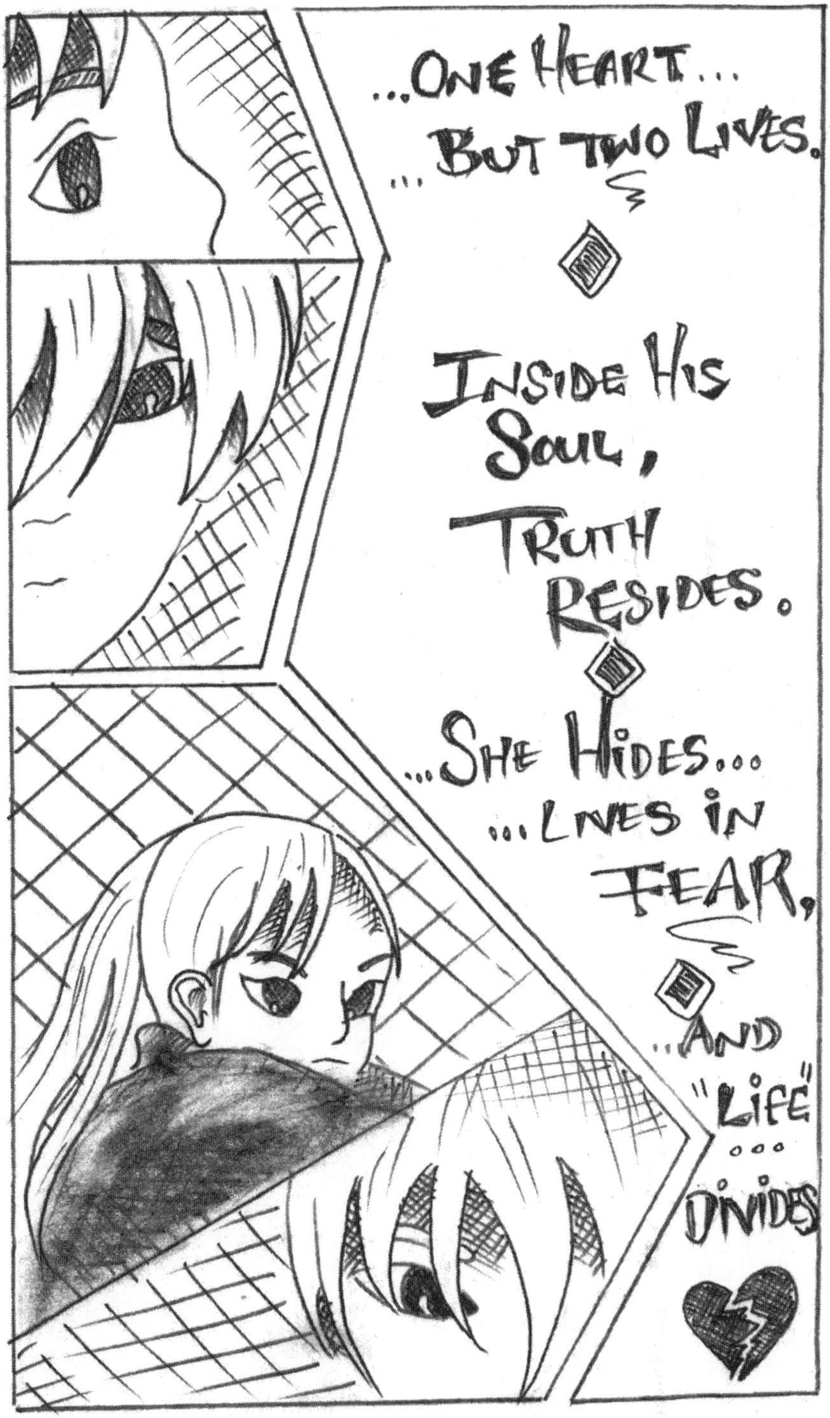

...ONE HEART...
...BUT TWO LIVES.
INSIDE HIS SOUL, TRUTH RESIDES.
...SHE HIDES...
...LIVES IN FEAR,
...AND "LIFE" ... DIVIDES

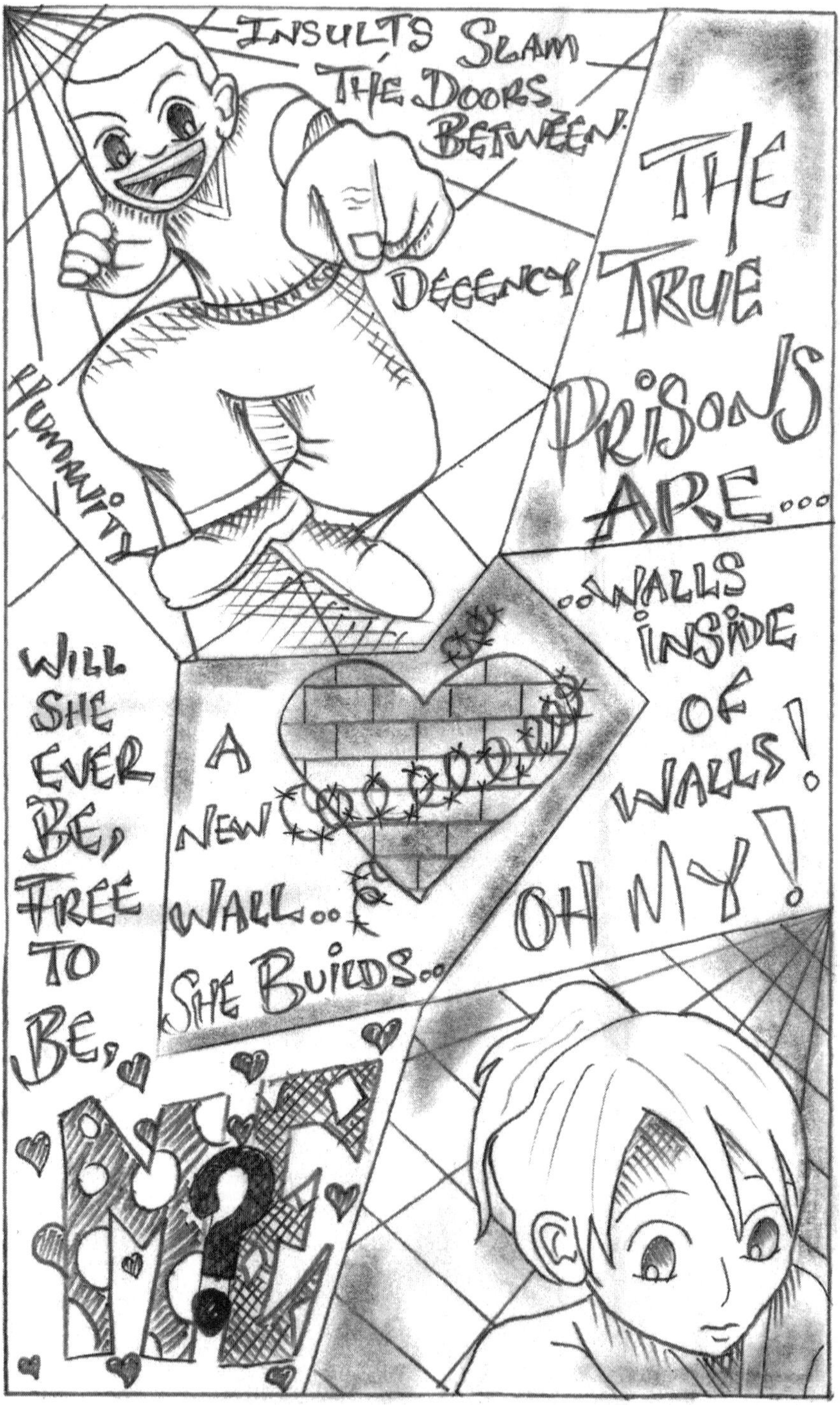
INSULTS SLAM THE DOORS BETWEEN:
DECENCY
HUMANITY
THE TRUE PRISONS ARE...
..WALLS INSIDE OF WALLS!
OH MY!
A NEW WALL... SHE BUILDS...
WILL SHE EVER BE, FREE TO BE,
ME?

Hard Candy
"Super Queer"

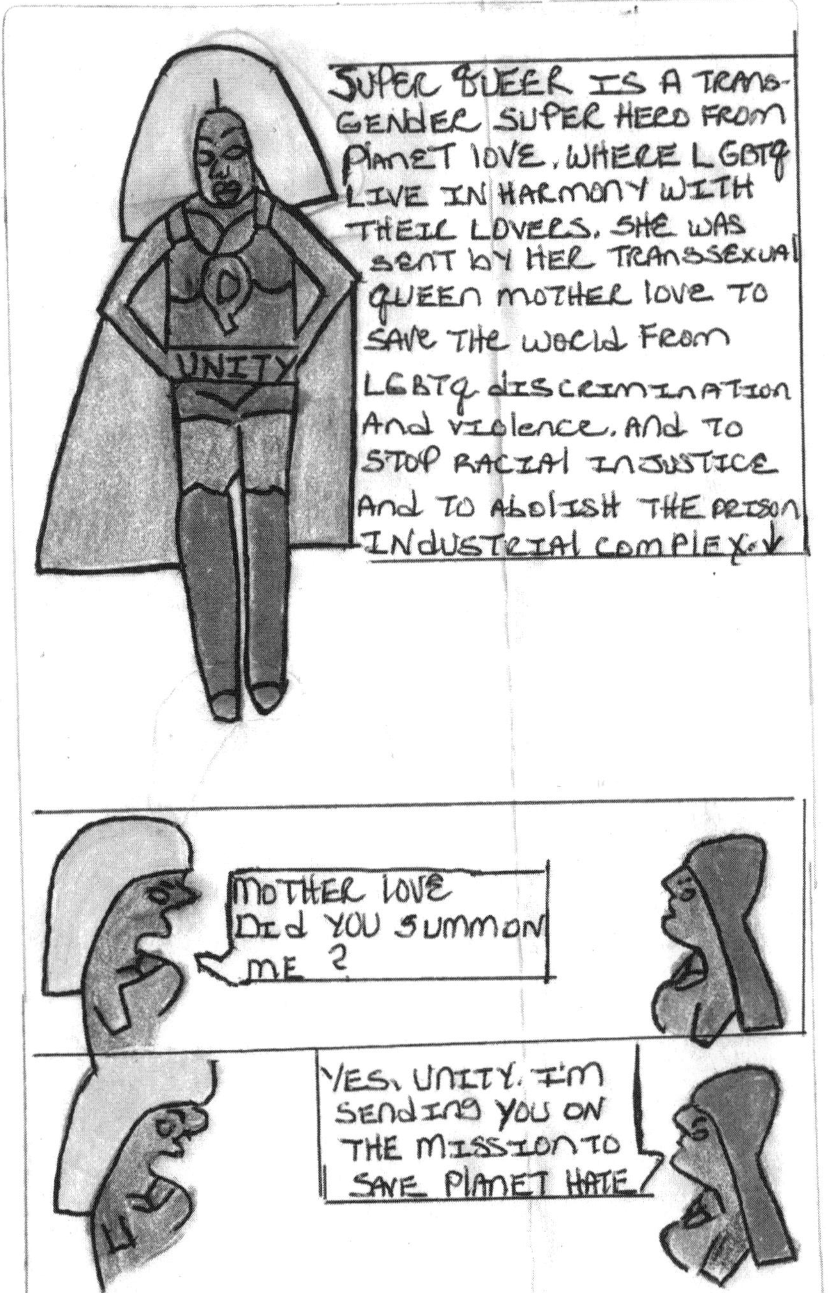
SUPER QUEER IS A TRANS-GENDER SUPER HERO FROM PLANET LOVE, WHERE LGBTQ LIVE IN HARMONY WITH THEIR LOVERS. SHE WAS SENT BY HER TRANSSEXUAL QUEEN MOTHER LOVE TO SAVE THE WORLD FROM LGBTQ DISCRIMINATION AND VIOLENCE. AND TO STOP RACIAL INJUSTICE AND TO ABOLISH THE PRISON INDUSTRIAL COMPLEX.
UNITY
MOTHER LOVE DID YOU SUMMON ME?
YES, UNITY. I'M SENDING YOU ON THE MISSION TO SAVE PLANET HATE!

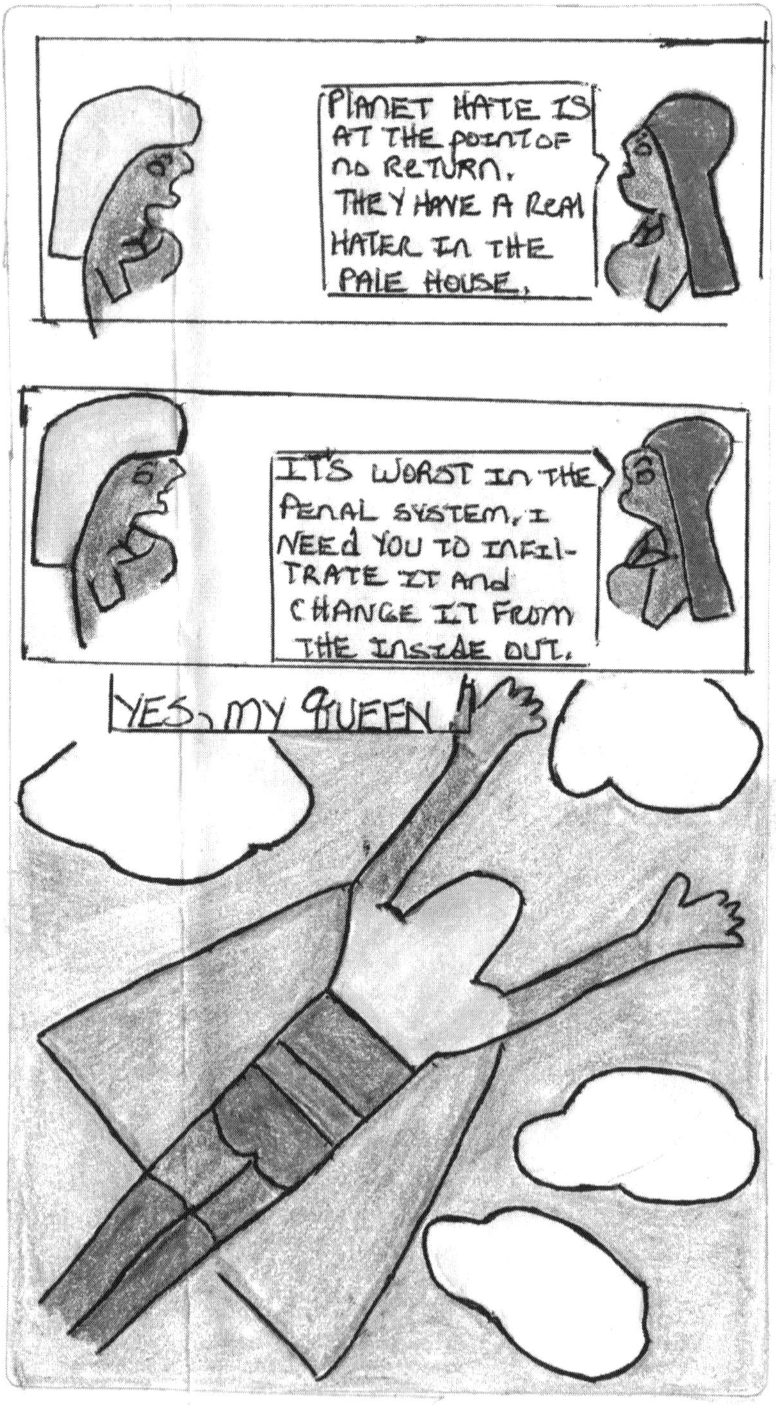
PLANET HATE IS AT THE POINT OF NO RETURN. THEY HAVE A REAL HATER IN THE PALE HOUSE.
IT'S WORST IN THE PENAL SYSTEM. I NEED YOU TO INFIL-TRATE IT AND CHANGE IT FROM THE INSIDE OUT.
YES, MY QUEEN!

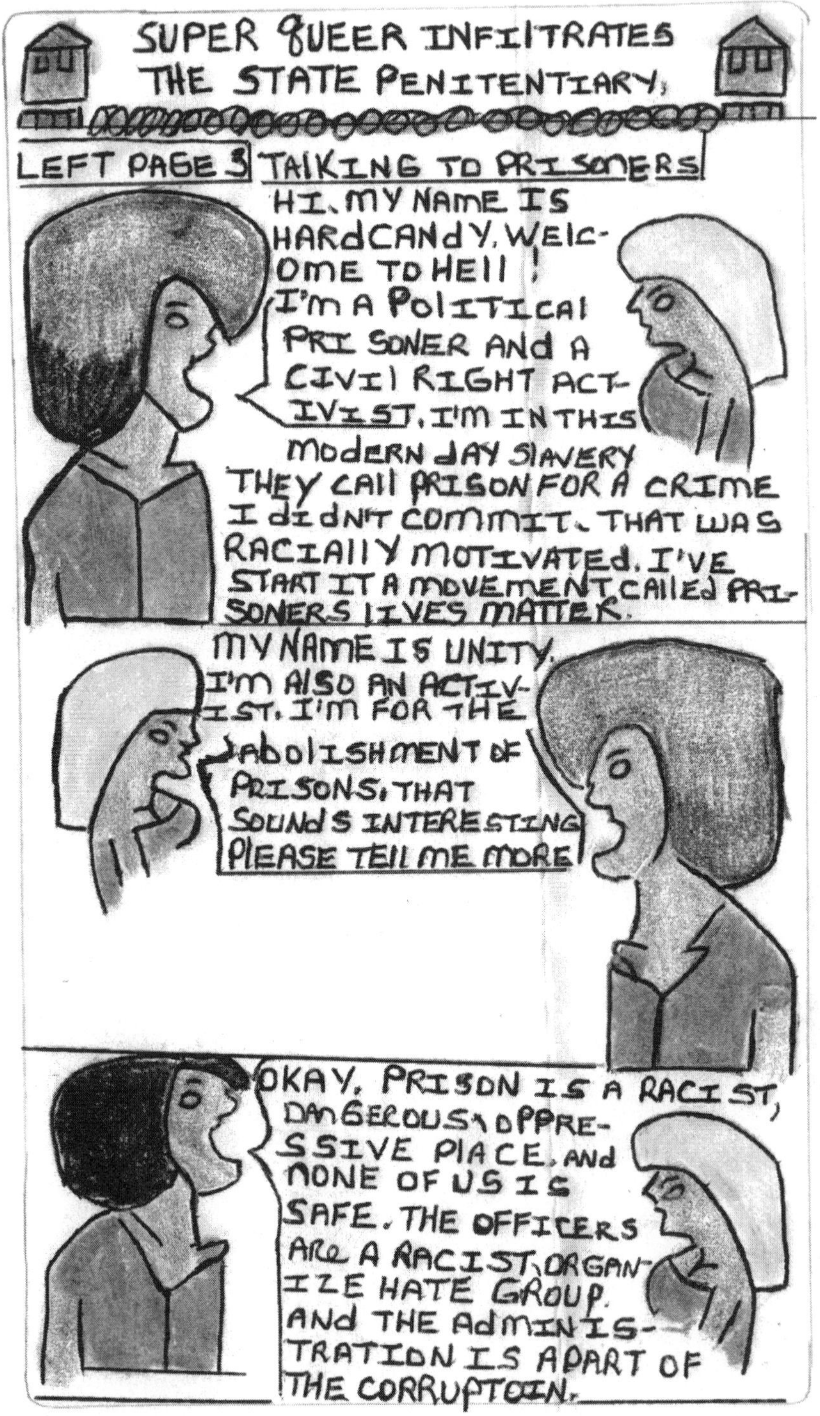
SUPER QUEER INFILTRATES THE STATE PENITENTIARY,
LEFT PAGE 3
TALKING TO PRISONERS
HI. MY NAME IS HARDCANDY. WELCOME TO HELL! I'M A POLITICAL PRISONER AND A CIVIL RIGHT ACTIVIST. I'M IN THIS MODERN DAY SLAVERY THEY CALL PRISON FOR A CRIME I DIDN'T COMMIT. THAT WAS RACIALLY MOTIVATED. I'VE START IT A MOVEMENT CALLED PRISONERS LIVES MATTER.
MY NAME IS UNITY. I'M ALSO AN ACTIVIST. I'M FOR THE ABOLISHMENT OF PRISONS. THAT SOUNDS INTERESTING PLEASE TELL ME MORE
OKAY, PRISON IS A RACIST, DANGEROUS, OPPRESSIVE PLACE, AND NONE OF US IS SAFE. THE OFFICERS ARE A RACIST, ORGANIZE HATE GROUP. AND THE ADMINISTRATION IS A PART OF THE CORRUPTOIN.

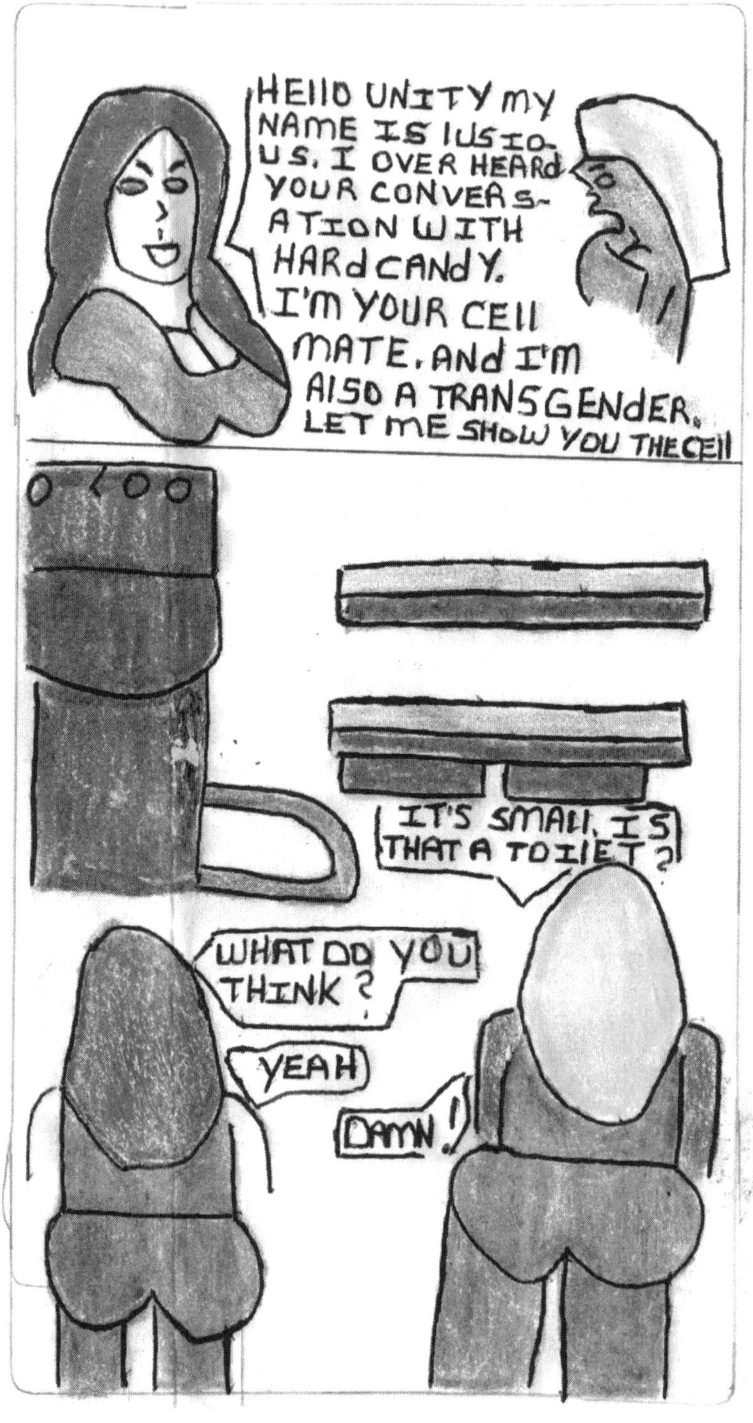
HEllO UNITY my NAME IS lUSIOUS. I OVER HEARd YOUR CONVERSATION WITH HARdCANdY. I'M YOUR CEll MATE. ANd I'M AlSO A TRANSGENdER. LET ME SHOW YOU THE CEll
IT'S SMAll. IS THAT A TOIlET?
WHAT DO YOU THINK?
YEAH
DAMN!

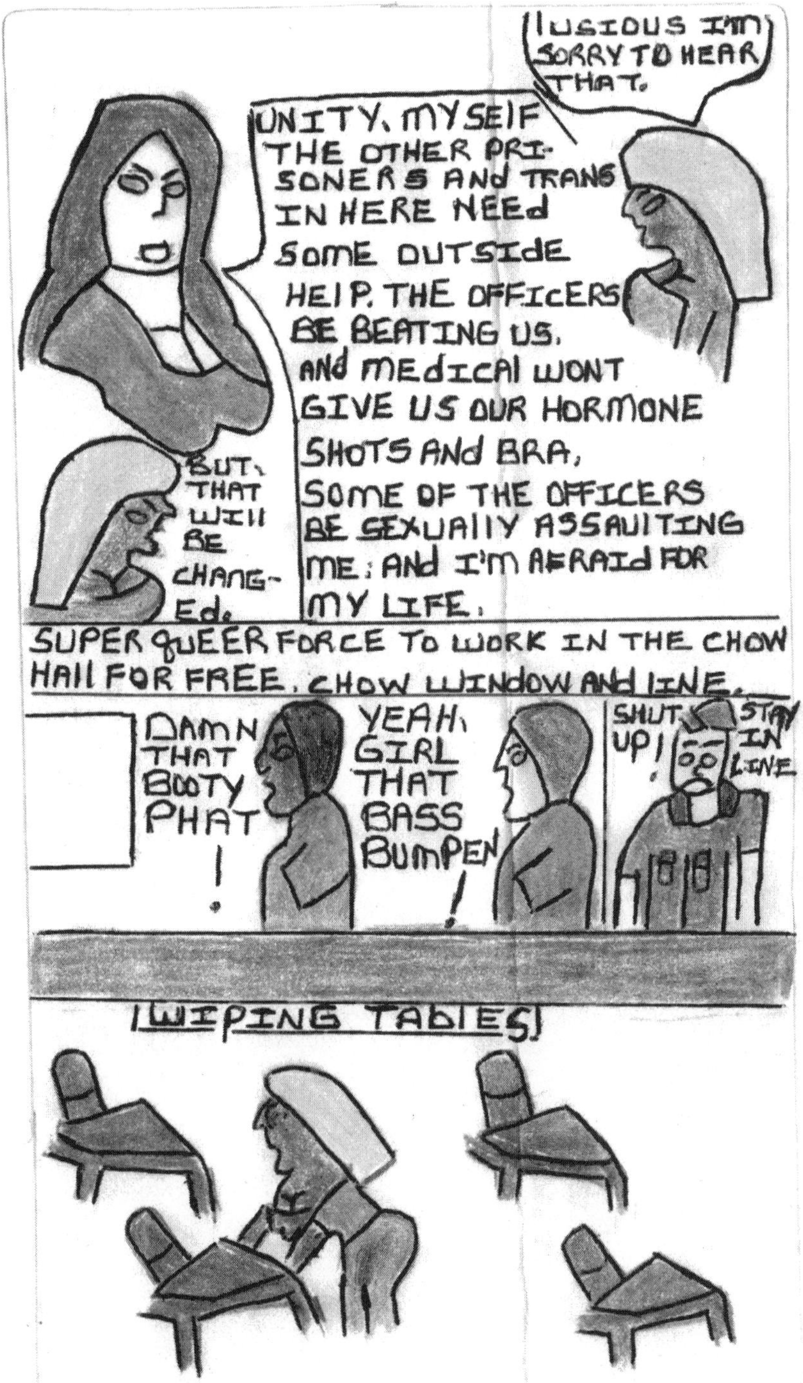
LUSIOUS I'M SORRY TO HEAR THAT.
UNITY, MYSEIF THE OTHER PRI-SONERS AND TRANS IN HERE NEEd SOME OUTSIDE HEIP. THE OFFICERS BE BEATING US. AND MEdICAl WONT GIVE US OUR HORMONE SHOTS AND BRA, SOME OF THE OFFICERS BE SEXUAllY ASSAUITING ME; AND I'M AFRAId FOR MY LIFE.
BUT, THAT WIll BE CHANG-Ed.
SUPER QUEER FORCE TO WORK IN THE CHOW HAll FOR FREE. CHOW WINdOW AND LINE.
DAMN THAT BOOTY PHAT!
YEAH, GIRL THAT BASS BUMPEN!
SHUT UP!
STAY IN LINE
WIPING TAbIES!

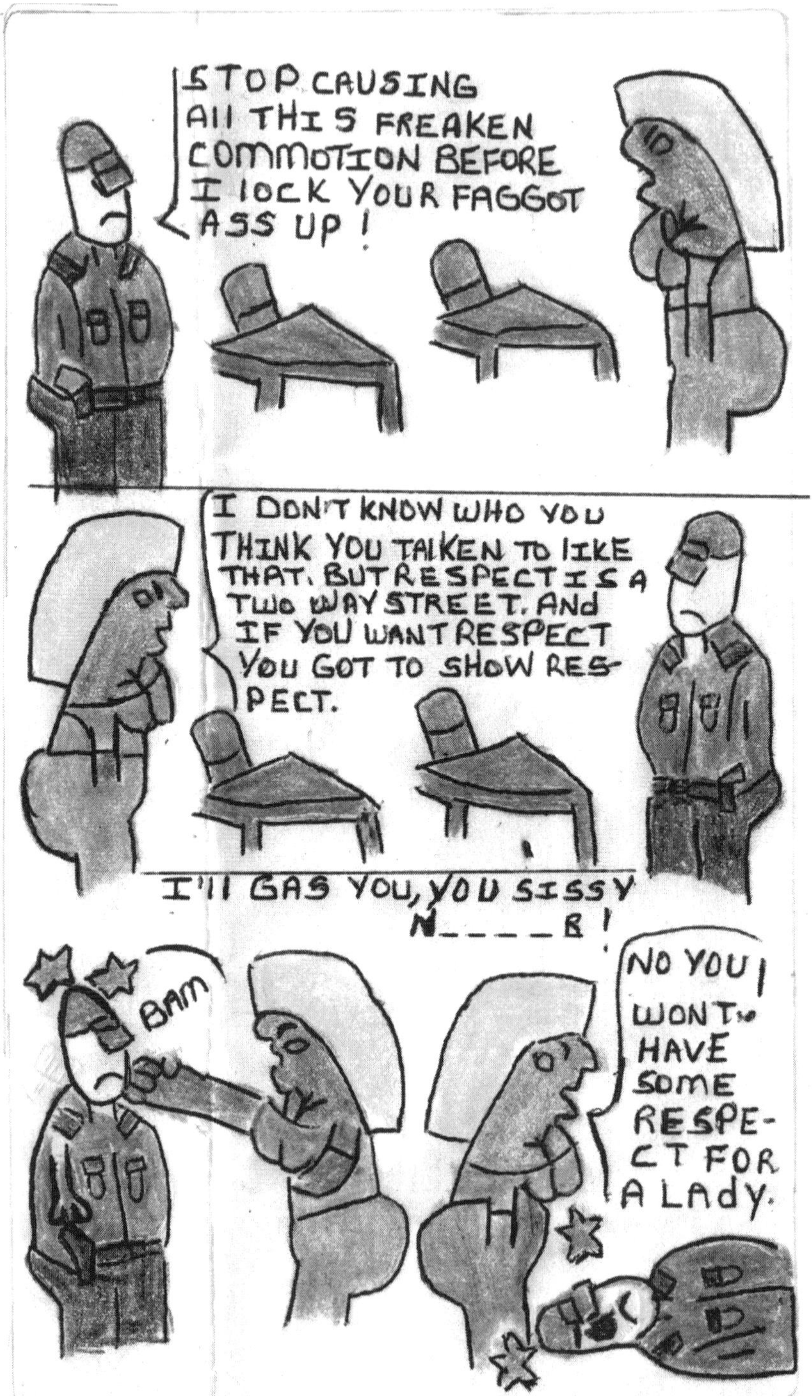
STOP CAUSING All THIS FREAKEN COMMOTION BEFORE I lock YOUR FAGGOT ASS UP!
I DON'T KNOW WHO YOU THINK YOU TAlKEN TO lIKE THAT. BUT RESPECT IS A TWO WAY STREET. And IF YOU WANT RESPECT YOU GOT TO SHOW RESPECT.
I'll GAS YOU, YOU SISSY N____R!
BAM
NO YOU WONT. HAVE SOME RESPECT FOR A Lady.

My Fight Club Status

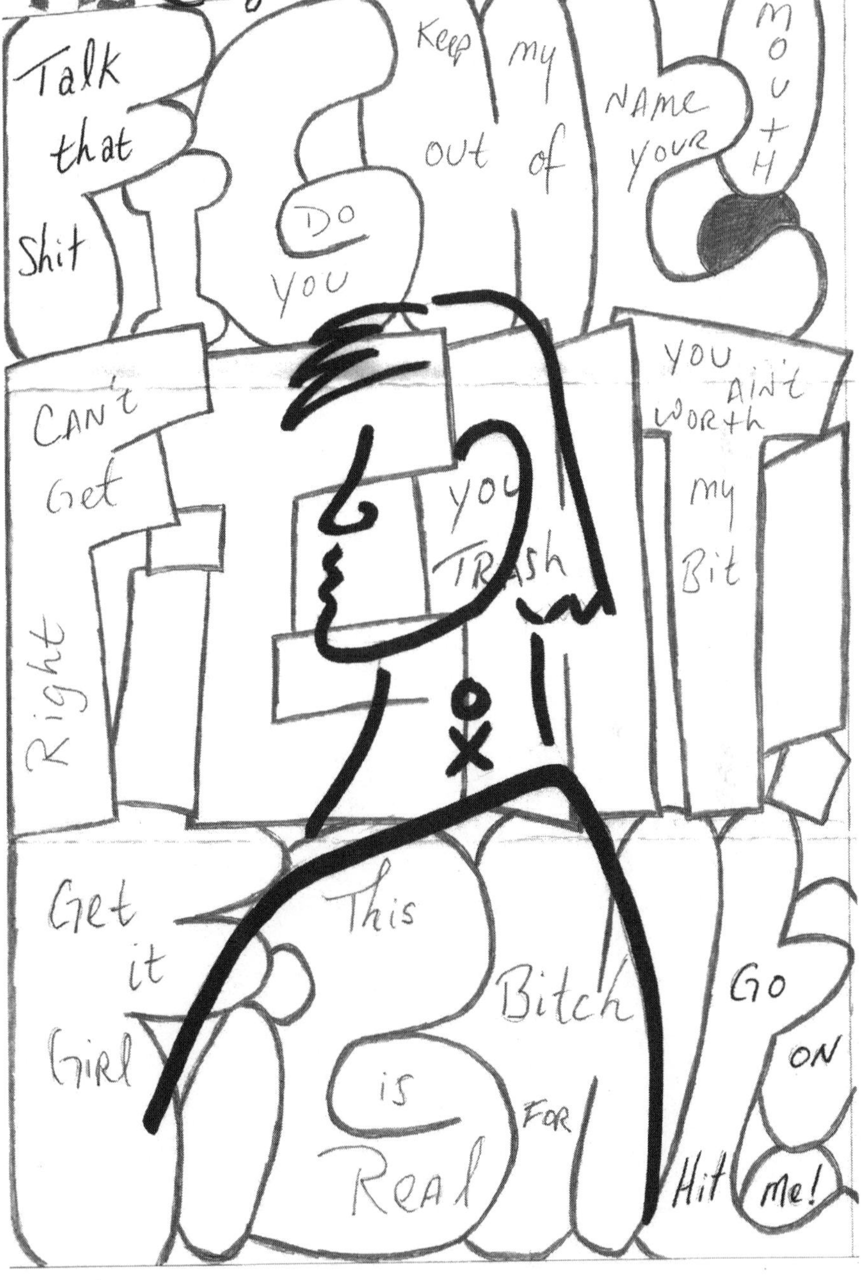

Talk that Shit
Do you
Keep my NAME out of your MOUTH
CAN'T Get Right
you TRASH
YOU AIN'T WORTH my Bit
Get it Girl
This Bitch is FOR Real
GO ON Hit me!

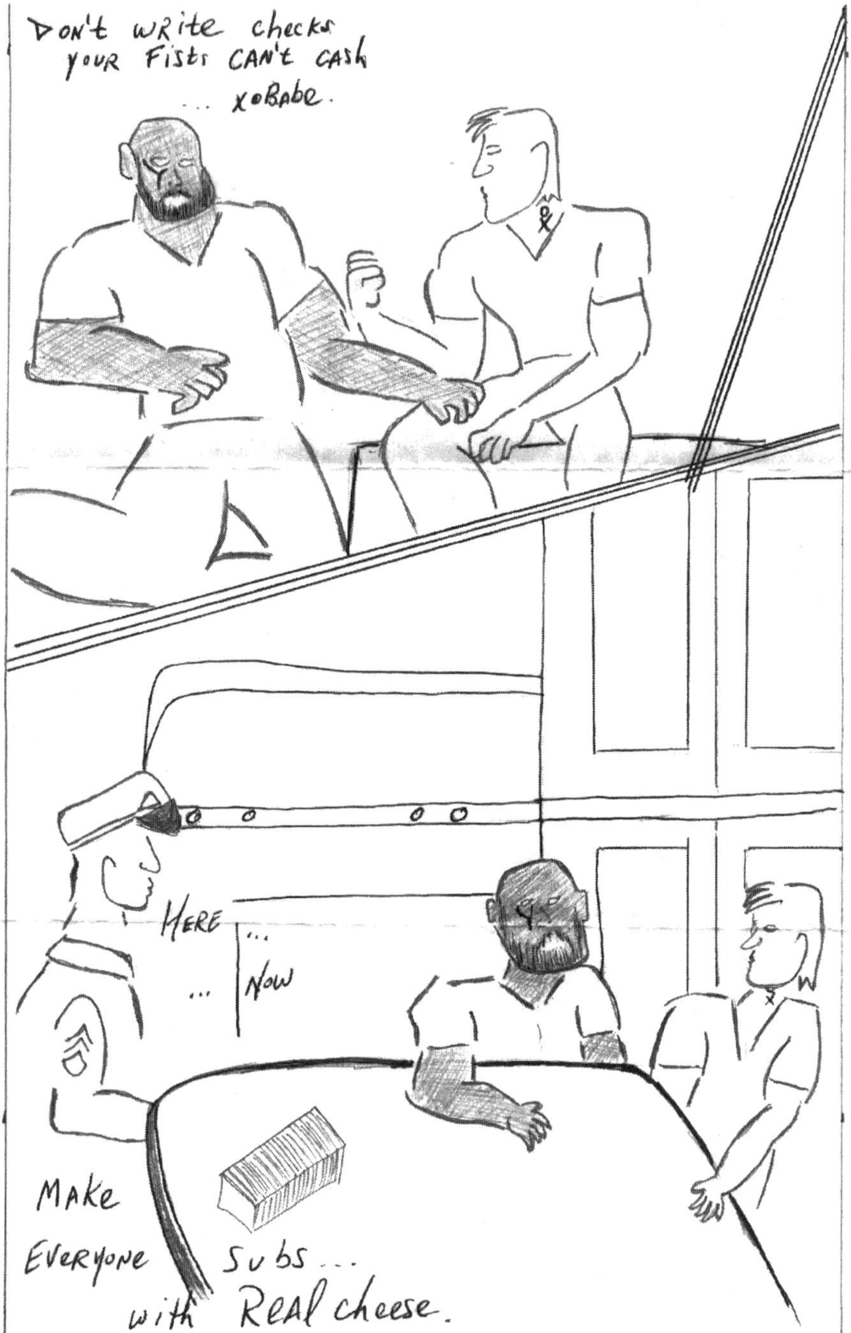
Don't write checks your Fists CAN't CASh ... xoBabe.
HERE ... Now ...
Make Everyone Subs ... with ReAl cheese.

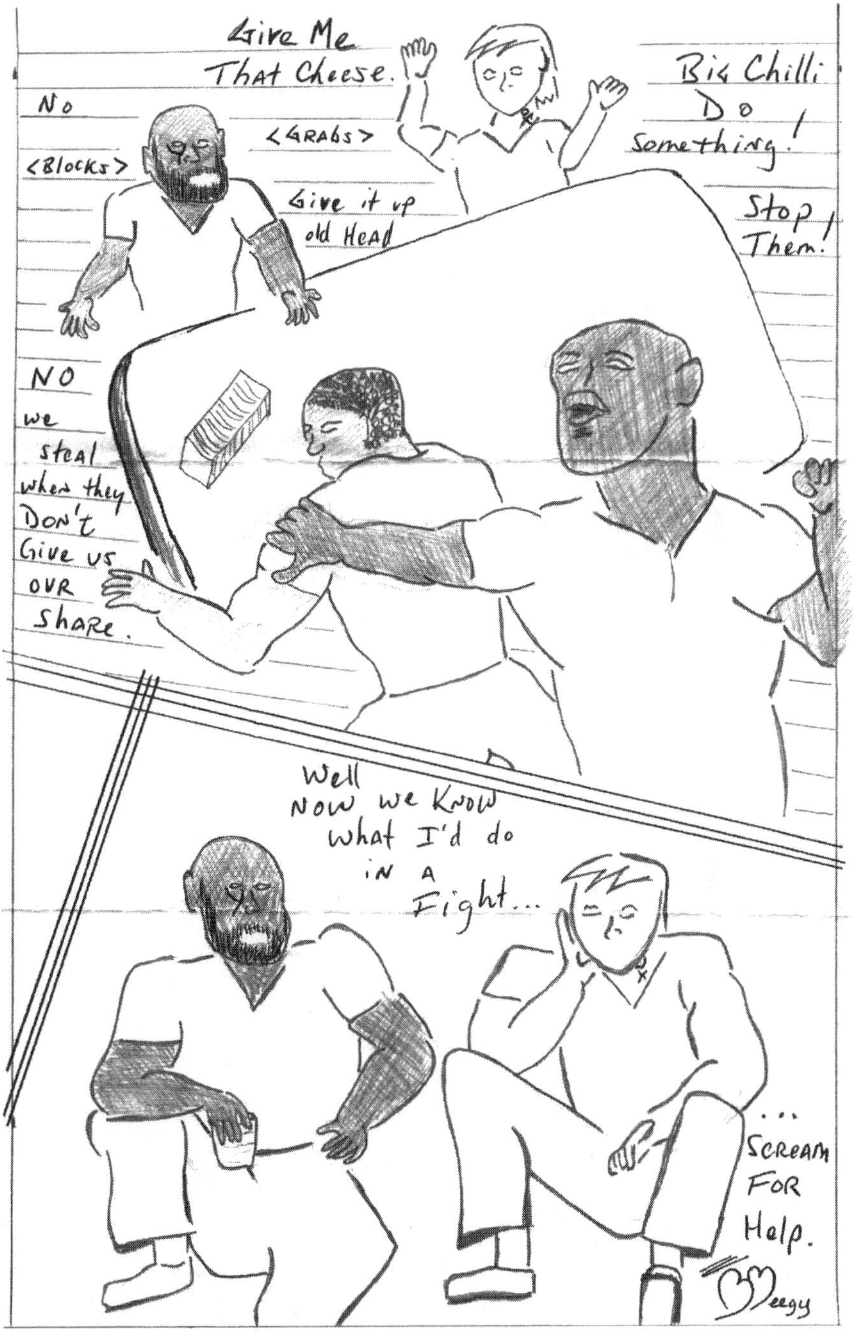

Give Me That Cheese.
<GRABS>
No
<Blocks>
Give it up old Head
Big Chilli Do something!
Stop Them!
NO we steal when they Don't Give us our Share.
Well now we Know what I'd do in a Fight...
... Scream For Help.
Meegy

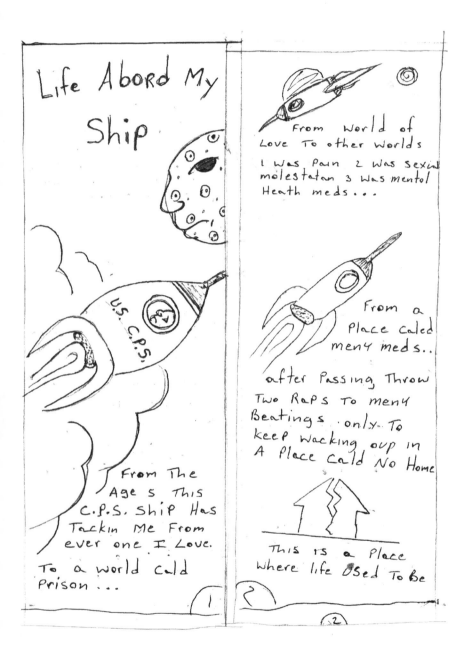

Life Abord My Ship

From world of Love To other worlds
I was Pain 2 was sexial molestaton 3 was mentol Heath meds...

From a Place caled meny meds..

after Passing Throw Two RaPs To meny Beatings .only. To keep wacking oup in A Place Cald No Home

This is a Place where life Osed To be

U.S. C.P.S.

From The Ages This C.P.S. Ship Has Tackin Me From ever one I Love.
To a world cald Prison ...

1

2

2

132

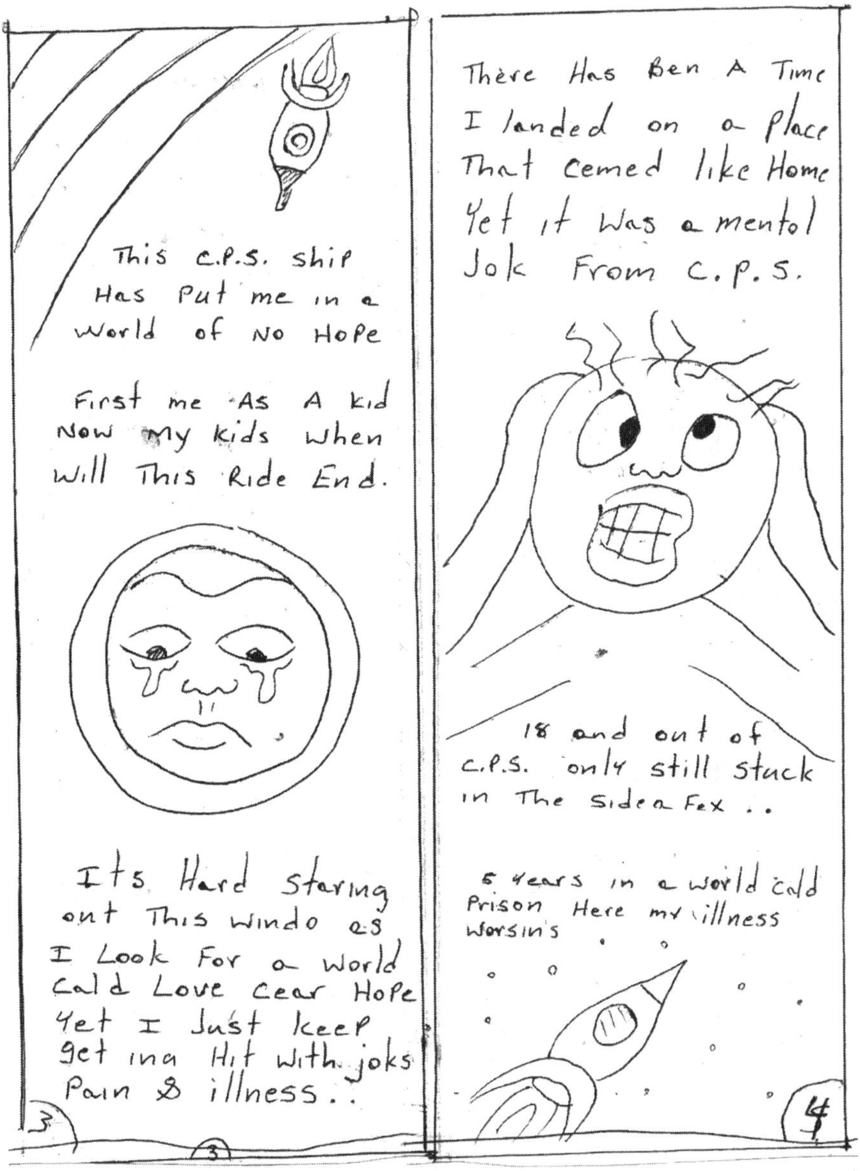
This C.P.S. ship
Has Put me in a
World of No HoPe
First me As A kid
Now my kids when
will This Ride End.
Its Hard Staring
out This windo as
I Look For a World
Cald Love Cear HoPe
Yet I Just keeP
get ina Hit with joks
Pain & illness..
There Has Ben A Time
I landed on a Place
That cemed like Home
Yet it Was a mentol
Jok From C.P.S.
18 and out of
C.P.S. only still stuck
in The Sidea Fex ..
5 years in a world cald
Prison Here my illness
worsin's

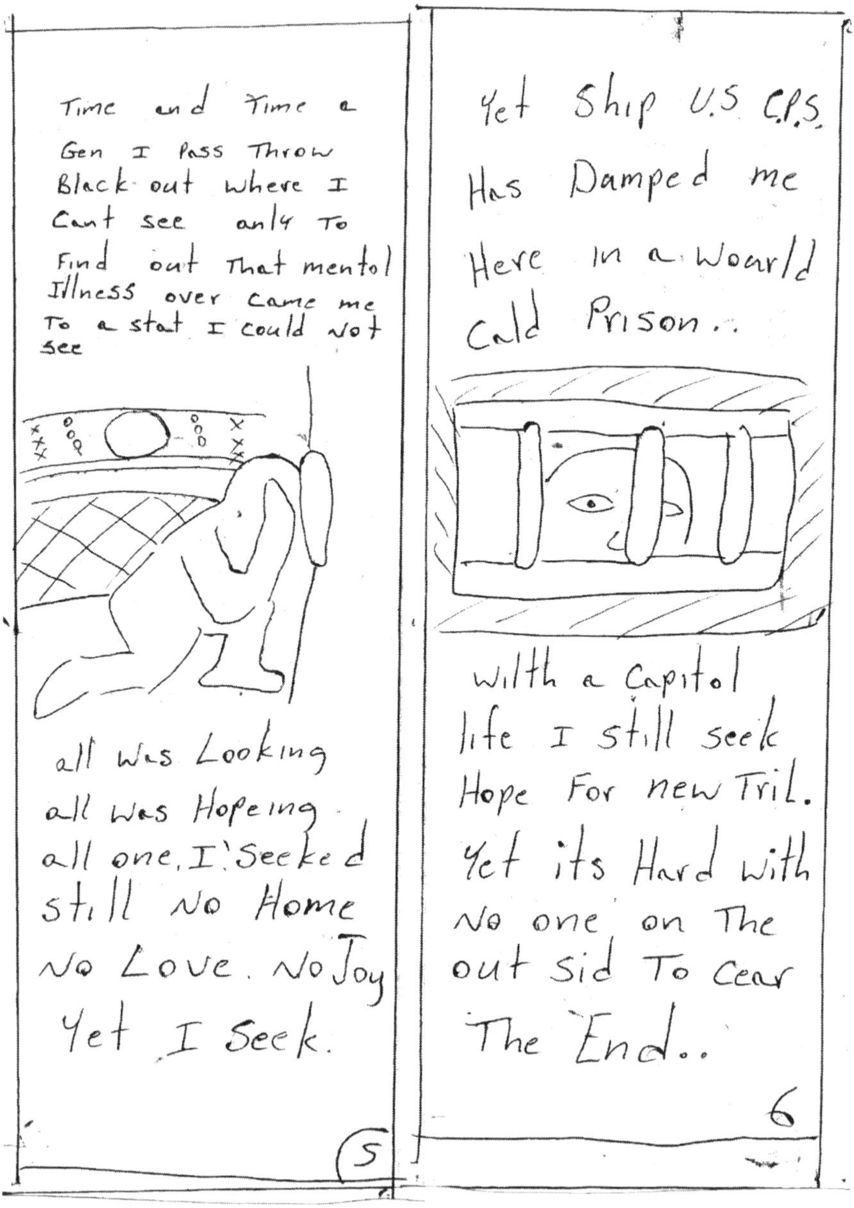
Time and Time a Gen I Pass Throw Black out where I Cant see anly To Find out That mentol Illness over came me To a stat I could Not see
all Was Looking all Was Hopeing all one, I Seeked still No Home No Love. No Joy Yet I Seek.
5
Yet Ship U.S C.P.S. Has Damped me Here in a Woarld Cald Prison..
wilth a Capitol life I still seek Hope For new Tril. Yet its Hard with No one on The out sid To Cear The End..
6

BIO Artist

I Billy, Thomas #1275621
age:46 still Doing
life in Prison after
a life of mentol &
Sexual Pain With
The Hard Ship of
over Comeing its
Sham ...

Yet in This Dark
Prison I Have Found
Hope. Hope in GoD
Hes Ben Here and
Sends Peppol That
Help Will That Be You
?

Billy D Thomas #1275621
AllRed Unit 2101 Fm 369N
Iowa Park. Tx 76367

135

H. Lee
"Pod Life"

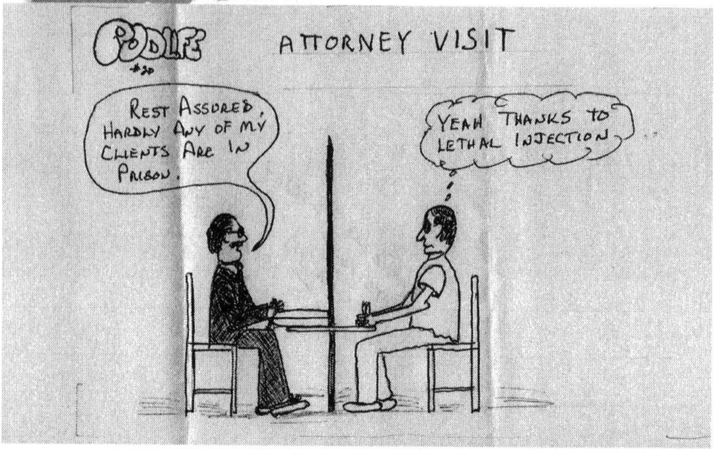
PODLIFE
ATTORNEY VISIT
REST ASSURED, HARDLY ANY OF MY CLIENTS ARE IN PRISON.
YEAH THANKS TO LETHAL INJECTION...

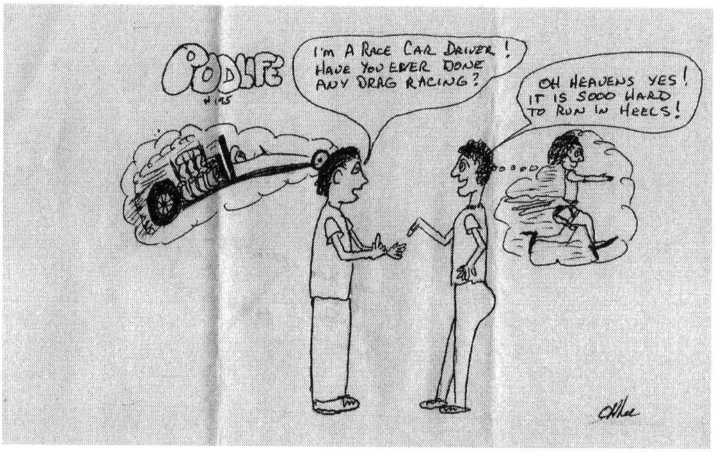
PODLIFE
I'M A RACE CAR DRIVER! HAVE YOU EVER DONE ANY DRAG RACING?
OH HEAVENS YES! IT IS SOOO HARD TO RUN IN HEELS!

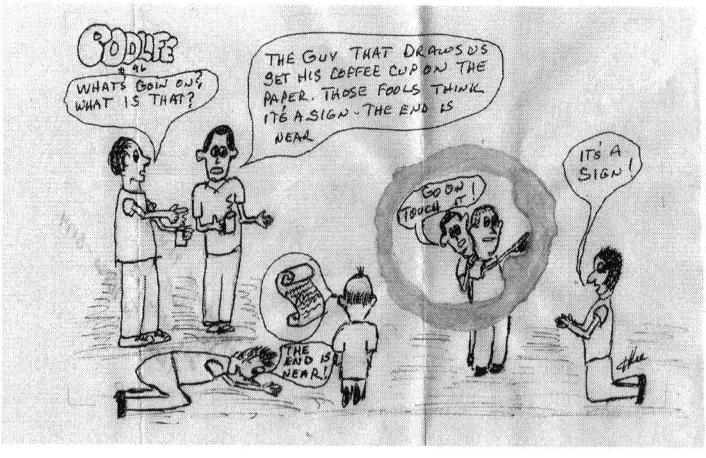
PODLIFE
WHATS GOIN ON? WHAT IS THAT?
THE GUY THAT DRAWS US SET HIS COFFEE CUP ON THE PAPER. THOSE FOOLS THINK ITS A SIGN - THE END IS NEAR
GO ON! TOUCH IT.
THE END IS NEAR!
IT'S A SIGN!

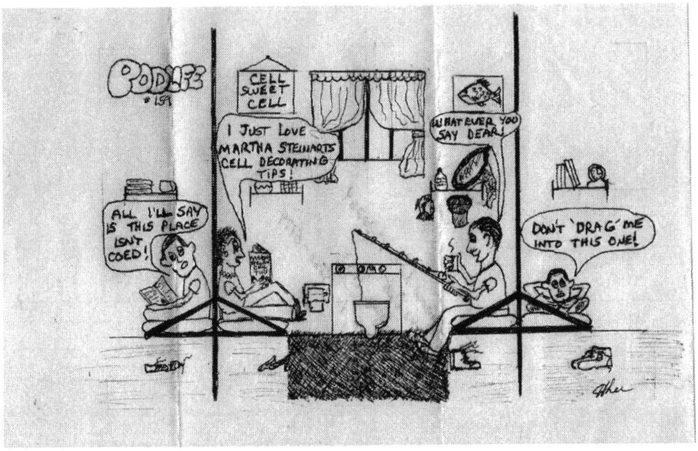
PODLIFE
159
CELL SWEET CELL
I JUST LOVE MARTHA STEWARTS CELL DECORATING TIPS!
WHATEVER YOU SAY DEAR!
ALL I'LL SAY IS THIS PLACE ISN'T COED!
DON'T 'DRAG' ME INTO THIS ONE!

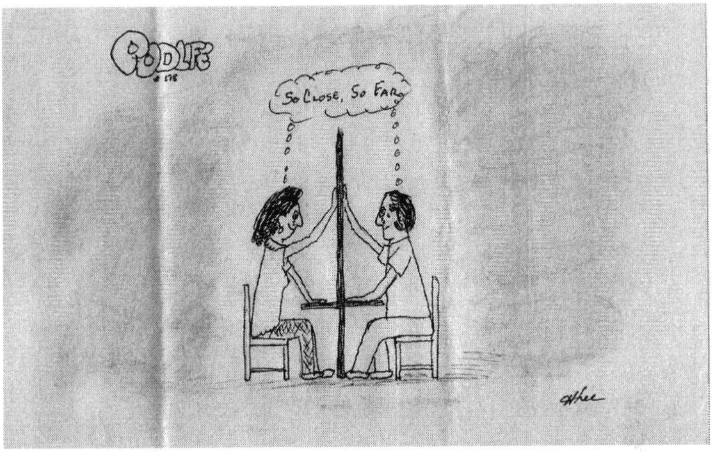
PODLIFE
178
SO CLOSE, SO FAR

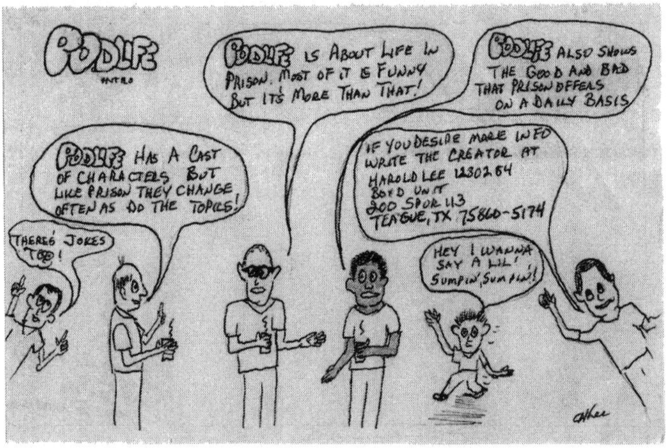
PODLIFE
INTRO
PODLIFE IS ABOUT LIFE IN PRISON. MOST OF IT IS FUNNY BUT IT'S MORE THAN THAT!
PODLIFE ALSO SHOWS THE GOOD AND BAD THAT PRISON OFFEAS ON A DAILY BASIS
PODLIFE HAS A CAST OF CHARACTERS BUT LIKE PRISON THEY CHANGE OFTEN AS DO THE TOPICS!
IF YOU DESIDE MORE INFO WRITE THE CREATOR AT HAROLD LEE 1230284 BOYD UNIT 200 SPUR 113 TEAGUE, TX 75860-5174
THERE'S JOKES TOO!
HEY I WANNA SAY A LIL' SUMPIN', SUMPIN'!

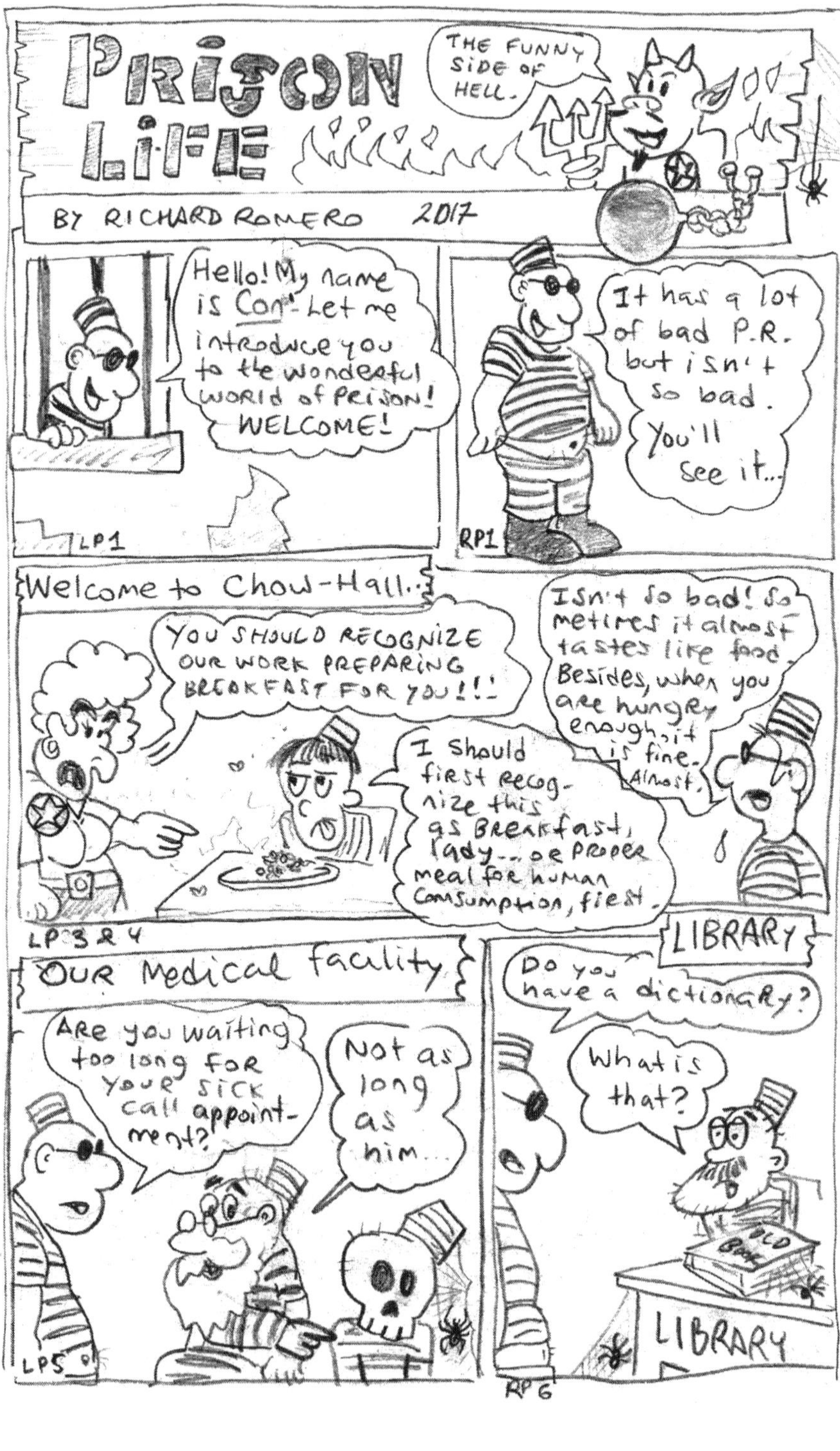
PRISON LIFE
THE FUNNY SIDE OF HELL.
BY RICHARD ROMERO 2017
Hello! My name is Con- Let me introduce you to the wonderful world of Prison! WELCOME!
LP1
It has a lot of bad P.R. but isn't so bad. You'll see it...
RP1
Welcome to Chow-Hall..
YOU SHOULD RECOGNIZE OUR WORK PREPARING BREAKFAST FOR YOU!!
I should first recognize this as Breakfast, lady... or proper meal for human consumption, first.
Isn't so bad! Sometimes it almost tastes like food. Besides, when you are hungry enough, it is fine. Almost.
LP 3 & 4
Our Medical facility
Are you waiting too long for your sick call appointment?
Not as long as him...
LP5
LIBRARY
Do you have a dictionary?
What is that?
OLD BOOK
LIBRARY
RP6

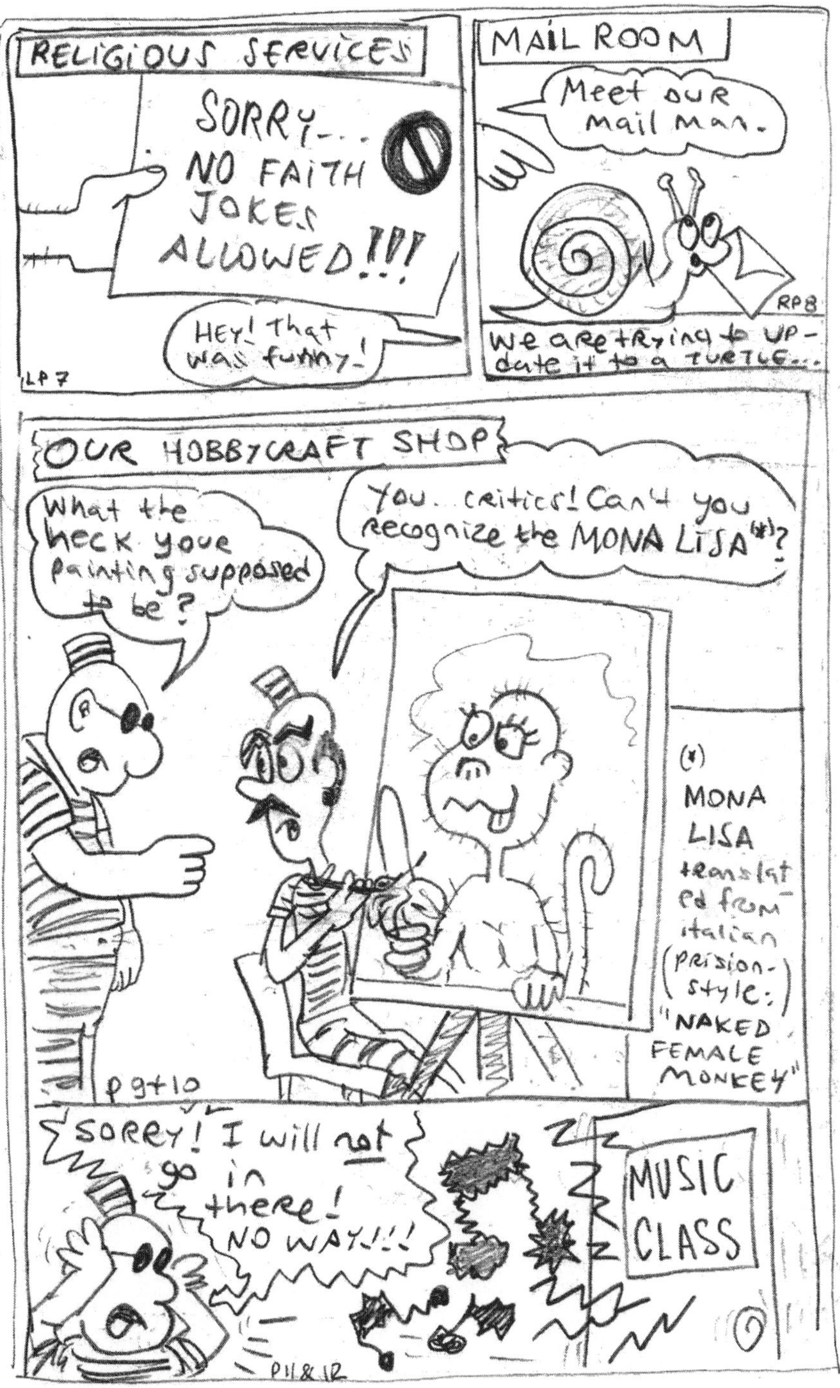
RELIGIOUS SERVICES
SORRY... NO FAITH JOKES ALLOWED!!!
HEY! That was funny!
LP 7
MAIL ROOM
Meet our mail man.
RP8
We are trying to up-date it to a TURTLE...
OUR HOBBYCRAFT SHOP
What the heck youre painting supposed to be?
You.. critics! Can't you recognize the MONA LISA(*)?
(*) MONA LISA translated from italian (prision-style): "NAKED FEMALE MONKEY"
pg+10
SORRY! I will not go in there! NO WAY!!!
MUSIC CLASS
P11&12

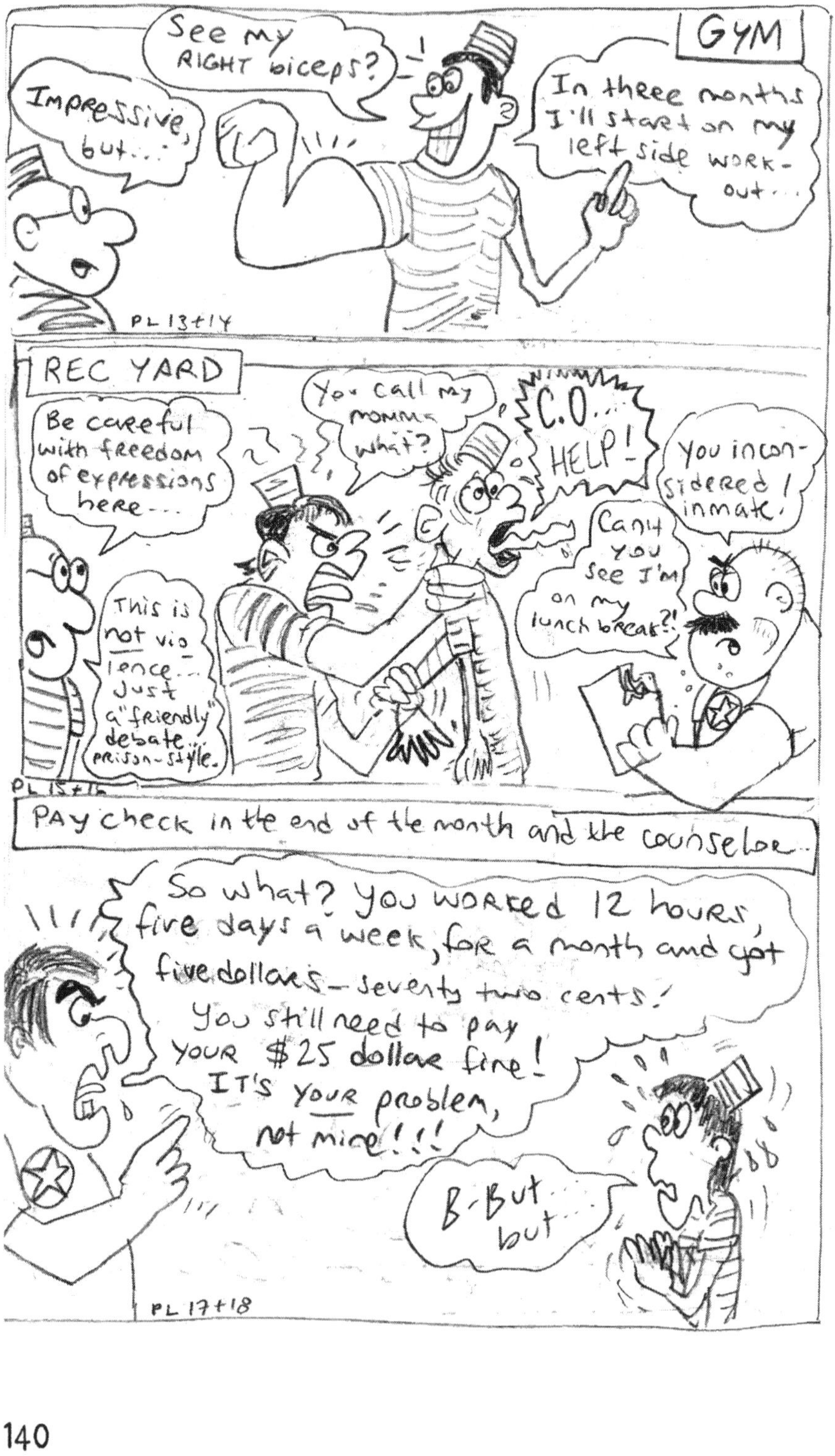
GYM
See my RIGHT biceps?
Impressive, but...
In three months I'll start on my left side work-out...
PL 13+14
REC YARD
Be careful with freedom of expressions here...
You call my momma what?
C.O... HELP!
You incon-sidered inmate!
Can't you see I'm on my lunch break?!
This is not vio-lence... Just a "friendly" debate... prison-style.
Pay check in the end of the month and the counselor...
So what? You worked 12 hours, five days a week, for a month and got five dollars — seventy two cents! You still need to pay your $25 dollar fine! IT'S YOUR problem, not mine!!!
B-But... but...
PL 17+18

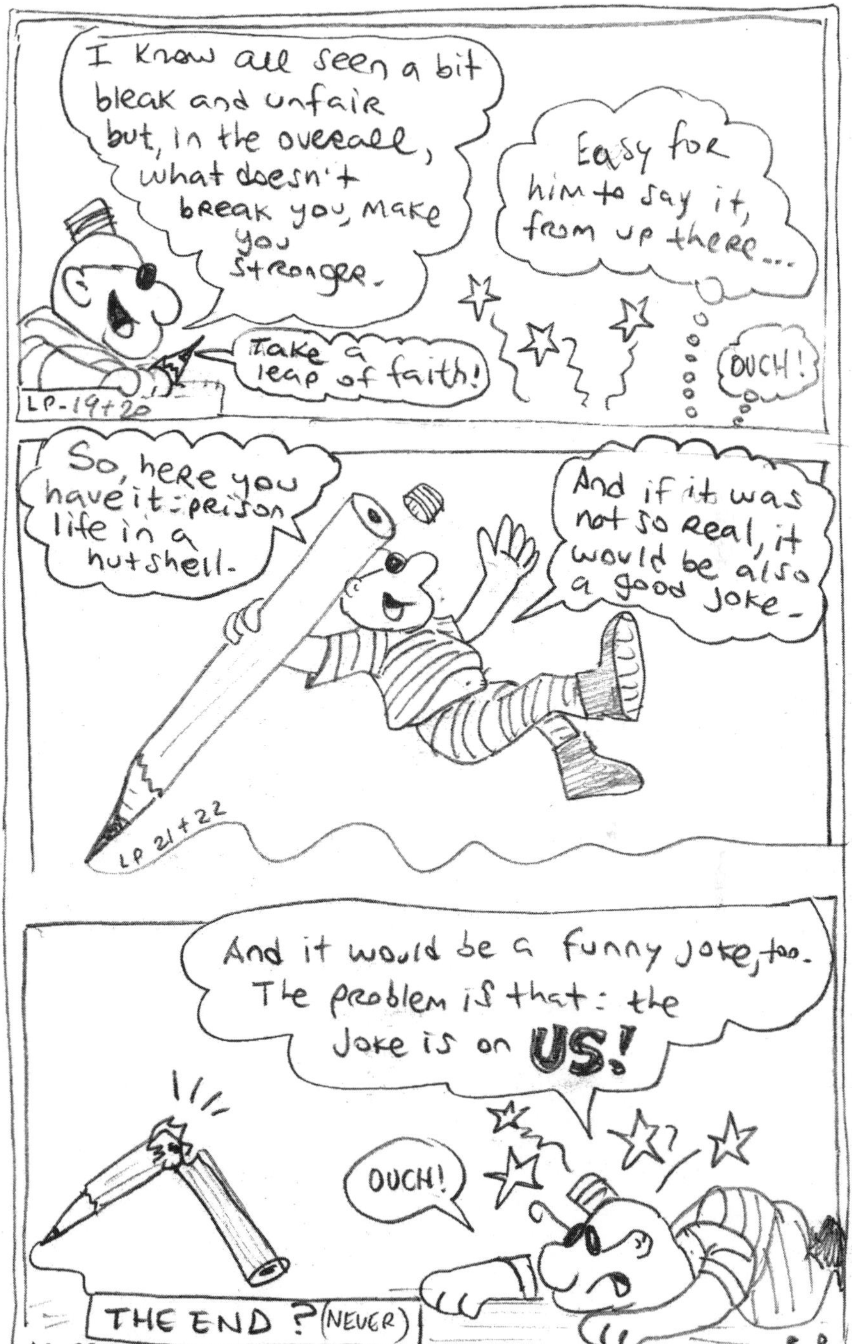
I know all seen a bit bleak and unfair but, in the overall, what doesn't break you, make you stronger.
Take a leap of faith!
Easy for him to say it, from up there...
OUCH!
LP-19+20
So, here you have it: prison life in a nutshell.
And if it was not so real, it would be also a good joke.
LP 21+22
And it would be a funny joke, too. The problem is that: the joke is on US!
OUCH!
THE END ? (NEVER)
LP 22+24
R.R.

The Diatribes
of a
Morning Starr
By: Krysta Morningstarr

AN AMERICAN MANGA 漫画

INCLUDES A BRAND NEW Alli Katz SHORT

THE ADVENTURES OF COSPLAY KRYSTA

BROUGHT TO YOU BY: ABO COMIX

EPISODE 2

142

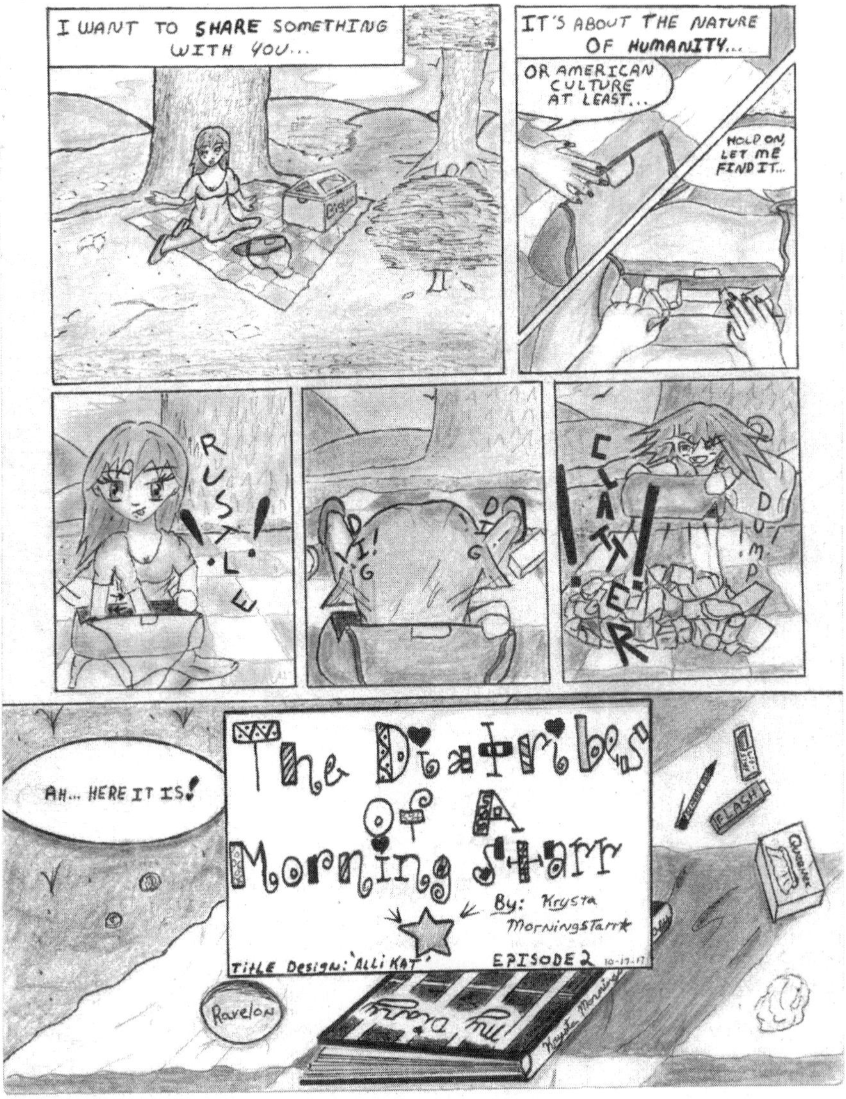
I WANT TO SHARE SOMETHING WITH YOU...
IT'S ABOUT THE NATURE OF HUMANITY...
OR AMERICAN CULTURE AT LEAST...
HOLD ON, LET ME FIND IT...
RUSTLE
DIG! DIG
CLATTER!
DUMP
AH... HERE IT IS!
The Diatribes of A Morning Starr
By: Krysta MorningStarr
TITLE Design: 'ALLI KAT'
EPISODE 2
FLASH
Revlon

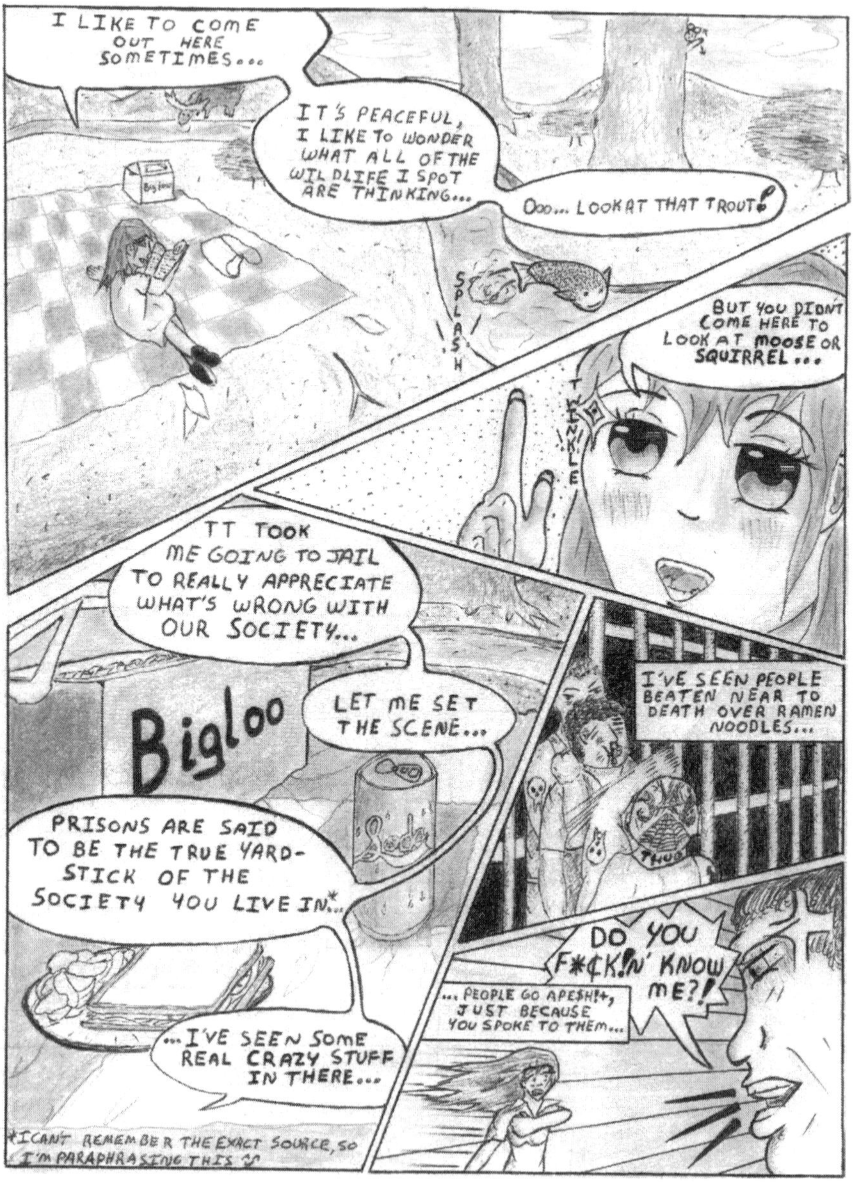
I LIKE TO COME OUT HERE SOMETIMES...
IT'S PEACEFUL, I LIKE TO WONDER WHAT ALL OF THE WILDLIFE I SPOT ARE THINKING...
Ooo... LOOKAT THAT TROUT!
SPLASH
BUT YOU DIDN'T COME HERE TO LOOK AT MOOSE OR SQUIRREL...
TWINKLE
IT TOOK ME GOING TO JAIL TO REALLY APPRECIATE WHAT'S WRONG WITH OUR SOCIETY...
LET ME SET THE SCENE...
Bigloo
PRISONS ARE SAID TO BE THE TRUE YARD-STICK OF THE SOCIETY YOU LIVE IN*...
...I'VE SEEN SOME REAL CRAZY STUFF IN THERE...
I'VE SEEN PEOPLE BEATEN NEAR TO DEATH OVER RAMEN NOODLES...
THUG
DO YOU F*¢K!N' KNOW ME?!
...PEOPLE GO APE$H!+, JUST BECAUSE YOU SPOKE TO THEM...
*I CAN'T REMEMBER THE EXACT SOURCE, SO I'M PARAPHRASING THIS

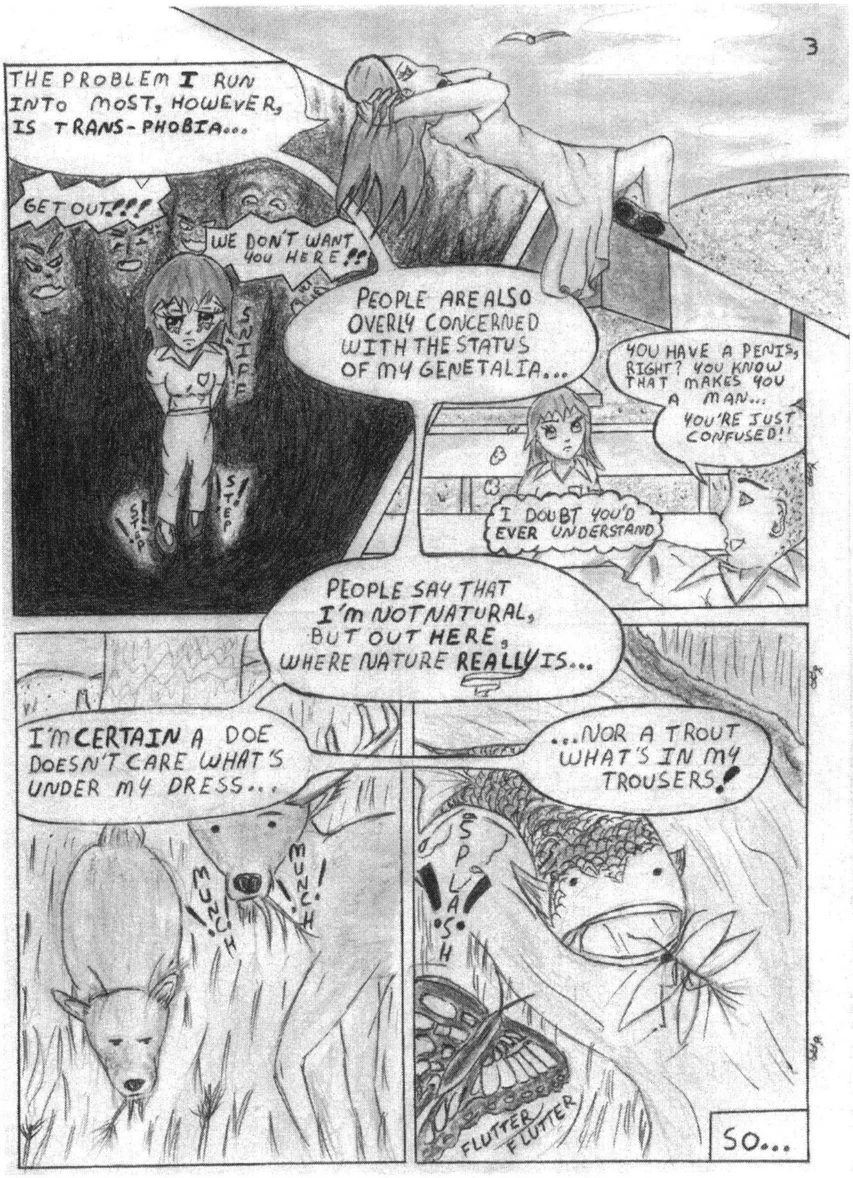
3
THE PROBLEM I RUN INTO MOST, HOWEVER, IS TRANS-PHOBIA...
GET OUT!!!
WE DON'T WANT YOU HERE!!!
SNIFF
STEP! STEP!
PEOPLE ARE ALSO OVERLY CONCERNED WITH THE STATUS OF MY GENETALIA...
YOU HAVE A PENIS, RIGHT? YOU KNOW THAT MAKES YOU A MAN... YOU'RE JUST CONFUSED!!
I DOUBT YOU'D EVER UNDERSTAND
PEOPLE SAY THAT I'M NOT NATURAL, BUT OUT HERE, WHERE NATURE REALLY IS...
I'M CERTAIN A DOE DOESN'T CARE WHAT'S UNDER MY DRESS...
MUNCH! MUNCH!
...NOR A TROUT WHAT'S IN MY TROUSERS!
SPLASH!
FLUTTER FLUTTER
SO...

My Diatribe

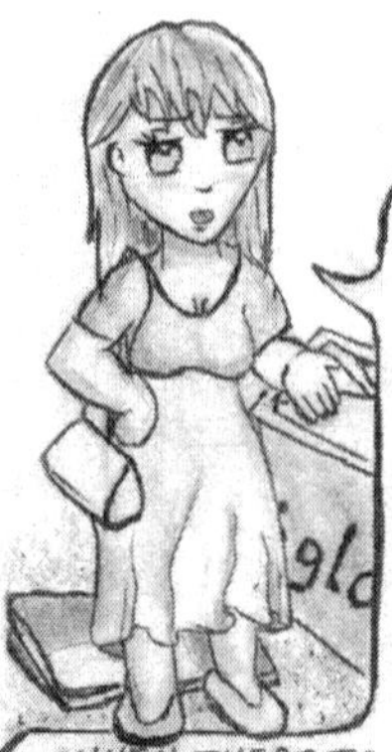

REMEMBER, I FIND THE BEST ANSWER TO SOLVING A PROBLEM IS TO FIRST ASK THE QUESTION "WHY?". WHY IS WHAT'S HAPPENING, HAPPENING?

IN THE FIRST ISSUE I EXPLORED THE ROOT OF THE TRANSPHOBIA PEOPLE EXPERIENCE, NOW I WISH TO EXPOUND UPON IT FURTHER.

THE REASON PRISONS ARE A GREAT MEASURING STICK OF SOCIETY IS THAT THESE PLACES CONCENTRATE & DISTILL THE EXTREMES OF BEHAVIOR & EMOTION.

BEHAVIORS ARE A CONDITIONED RESPONSE TO A STIMULUS. (i.e. CAUSE & EFFECT.)

WHEN THERE IS AN UPROAR ABOUT A TRANS-GENDERED PERSON, IT'S USUALLY BECAUSE THEY **LOOK** TRANS-GENDERED. SO...

THIS LEADS ME TO BELIEVE THAT THE CONDITIONING PEOPLE HAVE GONE THROUGH IS CAUSING THEM TO EXPERIENCE SOMETHING KNOWN AS **COGNITIVE DISSONANCE.**

IN A NUTSHELL, COGNITIVE DISSONANCE IS WHERE SOMEONE SEES ONE THING AND EXPERIENCES SOMETHING CONTRARY TO WHAT THEY EXPECT.

IMAGINE THIS: SOMEONE HANDS YOU AN ICE CREAM CONE FULL OF ICE COLD... **MASHED POTATOES!!!**
CONSIDER THE REVULSION YOU'D FEEL UPON TASTING IT.

THE GOOD THING IS THIS: AS IT IS A **CONDITIONED** RESPONSE, COUNTER-CONDITIONING HAS A **POSSABILLITY** TO FIX IT.

I'VE TRIED TO EMPLOY A LITTLE COGNITIVE DISSONANCE IN THIS ISSUE BY COMBINING THE PEACEFUL PIC-NIC SCENES WITH HORRIFIC, EMOTION LADEN PRISON SCENES. IF YOU UNDERSTAND YOURSELF, AND YOU UNDERSTAND YOUR ENEMY, YOU CAN CONTROL THE OUTCOME OF THE BATTLE.

Thanks for reading! ♡

THANKS FOR HAVING LUNCH WITH ME!

I DON'T JUST STAND BY MY WORDS, I STAND **ON** THEM. IF ANYONE CAN PROVE A SINGLE ONE OF THEM FALSE*, COME TO MY NEXT PIC-NIC & I'LL EAT THEM FOR LUNCH!

Much Love~

~ Krysta Marie Morningstar ☆

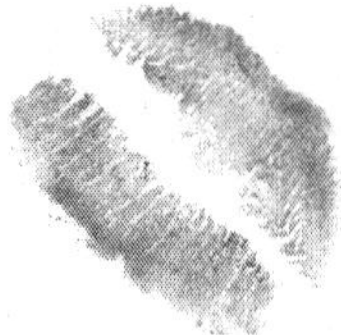

*EXCEPT THIS ONE!

CALIGRAPHY BY: HILLTOP

how to get involved

We hope these stories have inspired you to get involved in the fight for prison abolition. Whether it be writing someone on the inside, linking up with an abolitionist organization, or running a bulldozer into your local penitentiary, we always need more people on board. Here are some ways you can get involved. And remember kids: accomplices not allies.

ABO Comix - Hey that's us!
If you are in the SF Bay Area and would like to help out shoot us an email! Otherwise, please give us all your $$$ so we can continue publishing our queer buds behind bars. If you would like to send mail to any of our contributors or become penpals with them, write to us and we'll get you introduced: abocomix@gmail.com // facebook.com/abocomix
PO Box #11584, 195 41st Street, Oakland, CA 94611

Black & Pink
Find yourself an LGBTQ or HIV+ penpal in prison through Black and Pink. Or team up with your local chapter/make a new one @ blackandpink.org

Critical Resistance
Critical Resistance is a "member-led organization with volunteer members and supporters across the country. (Their) mission is to fight against the interlocking systems of policing, imprisonment and surveillance that make up the prison industrial complex (PIC)."
Volunteer, donate or start a chapter @ criticalresistance.org

Anarchist Black Cross Federation
The ABCF is "an organization based on work and ongoing organizing efforts to support and defend political prisoners/prisoners of war using anarchist and anti-authoritarian organizational structures."
Volunteer, donate or help organize @ abcf.net

Incarcerated Workers Organizing Committee (IWOC)
IWOC is a "a prisoner-led section of the Industrial Workers of the World. (They) struggle to end prison slavery along with allies and supporters on the outside."
Become a member, sponsor or subscribe @ incarceratedworkers.org

Books through Bars
Books through Bars is a collection of unaffiliated projects with the same goal of getting books to prisoners. To donate books to a chapter near you or get inspiration to start your own Books 2 Prisoners program visit booksthroughbars.org

Transgender, Gender Variant, and Intersex Justice Project (TGIJP)
"TGI Justice Project is a group of transgender, gender variant and intersex people-inside and outside of prisons, jails and detention centers-creating a united family in the struggle for survival and freedom."
Donate @ tgijp.org

California Coalition for Women Prisoners (CCWP)
"CCWP is a grassroots social justice organization, with members inside and outside prison, that challenges the institutional violence imposed on women, transgender people, and communities of color by the prison industrial complex."
Donate or ask to get involved @ womenprisoners.org

Prison Activist Resource Center (PARC)
"PARC is a prison abolitionist group committed to exposing and challenging all forms of institutionalized racism, sexism, able-ism, heterosexism, and classism, specifically within the Prison Industrial Complex (PIC)."
Volunteer or donate @ prisonactivist.org

Decarcerate Alameda County
An Oakland-based coalition fighting the construction of a new $66M "mental health" unit at Santa Rita Jail. Mental health in a jail or prison is an oxymoron because cages only exacerbate mental health issues. Learn more about @alamedacountyjailfight.wordpress.com and on Facebook /santaritajailfail/.

Was so glad to receive your letter today! It made my day.

One thing, I want others on the outside to know is

this is a Lonely and hard way of doing time. I wouldn't wish this on my worst enemy.

I am a hard worker not only did I work for 17 years to become incarcerated. I worked hard for twenty years to end up in

solitary confinement....

doing this gives me a whole new sense of purpose. The brightest blessings to you for coming into my life!!! ♥

Thank You so much for your encouraging letter. The information you sent on how to make a home-made zine, was awsome! I've got to tell you this has been the most fun I've had in a while.

148

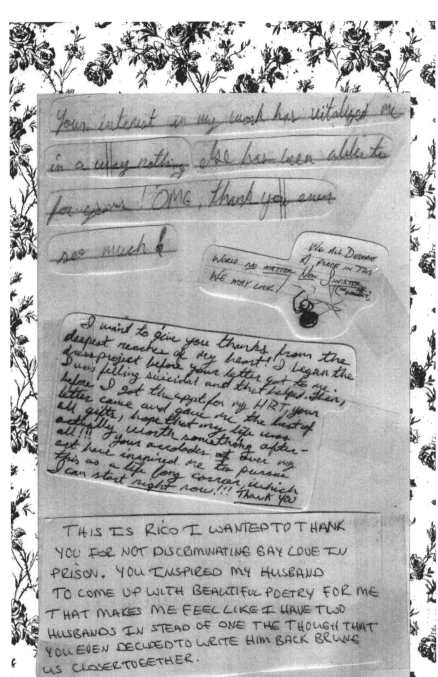

Your interest in my work has vitalized me in a way nothing else has been able to for years! OMG, thank you ever so much!

WORLD NO MATTER HOW WE MAY LOOK! We all deserve a place in this world no matter how sinister (or different)

I want to give you thanks from the deepest recolee of my heart! I began the dress project before your letter got to me. I was feeling suicidal and that helped. Then, before I got the appl. for my HRT, your letter came and gave me the best of all gifts, hope that my life was actually worth something after all!!! Your accolades over my art have inspired me too pursue this as a life long career, which I can start right now!!! Thank you

THIS IS RICO I WANTED TO THANK YOU FOR NOT DISCRIMINATING GAY LOVE IN PRISON. YOU INSPIRED MY HUSBAND TO COME UP WITH BEAUTIFUL POETRY FOR ME THAT MAKES ME FEEL LIKE I HAVE TWO HUSBANDS IN STEAD OF ONE THE THOUGH THAT YOU EVEN DECIDED TO WRITE HIM BACK BRINGS US CLOSER TOGETHER.

I have been drawing for a while but I have a new and profound respect for professional comic artist!

I don't have access to the most professional tools to attempt this endeavour. I am using whatever I can make, beg, borrow, or steal to get this done. Instead of India Ink for black fills I am using modified "home-made" ink that is usually used for prison tattoos. It works OK, but likes to smudge.

• PPl used to make fun of me for drawing comics when the typical prison art format is portraits. Let them laugh now!

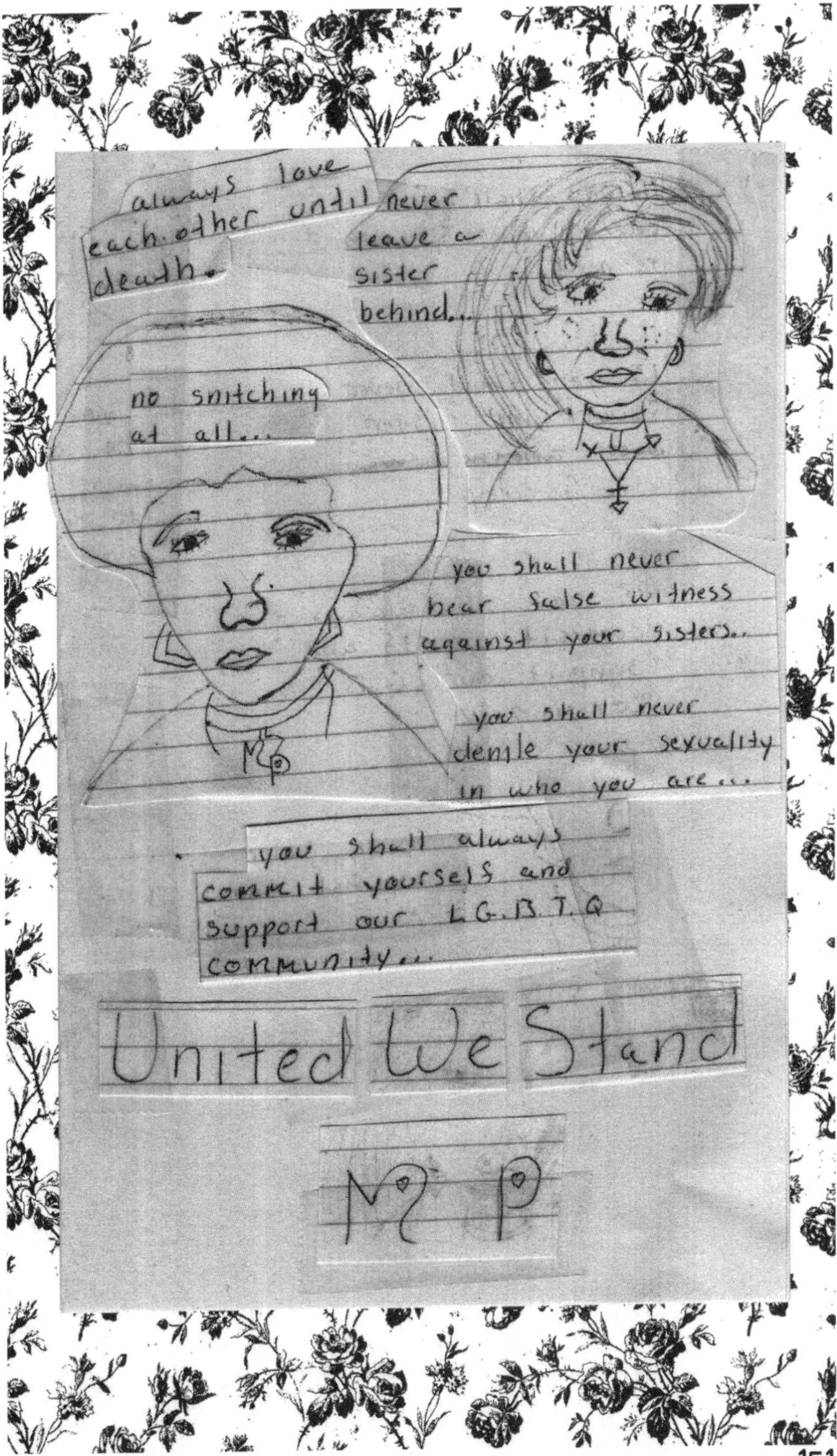
always love each other until death.
never leave a sister behind...
no snitching at all...
you shall never bear false witness against your sisters..
you shall never denie your sexuality in who you are...
you shall always commit yourself and support our L.G.B.T.Q community...
United We Stand
M P

Thankyou for giving people such as myself the chance to do something with my/our time.

Oh, My, F'ing, Gawd!

I've been looking for you FOREVER!

Working on this keeps my mind off of this stuff for the most part.

I really respect what you guys are doing for not only fellow queers, etc. but prisoners as well. I hope this project/anthology is successful. I'm all for queer awareness & prison abolition. I am 100% queer & I'm 100% incarcerated...